UNITED
STATES

Published in 1980 by Grisewood and Dempsey Limited, Grosvenor House, 141/143 Drury Lane, London WC2.

Printed and bound by South China Printing Co, Hong Kong.
ISBN 0 906279 06 2

RAINBOW

Science Encyclopedia

this edition produced exclusively for WHSMITH

Contents

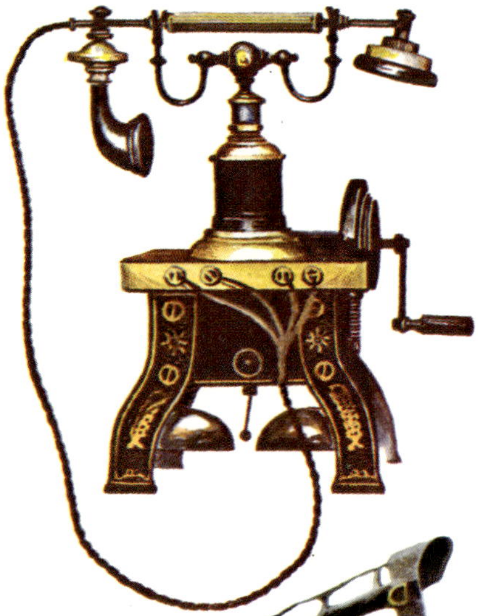

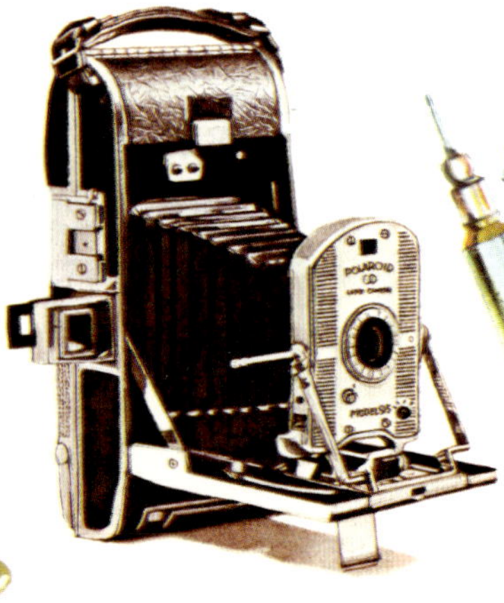

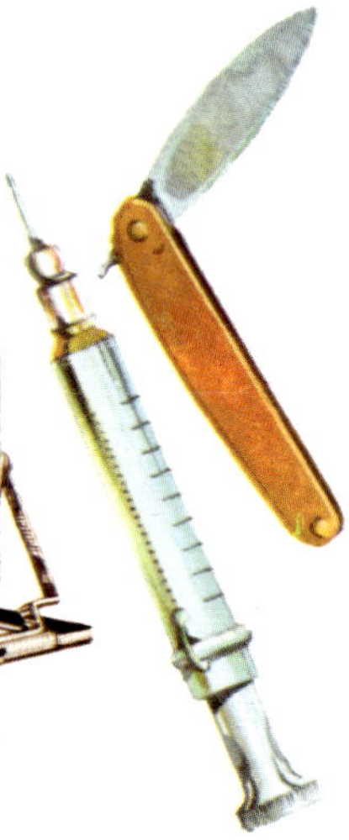

EDITORIAL
John Paton
Simon Franklin
Cover: Denise Gardiner

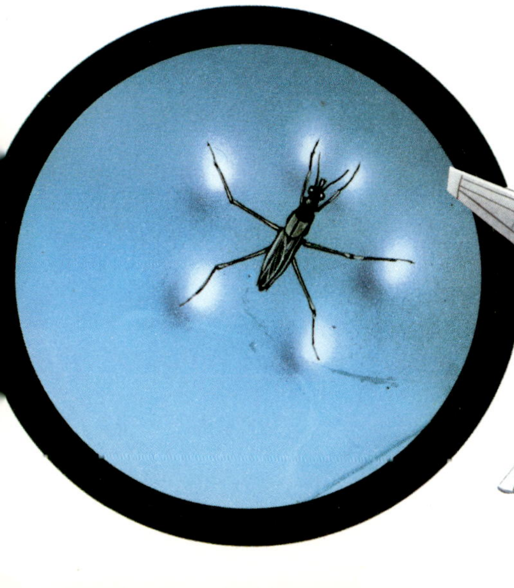

The First Inventors

Man's first discoveries were concerned mainly with survival. He learned to hunt animals for food, and he found that he could keep warm by wearing clothes made from the skins. He kept fires burning all the time, having lit them first of all from natural fires. These were caused, from time to time, by lightning, or by red-hot lava gushing from an erupting volcano. Sometimes, the heat produced by chemical reactions in rotting plants would be enough to start a fire. If a man let his fire go out by mistake, he would relight it from a neighbour's fire. And, if a group decided to move to a new area, they would take fire with them. For they might have to wait a long time before finding another natural fire.

This problem was solved about half a million years ago, when man discovered how to make fire by friction. Rubbing two sticks together eventually made them so hot that they would set fire to a pile of dry grass. The art of firemaking must rank as one of man's greatest discoveries. For it was essential in enabling him to survive the Ice Ages that came some 300,000 years ago.

Sticks and stones were man's first weapons and tools. For fighting and hunting, he threw rocks. And branches ripped from trees served as clubs. The earliest stone tools discovered by scientists have proved to be over 2 million years old. These crude implements were used by our ape-like ancestor known as *Homo erectus* (upright man). Over hundreds of years, man learned to improve his tools by shaping them to make them more effective and easier to use.

Flint was an important material, as it could be chipped with another stone to give a hard, sharp cutting edge. Many flints were used for axes and knives, while others were shaped into spear heads. Then, at some unknown time and place, the bow and arrow were invented, and flints were used for arrow heads too. Because stone tools were so widely used, this early period in man's history is known as the Stone Age.

Stone Age man generally hunted in groups. When an animal had been killed, it would be taken back to the camp, cut up and eaten raw. The skin would be removed carefully, scraped clean and sewn to make simple clothes. Needles were made from the bones of the animal. And its fine, tough tendons served as thread.

The advantage of cooking food was probably discovered when someone accidentally left their meat near to a fire. Finding the roasted meat more tender would have encouraged man to experiment further.

Early men, with no fur or hair to keep out the cold, wrapped themselves in animal skins for warmth. Then someone, bolder than the rest, picked up a burning branch from a natural forest fire. He found that he could use and control fire. Later, men found that they could make fire by rubbing sticks together and by striking sparks from flints.

About 10,000 years ago, the last Ice Age ended. Most of the ice that had covered so much of the northern hemisphere melted, exposing the land and leaving rivers and lakes. This marked the start of a new period in man's history. He discovered how to grow crops and to catch fish using hooks and nets. He made boats from hollowed logs. He learnt how to make pottery, and to spin thread and weave cloth. And, some time before 3000 BC, man made his most important invention of all time — the wheel. By now, the Stone Age was ending, and metals were being used for weapons, tools, ornaments and utensils.

Thousands of years ago, man learnt to twist fibres together to make twine. This was used for many purposes. Fishing nets were made by knotting lengths of twine together at regular intervals. In the print shown here, Japanese fishermen are using a dip net. Until reliable boats were developed, fishing was confined to rivers and shallow coastal waters. Nets were not used only for fishing. The Egyptians, for example, often used nets to catch ducks and geese.

Right: Japanese fishermen with a dip net. Stone Age men made nets by knotting fibres. When man first learned how to tie knots he had added an important tool-making skill.

The Wheel

The wheel was probably invented in several places at about the same time. It was certainly in use in the Middle East around 3000 BC. Wheels may have been used to make pottery before anyone thought of using them to make transport easier. The use of the wheel led to increased trade between villages and towns. The traders took new ideas and products with them and in this way civilization spread and grew.

Before the wheel, heavy loads had to be carried or dragged. Putting wooden rollers beneath a load reduced the friction. This was a step towards inventing the wheel.

The first wheels were made either from sections of tree trunk or from three planks clamped together. Spoked wheels appeared around 2000 BC. The wheel also gave man a useful lifting device, the pulley, invented around 800 BC.

The Builders

The cave dwellings used by early man provided good shelter. But it was a disadvantage being able to live only where there were caves. So man learnt to build huts and tents. These enabled him to live almost anywhere. This was important when he started to farm the land. For the best land might be a long way from the nearest caves.

Simple tents were made by tying branches together and covering them with skins, bark or leaves. Huts were made from mud. This was first mixed with straw, shaped into blocks and then left in the sun to dry and harden. The straw helped to hold the mud together, and prevented the blocks from cracking as they dried. Walls made from the bricks were held together by mortar. Like the bricks, this was made from a mixture of mud and straw. Sun-baked bricks were used to build houses from about 5000 BC. And better bricks, made by being heated in high-temperature kilns, were being produced by about 2500 BC.

By this time, great advances had been made in building techniques. In many places, houses had become more complicated in structure, and more attractive in appearance. As well as bricks, many types of stone were used in building. And the walls inside were often sealed with plaster.

Above: In North America, the early Indians cut birch poles to make the frameworks for their tents. To cover the frames, they used strips of bark or animal skins.

Below and left: In the region we now call the Middle East, the ancient Sumerian builders used bricks made from mud and straw. These were hardened by baking in the sun.

Right: The pyramids in Egypt are spectacular feats of building. They are made from massive blocks of stone. The Egyptians did not use cement to hold the blocks together. Instead, they carefully shaped the blocks so that they fitted together perfectly. Set squares and plumb lines were used to check the shape of the blocks. When a block was finished, it was lifted onto a sledge. A team of slaves hauled the sledge up the pyramid and the block was then placed in position.

The most spectacular work was to be seen in the monuments, palaces, temples and tombs. Outstanding among these were the Egyptian pyramids, which became known as one of the seven wonders of the world. The pyramids were built as tombs for the pharaohs around 2600 BC. The largest of these structures, known as the Great Pyramid, is as high as a forty-storey skyscraper. It is estimated to weigh about 6 million tonnes, and its construction must rank as a major feat of civil engineering. The Great Pyramid was built from carefully shaped blocks of stone, each weighing several tonnes. These were put on sledges, hauled up ramps and pulled into position by hand.

The ancient Greeks were particularly concerned with the proportions of buildings and laid down mathematical rules for producing pleasing effects. The Romans used pulleys, cranes and wooden scaffolding on their building sites. They developed the use of the arch in buildings and bridges. And they provided piped water in many towns.

In the Middle Ages, most houses in Europe were made of wood. Then, in the 1500s, a renewed interest in design led to greater use of brick and stone. The only tall buildings were the cathedrals. For the walls of ordinary houses were too weak to support heavy loads.

Skyscrapers first appeared in the United States in the 1880s. These buildings were made possible by a new building technique. The use of reinforced concrete slabs held in a steel framework provided great strength with relatively low weight. Today skyscrapers dominate the skyline in New York and other major cities around the world.

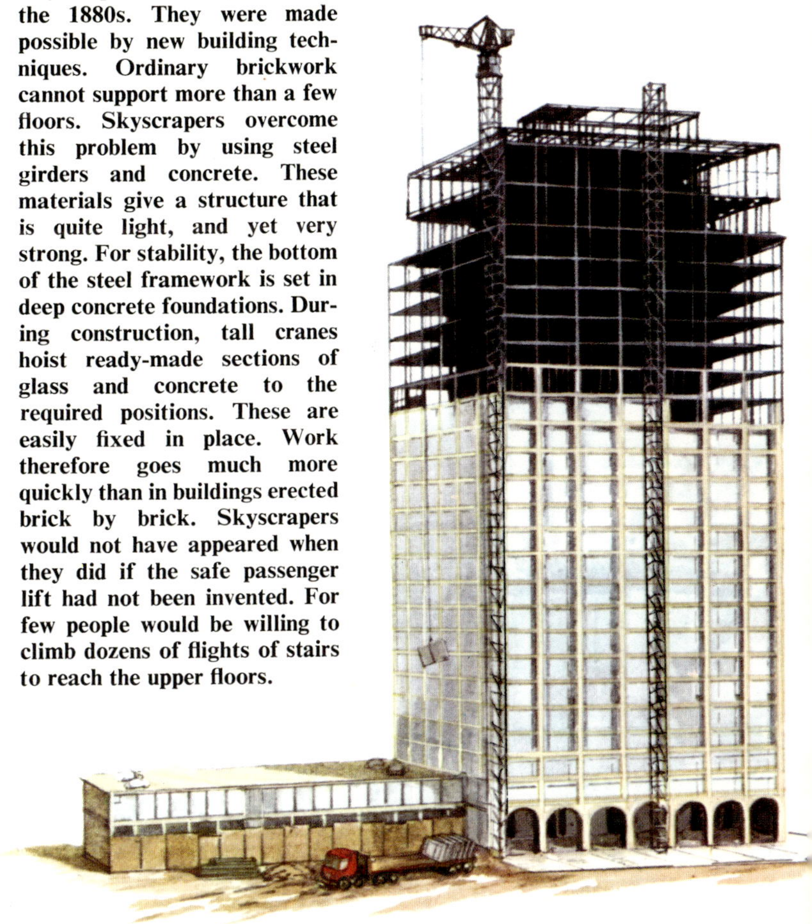

Skyscrapers first appeared in the 1880s. They were made possible by new building techniques. Ordinary brickwork cannot support more than a few floors. Skyscrapers overcome this problem by using steel girders and concrete. These materials give a structure that is quite light, and yet very strong. For stability, the bottom of the steel framework is set in deep concrete foundations. During construction, tall cranes hoist ready-made sections of glass and concrete to the required positions. These are easily fixed in place. Work therefore goes much more quickly than in buildings erected brick by brick. Skyscrapers would not have appeared when they did if the safe passenger lift had not been invented. For few people would be willing to climb dozens of flights of stairs to reach the upper floors.

Below: The Romans used cranes when building aqueducts to carry water.

Medieval builders used cranes and wooden scaffolding. They had two useful machines: the winch and pulley for hoisting small loads, and the wheelbarrow. Wheelbarrows appeared in Europe about 1200 and have since then remained more or less unchanged.

Toolmakers and Craftsmen

Man's total dependence on stone tools ended around 4000 BC, when he discovered how to use metals. Lumps of copper, silver or gold found in the ground could be shaped by beating with a stone. Many uses were found for metal, which had quite different properties from stone. And so a whole new range of tools and utensils gradually evolved.

Not all metal was found in a ready-to-use form. Sometimes, blobs of molten metal ran from the earth near fires as it was baked. Even earth that appeared to have no metal in it could yield the glimmering liquid when heated. For the earth was often rich in ores — chemical compounds with a metallic content. This heating process, called smelting, did not always yield pure metal. If, for example, both copper and tin ores were present, the resulting metal was an alloy (mixture) called bronze. Gradually, metal workers became familiar with the various types of ores. And they learned to make alloys for quite different uses by mixing metals in various proportions.

The introduction of metal tools enabled many new crafts to develop. Besides hammers and axes, there were soon saws, drills and chisels. Some craftsmen used the new tools to make objects of great beauty. Other workers invented and built instruments and simple machines. Thus the age of metals, and their use, brought about changes that, in the end, affected all mankind.

CASTING BY THE LOST WAX PROCESS

1. In the lost wax process, the object to be cast was first carved from a block of wax, using a metal tool.

2. The finished wax model was placed in a container. Then, wet, runny clay was poured around it and allowed to set.

3. The clay was heated until the wax ran out of a drainage hole. Molten metal was then poured into the hollow mould.

4. The mould was left to cool, and the metal became solid. The clay mould was broken open to extract the metal casting.

The spinning wheel (centre) twisted fibres into yarn, and wound it on a spindle. In the medieval frame loom (left), pressing the pedals parted the threads. This allowed the shuttle to be passed through. The woven cloth was coloured by boiling in dyes (right).

Left: Chinese blacksmiths forging a sword. The blade is held on the anvil by pincers, and two sizes of hammer are being used. A less skilled workman, right, worked the bellows. The Chinese developed very efficient bellows and so were able to smelt iron far earlier than the rest of the world. In the 5th century BC they made cast iron cauldrons and iron moulds for the casting of spades, chisels and chariot parts.

Right: The Romans were great builders and stone was an important building material. Their stone masons cut and carved blocks of stone with many tools that are familiar to us today. Saws, mallets and chisels were used to cut and carve the stone, a compass and measuring stick to size it and a wooden pattern to check the shape.

Left: Medieval carpenters secured wooden joints with dowels or pegs and glue made from boiled bones. The auger was used for drilling. And an all-purpose tool for shaping wood was the adze (centre). Other tools had changed little since Roman times. The pole lathe (right) was worked by 'pumping' the pole. The turner could hold his chisel with both hands for as long as the lathe kept spinning.

Wheels at Work

By 3000 BC, wheeled carts were being made in the Middle East. But this was not the first use of the wheel. For it was in use at least 1000 years earlier for making pottery. Wet clay was turned on a horizontal wheel and shaped with the hands to form beautiful pots and jugs. These were then baked hard. Examples of work produced in this way some 6000 years ago have been found in the Middle East. And the same technique is still used today. The first potter's 'wheel' may not have been round — the turning platform could have been any shape. But sharp corners would have made it difficult to get close to the work. So these would soon have been cut off and the platform made round.

Throughout the ages, man gradually found more and more uses for the wheel. Water was sometimes scooped from rivers by turning a large, vertical wheel with buckets fixed to the rim. This simple device may have led to the invention of the waterwheel. For it must have been noticed that the force of the moving water would, itself, sometimes turn the wheel. Some form of waterwheel may have been used as early as 3000 BC, in south-west Asia. But it was the Romans who, in the first century BC, developed it into an efficient machine. At last, man was learning to make use of the forces of nature. Surprisingly, the windmill was not invented until the seventh century AD.

Originally, water and wind power were used to turn millstones, which ground corn into flour. And water power was used to operate some machines when the industrial revolution started in the 1750s. The many clever attempts at making machines turn by themselves had not worked out.

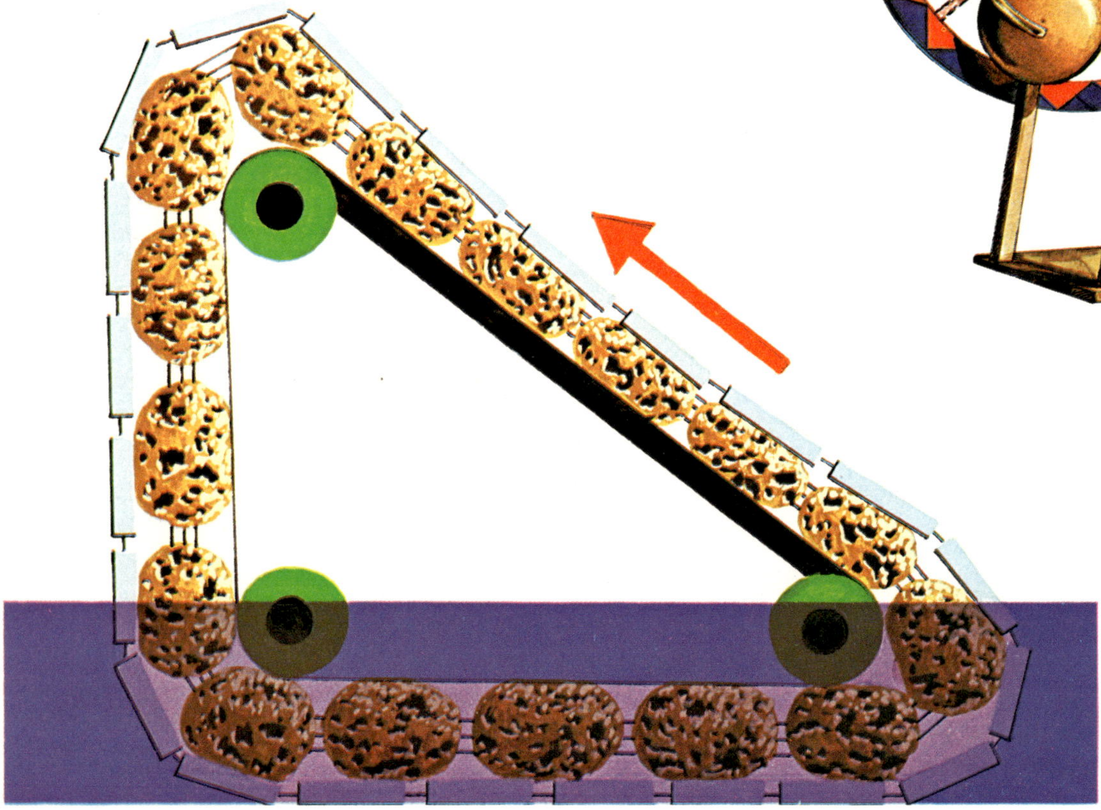

Left: British engineer Sir William Congreve designed this perpetual motion machine in the 1800s. Sponges on the left absorb water when they touch the surface. Congreve thought that the weight of the water would make the sponges descend right into the water and start the belt turning. The weights were supposed to squeeze the water from the sponges on the right, thus making them lighter. Unfortunately, the force produced on the left was never enough to make the belt turn.

Far left: Many designs were made for perpetual motion machines. It was hoped that they would turn for ever, giving free energy for driving other machines. In the design shown here, water from the trough passes down a pipe on the right and falls on a waterwheel. This is coupled to an Archimedean screw—a shaft with a pipe coiled around it. The falling water is supposed to turn the waterwheel. At the same time, the screw would lift water back to the trough. This would give a continuous supply for perpetual motion. However, the machine would not work. The problem is that the energy produced by the falling water could never be enough to raise the same amount of water, let alone turn the machinery.

Far left: The Italian inventor and artist Leonardo da Vinci (1452-1519) designed this perpetual motion machine. The four globes were half filled with mercury. This liquid metal is more than 13 times as heavy as the same volume of water. Leonardo thought that, if the globes were started spinning, the movement of the heavy mercury would keep them turning. The globes were attached to a spindle by four rods. Rotation of the spindle was transmitted to a large wheel by means of cogs. These were arranged so that one rotation of the globes would make the large wheel turn many times. But, like all other perpetual motion machines, Leonardo's invention was doomed to failure. With no outside energy source, there was nothing to overcome the friction in the machine. So it soon slowed down and stopped. Eventually, Leonardo gave up all hope of making a perpetual motion machine. Unlike many other inventors, he came to realize that it was impossible.

Above: Man's first success in harnessing the forces of nature came when he invented the waterwheel. This early example, at Hama in Syria, dates from Roman times. The River Orontes flows under the wheel, making it turn. The movement is used to raise water from the river to an aqueduct. The water in the aqueduct is used to irrigate the fields and to supply homes in the area.

Right: This machine for raising water was first used for irrigating land in the Nile valley. It was probably invented by a Greek mathematician and scientist called Archimedes, who lived in the second century BC. For this reason, it is known as the Archimedean screw. It consists of a large screw in a long cylinder. The bottom end dips in the water supply. The screw is turned by means of a handle at the top. As the screw rotates, water trapped between its thread and the cylinder wall rises steadily. At the top of the cylinder, the water gushes out into a tank. The extra height of the water gives pressure for making it flow along pipes to wherever it is needed.

A huge steam engine provides power for the looms in one of the new textile factories of the late 1700s. High-pressure steam from a boiler pushes a piston up a cylinder. Then the steam is condensed back into water. This causes the piston to be sucked back down the cylinder again. The rocking beam and gear wheels turn the up-and-down movements of the piston into round and round motion. This is transmitted to the looms by means of a system of pulleys and belts.

From the mid-1700s, many factories were built to house the new, large machines devised by various inventors. The machines enabled all kinds of work to be carried out much more quickly than had previously been possible. At first, many of the machines were turned by water power. But steam power was to prove more satisfactory. For it meant that factories could be built anywhere—not just beside fast-flowing rivers.

Steam and the Industrial Revolution

The mid-1700s saw the start of a rapid expansion in European agriculture and industry. So marked was this change that it was given a name of its own — the Industrial Revolution. In previous years trade had increased, new companies had been set up and fortunes made by a few enterprising people. A greater variety of goods was available, and more and more were demanded. So inventors tried hard to design new machines that could be used in industry. Before, most goods had been made by individuals or families working at home with hand tools. But now, people with money used it to build and equip factories. Many of these were situated next to rivers where they could use waterwheels to harness the energy of the moving water. The waterwheels drove all kinds of factory machinery, enabling goods to be produced much faster than ever before.

Before the Industrial Revolution, many people farmed to obtain food and other products mainly for their own use. Now industry needed large amounts of raw materials for the factories. So farming developed in response, and gradually became more mechanized. The plough, which had been in use for thousands of years, was improved. And more use was made of the seed drill, invented in 1701 by Jethro Tull. Some attempts at harvesting by machine were made at the end of the century. But the first practical reaper, invented by Patrick Bell, did not appear until 1826.

At the start of the Industrial Revolution, horses provided pulling power for agriculture. And industry depended largely on water power. But steam power was already on the way.

The Age of Steam

The fact that steam could produce motion was known to the ancient Greeks. In a device built by Hero of Alexandria, steam was piped to a metal sphere (ball). When the steam escaped through two jets it caused the sphere to turn. But little useful energy was produced, and the machine was really only regarded as an interesting toy.

The steam engine, as we know it, started to develop in 1698 when Thomas Savery invented a machine to pump water from mines. Steam from a boiler filled a cylinder, which was then cooled. This cooling turned the steam into a small volume of water, but also left a partial vacuum (pressurized space) in the cylinder. The pressure of the vacuum was used to suck up water from the mineshafts. In 1712, Thomas Newcomen built a better steam engine, with a piston in the cylinder. The expansion and contraction of the steam in the cylinder caused the piston to move up and down and, in turn, to operate a separate pump.

Although reliable, Newcomen's engine was very inefficient, using large amounts of fuel to do relatively little work. James Watt made great design improvements in the 1760s, and he converted the up-and-down motion of the piston into round and round movement. Watt's steam engines were capable of driving all kinds of factory machinery. They began to take the place of water power, enabling factories to be sited away from the rivers. Steam engines were also used to power farm machinery. They completely changed people's lives and steam-driven vehicles were soon to revolutionize transport by sea and land.

Writing and Printing

We do not know when man first learned to draw and paint. For the earliest examples of this art must have disappeared long ago. But various engravings and paintings found in caves have proved to date from before 20,000 BC. Early man made pictures on stone to keep records of important information, such as ways of hunting. Later, as his activities expanded, he recorded other information, such as the number of animals he owned. In order to communicate information to others, he could draw a series of pictures in the form of a story. Gradually, the pictures became less lifelike, and developed into a set of standard symbols. A single symbol would represent an object or an action. Messages could be passed on by arranging such symbols in a line to form a simple sentence. This form of picture writing is called pictography.

Pictography was probably first developed in the Middle East by the Sumerians, some 5000 years ago. Egyptian writing developed around the same time, but each symbol had its own sound. Also, instead of using thousands of symbols to represent different objects, various words were built up from a much smaller alphabet of symbols. Simplification of this system by the Phoenicians and the Greeks resulted in an alphabet similar to the one we use in the western world today.

Sumerian writing was often done by making marks in soft clay tablets, which later hardened. Then, as written works became longer, the scribes tried to find less bulky materials to write on.

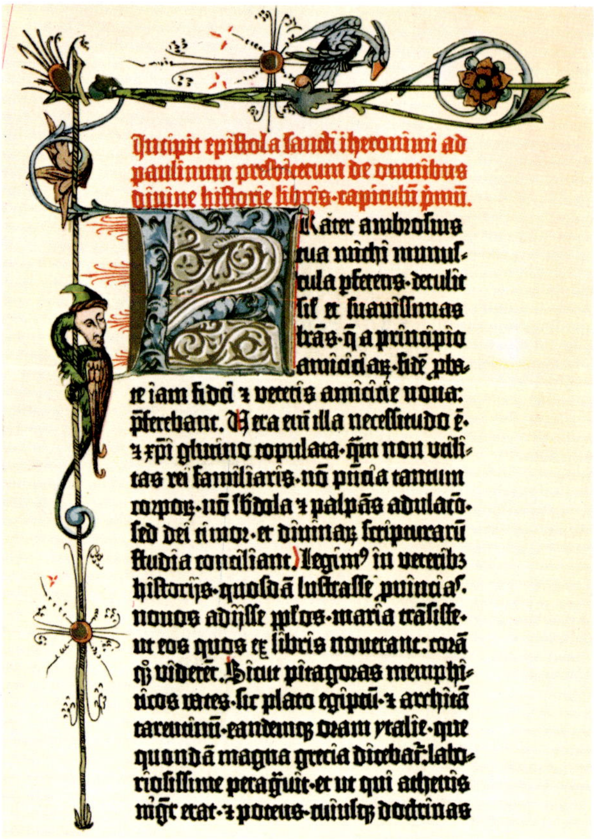
Incipit epistola sancti iheronimi ad
paulinum presbiterum de omnibus
divine historie libris-capitulu primu.
Frater ambrosius
tua michi munus-
cula perferens detulit
sil et suavissimas
lras-q a principio
amicicias-fide pba
te iam fidei et veteris amicicie nova:
preferebant. Vera eni illa necessitudo e.
et xpi glutino copulata-qm non utili-
tas rei familiaris-no pntia tantum
corpor-no subdola et palpas adulacio.
sed dei timor-et divinaz scripturaru
studia conciliant. Legim in veteribz
historiis-quosda lustrasse provincias.
novos adiisse ppls-maria transisse-
ut eos quos ex libris noverant: cora
q viderent. Sicut pitagoras memphi-
ticos vates-sic plato egiptu-et archita
tarentinu-eandemq ora ytalie-que
quonda magna grecia dicebat: labo-
riosissime peragravit-et ut qui athenis
migr erat-et potens-cuiusq doctrinas

Above: A page from the Bible printed in Latin by the German printer, Johannes Gutenberg. He used a crude wine press to produce this breathtakingly beautiful Bible. Gutenberg could print up to 300 sheets a day in his press.

Below: A page from an early book printed in England in 1480 by William Caxton.

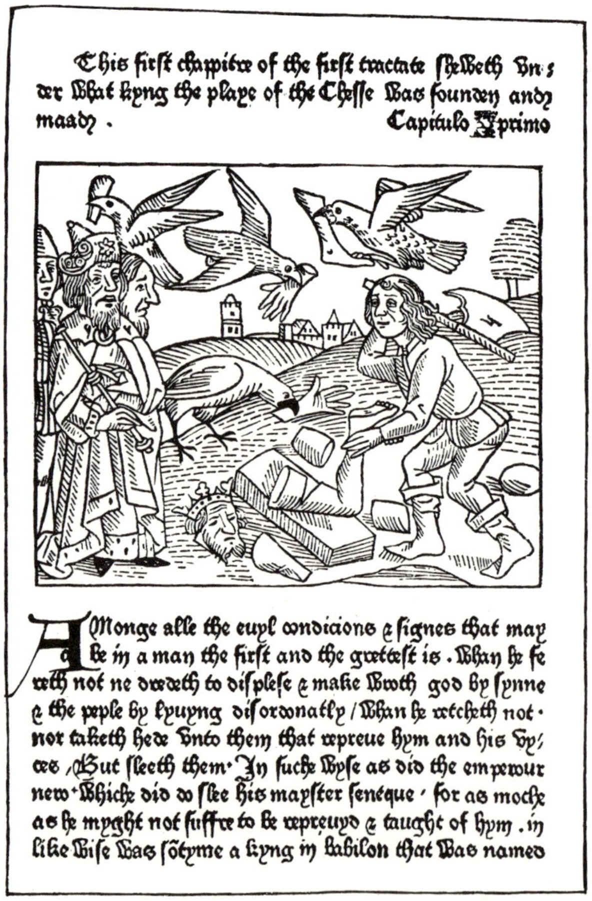
This first chapitre of the first tractate sheweth vn-
der what kyng the playe of the Chesse was founden and
maad . Capitulo primo

Amonge alle the evyl condicions & signes that may
be in a man the first and the grettest is . Whan he fe
reth not ne dredeth to displese & make wroth god by synne
& the peple by lyvyng disordynatly / Whan he retcheth not .
nor taketh hede unto them that repreue hym and his vy-
ces / But sleeth them . In suche wyse as did the emperour
nero . Which did do slee his mayster seneque . for as moche
as he myght not suffre to be repreuyd & taught of hym . in
like wise was somtyme a kyng in babilon that was named

Left: Johannes Gutenberg 1400?-68? is generally regarded as the man who invented printing as we know it today. Born in Mainz, Germany, he was a skilled metal worker. He devised a mould for casting type. This made printing from movable type practicable for the first time. He produced the Gutenberg Bible and many other beautiful books.

1.Wheel-driven trip hammers, fitted with spikes, shred rags mixed with water to a pulp. 2.The pulp was transferred to a vat and stirred. Then a wire screen or sieve was dipped into the pulp, lifted out, shaken and laid on a piece of felt. The paper then stuck to the felt. 3.The wet sheets were screw-pressed to squeeze out the moisture and compress the fibres. 4.The finished paper was peeled from the felt and hung to dry.

Printing in the 1500s. The man composing (setting) the type picks out letters and arranges them in a composing stick held in his left hand. The lines of type are arranged in a tray and inked. To check that no mistakes have been made, a 'galley proof' is taken before the type is tapped firmly into the forme ready for printing. The screw press itself is hand operated and after being printed, the wet sheets are hung up to dry.

The Chinese made a form of paper by beating plant fibres into a pulp. The pulp was then pressed into sheets and left to dry. Inks were made from various plant and animal fluids and, later, from a mixture of lamp black (soot) and gum. The Egyptians made their paper from the papyrus plant in a similar way. Parchment, made from specially prepared animal skins, was used by the Romans.

The first books, made some 5000 years ago, were written on scrolls. These consisted of numerous sheets of papyrus, stuck end to end and rolled up on sticks. But the Romans' parchment sheets were quite tough, so could be stitched. This enabled them to be bound together between two covers to form the kind of book with which we are familiar today. The first bound books were made around 200 BC, and soon became more popular than scrolls.

Words in Print

Before printing was invented, books had to be written by hand. This was a slow process, so few books were produced.

Printing was invented over 1000 years ago, probably in China. The earliest printed book known to exist is a Chinese work on Buddhism, dated 868. All the words for each page were carved in a single block of wood. Printing was simply a matter of inking the block and pressing it onto paper. Drawings were printed in this way too. Woodblock printing enabled many copies of a book to be produced quickly — once the blocks had been made. But the initial process took a considerable time.

The great advance in printing came with movable type. Small blocks, representing one for each individual letter or symbol, were arranged to form the words. Once a number of blocks had been made, they could be used over and over again for different books. The Chinese may have used movable type in the 1300s. But it was the German Johann Gutenberg who made the process popular in the 1450s. Gutenberg's printing press used metal type. The 1800s saw the introduction of steam-driven printing presses, and machines to cast type, from liquid metal, when it was needed. Today, photographic processes are used to make plates for printing.

A woodcut printed by Caxton in the 1480s. A picture was cut into a wooden block, inked and stamped on to the paper.

To make a colour picture, it is first photographed through four colour filters. Then a printing plate is made for each colour. The yellow plate is printed first; then come the red and blue plates. The black is printed last and the paper then goes through a drying, folding and cutting unit. It comes out as a finished magazine, newspaper or book section.

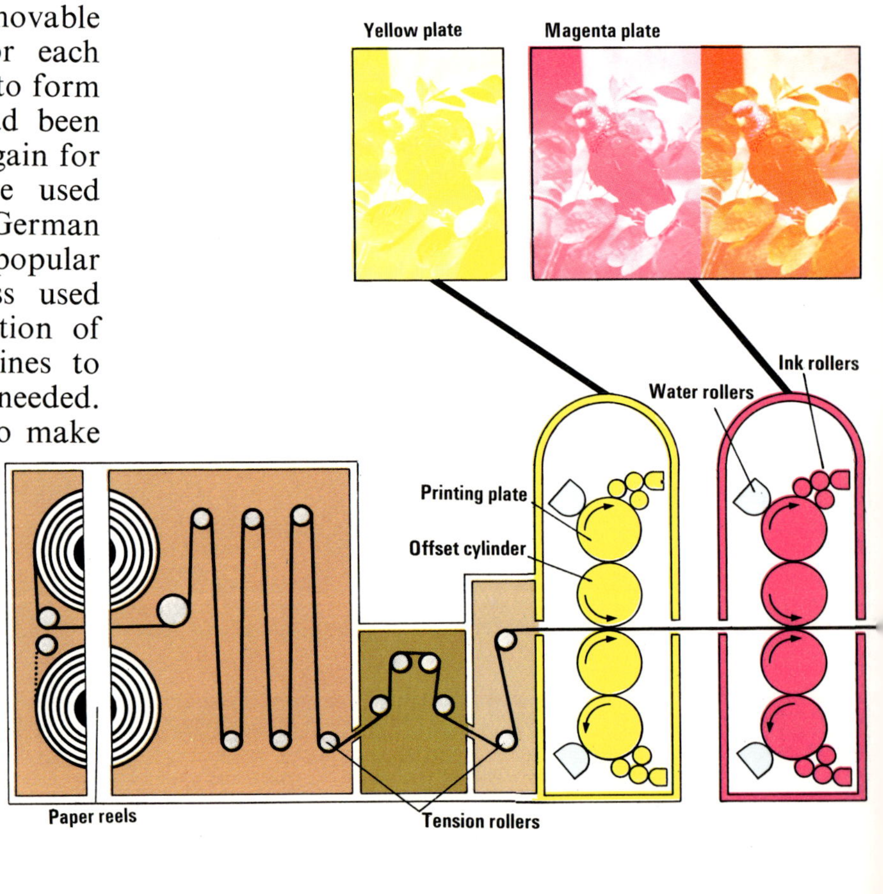

Right: The printing process invented by Gutenberg is known as letterpress or relief printing. Today much printing is done by offset lithography, often called offset litho. This uses printing plates that are prepared photographically from type set either in hot metal or on film.

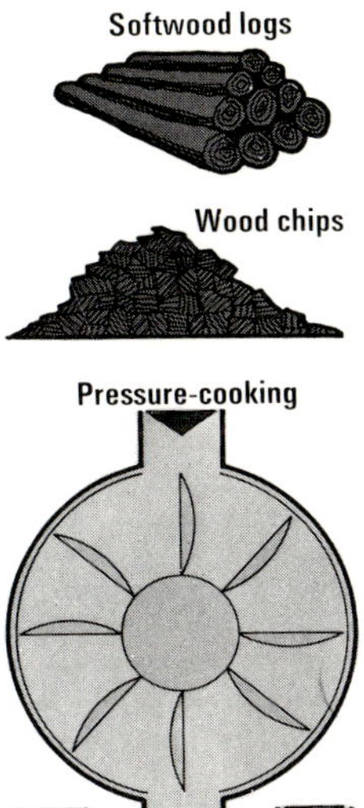

Left: When logs arrive at a paper mill, their bark is removed in revolving drums. Then they are cut into small chips. The chips are cooked with chemicals to break down the fibres. The pulp is washed, bleached and beaten into even finer fibres. It is then mixed with resins and perhaps dyes, depending on the kind of paper required. Then the pulp goes into the paper-making machine. The wet mass is laid down to form a long mat. It is dried in steam-heated cylinders and polished in calender rollers. Finally, it is wound on large reels.

Right: In modern printing, the printing surface of the plates is fitted around a cylinder in a high-speed rotary press.

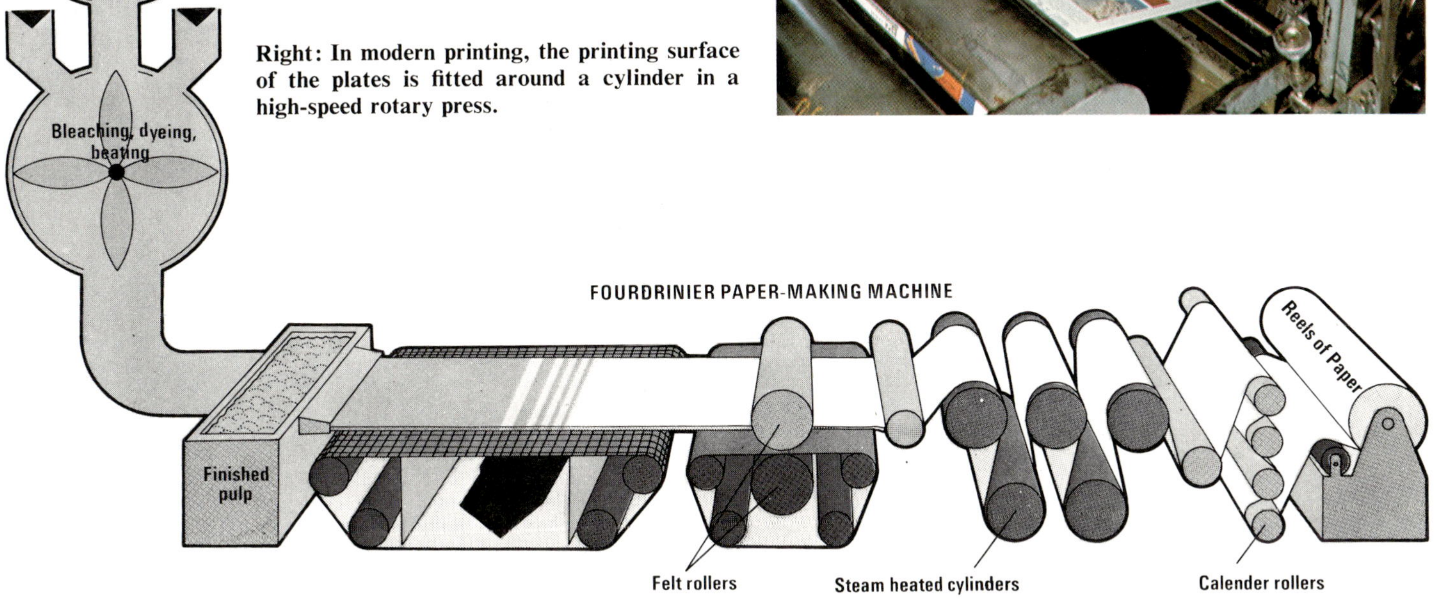

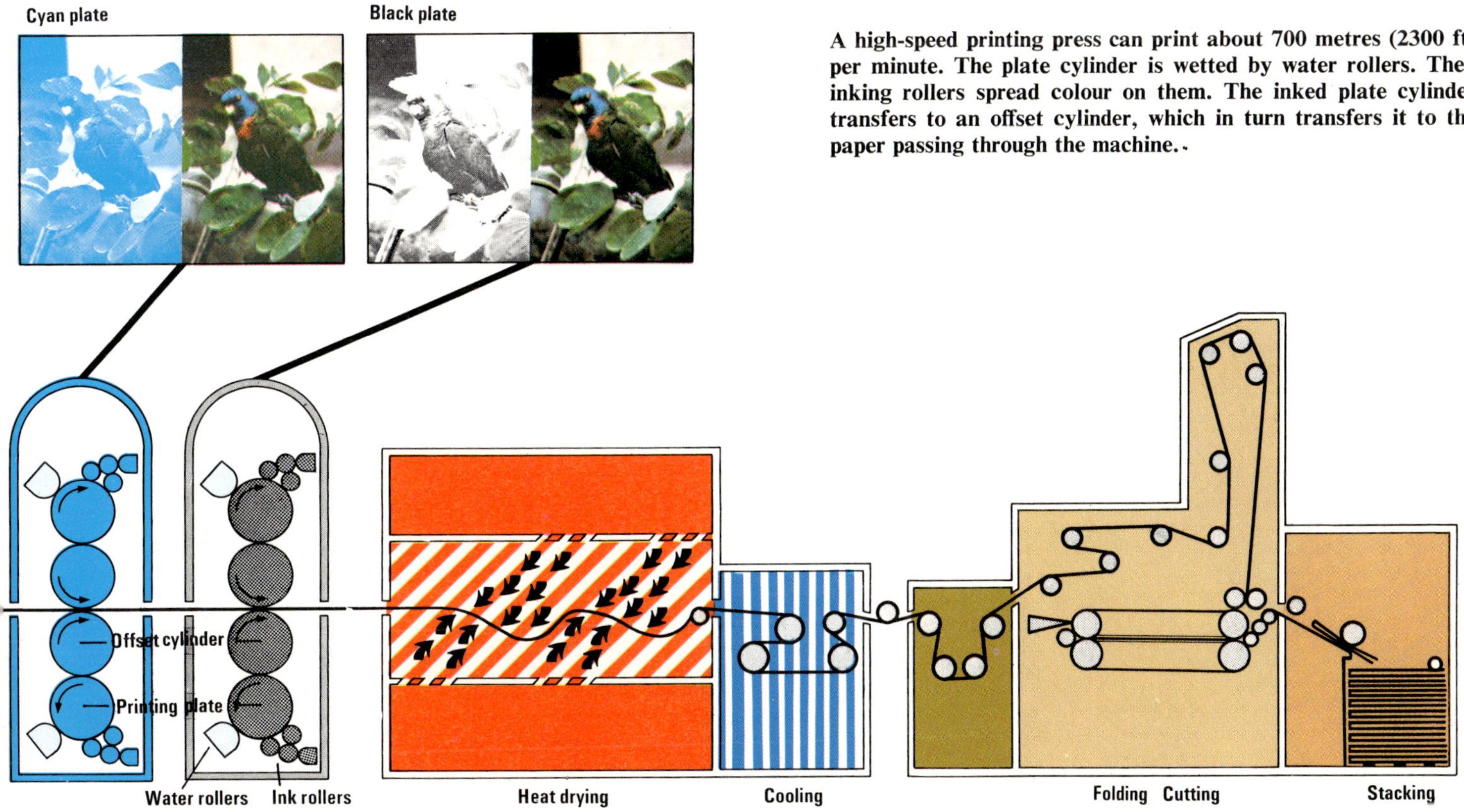

A high-speed printing press can print about 700 metres (2300 ft) per minute. The plate cylinder is wetted by water rollers. Then inking rollers spread colour on them. The inked plate cylinder transfers to an offset cylinder, which in turn transfers it to the paper passing through the machine.

Man the Inventor

Besides being a very famous artist, Leonardo da Vinci (1452-1519) was a clever inventor. The sketches he made of various machines showed a great deal of understanding of scientific principles. But the technology of the time was not advanced enough to make full use of da Vinci's ideas. For example, he designed a machine for vertical flight. It might have spun slowly to the ground if some extremely strong, light material had been available to make its large, spiral propeller. The machine might also have been capable of vertical take-off if an engine had been available to turn the propeller.

Modern inventors are much luckier. Advances in metallurgy have given them a vast range of alloys to use for particular purposes.

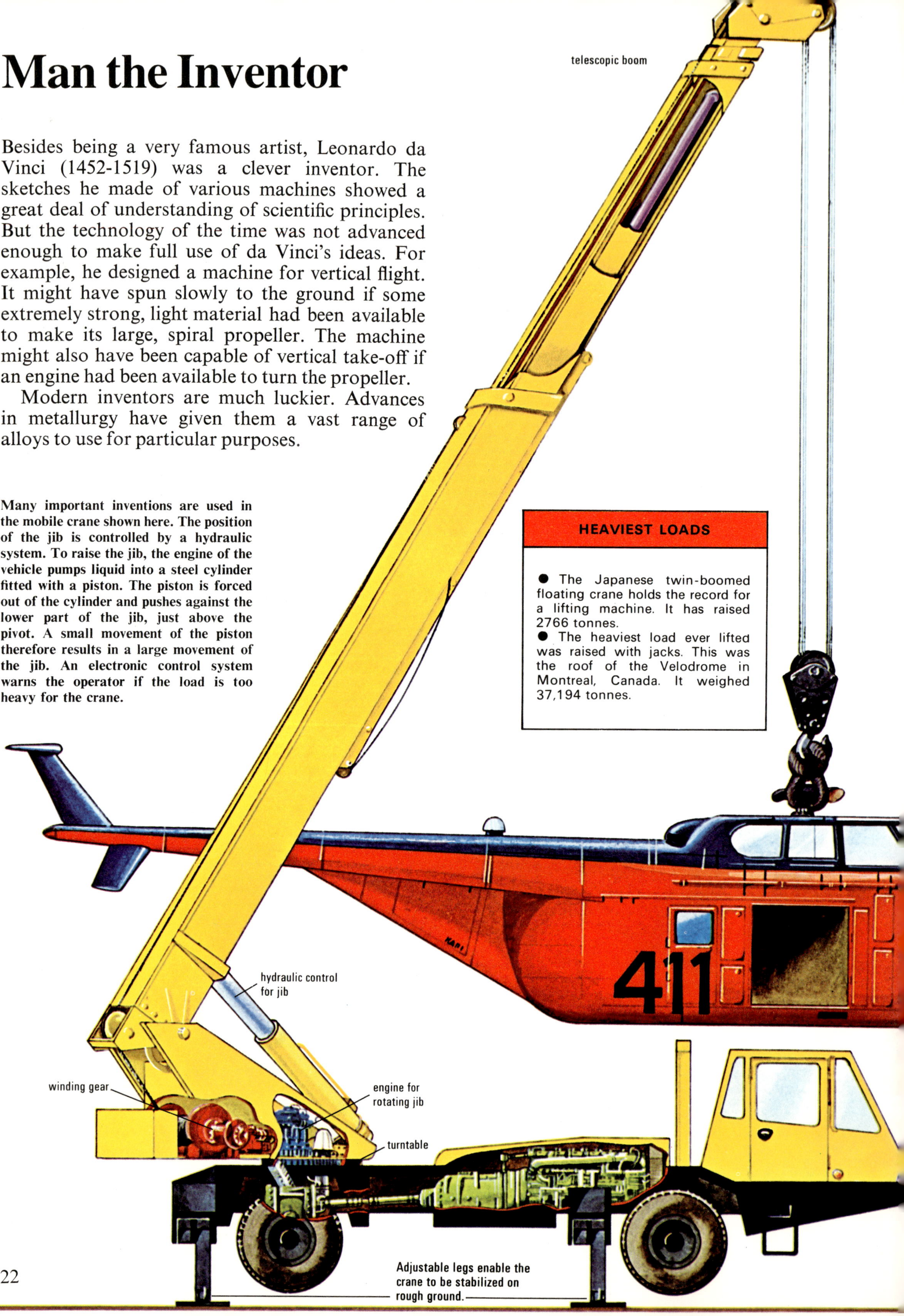

Many important inventions are used in the mobile crane shown here. The position of the jib is controlled by a hydraulic system. To raise the jib, the engine of the vehicle pumps liquid into a steel cylinder fitted with a piston. The piston is forced out of the cylinder and pushes against the lower part of the jib, just above the pivot. A small movement of the piston therefore results in a large movement of the jib. An electronic control system warns the operator if the load is too heavy for the crane.

Adjustable legs enable the crane to be stabilized on rough ground.

HEAVIEST LOADS

- The Japanese twin-boomed floating crane holds the record for a lifting machine. It has raised 2766 tonnes.
- The heaviest load ever lifted was raised with jacks. This was the roof of the Velodrome in Montreal, Canada. It weighed 37,194 tonnes.

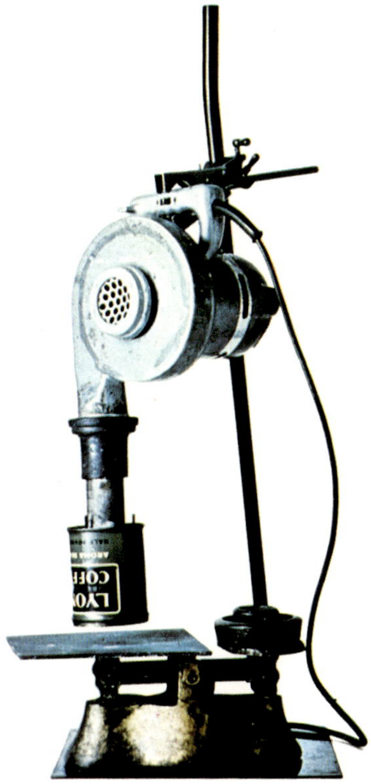

Above: Inventor Christopher Cockerell used this simple apparatus to test one of his theories. He bolted one tin inside another and connected them to an electric air blower. In this way, he obtained an annular (ring-shaped) jet of air. It produced a much greater thrust than an ordinary air jet. Cockerell measured the downward thrust on one side of a pair of scales by finding what weight was needed on the other side to balance it. Cockerell used the principle of the annular jet to work his invention—the hovercraft.

Above: The overhead cable car is a very useful form of transport in mountain regions. The car is attached to an endless cable running between two stations. The cable is driven by an engine in one of the stations. The cable cars work in pairs. As one goes down, the other goes up. By operating in this way, the weights of the two cars balance each other. So the engine does not have to exert so much force to make the cars move.

Left: At Charles de Gaulle Airport, near Paris, covered escalators carry passengers from one level to another. And moving walk-ways are provided for transportation of passengers and their luggage along the same level.

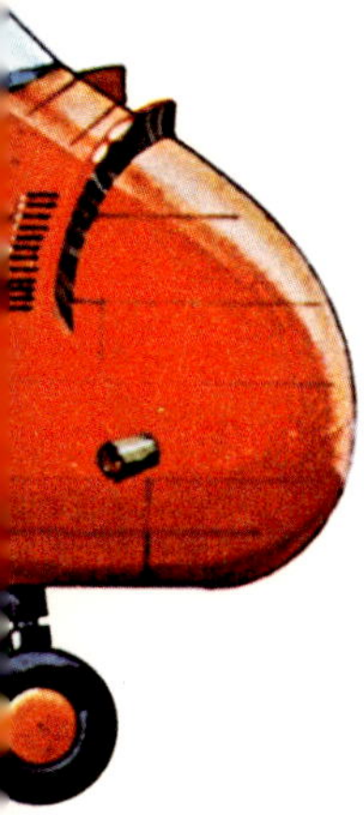

A movable source of power first became available in the 1700s with the invention of the steam engine (see page 17). From this sprang designs for steam-powered carriages and boats. Steam locomotives followed in the early 1800s. Balloons with steam-driven propellers did not work well as the engines were so heavy. The internal combustion engine provided power for motor cars in the late 1800s, and for aeroplanes early this century. It also made possible one of Leonardo da Vinci's dreams — the helicopter.

Today, aluminium alloys combine strength with lightness, and are widely used in aircraft. Various forms of steel are also available where extreme strength or hardness is of utmost importance. Plastics, which are all man-made, play a vital role in modern technology, and thousands of different types are available. They are used for numerous purposes, from artificial heart valves to motor-car bodies, furniture and bullet-proof vests.

Below: The Earth was formed about 4600 million years ago. The picture shows how its appearance has changed in that time.

Planet Earth

The Earth formed about 4600 million years ago. For millions of years, it must have been an extremely hot, molten body. Denser (heavier) materials, such as iron, sank towards the centre of the Earth, while lighter materials rose. As a result, the Earth now has a thin, light *crust*, which rests on a denser *mantle*. The mantle encloses the extremely dense *core*.

Constant volcanic action released gases and water vapour from the rocks. These substances formed a poisonous atmosphere. The water vapour accumulated in the air until, finally, it fell as rain during great storms. The water collected in hollows and formed the first oceans.

Left: A view of the Earth's surface taken from a spacecraft.

The Changing Earth

Even after the crust hardened, powerful forces inside the Earth kept changing its appearance. The crust split into large blocks, called *plates*, which moved slowly around because of movements in the partly molten upper mantle. When plates pushed against each other, rocks were squeezed up to form new land masses and mountains. Plate movements continue today. They can cause earthquakes.

Recent discoveries by American scientists suggest that the first living cells, bacteria, may have appeared about 3800 million years ago. Other life forms developed from these simple beginnings. Around 1900 million years ago, advanced plants began to produce oxygen in quantity. This made the evolution of animals possible. Some oxygen was changed into another gas, *ozone*. Ozone in the air blocks out most of the Sun's harmful ultraviolet rays. Guarded by this ozone shield, living things were able to spread from the seas on to the land. The first land animals, amphibians, appeared around 350 million years ago. Man was a late-comer. He developed in the last two million years.

Above: The Apollo 11 astronauts, the first men to land on another world, took this photograph of the Earth when they were about halfway to the Moon.

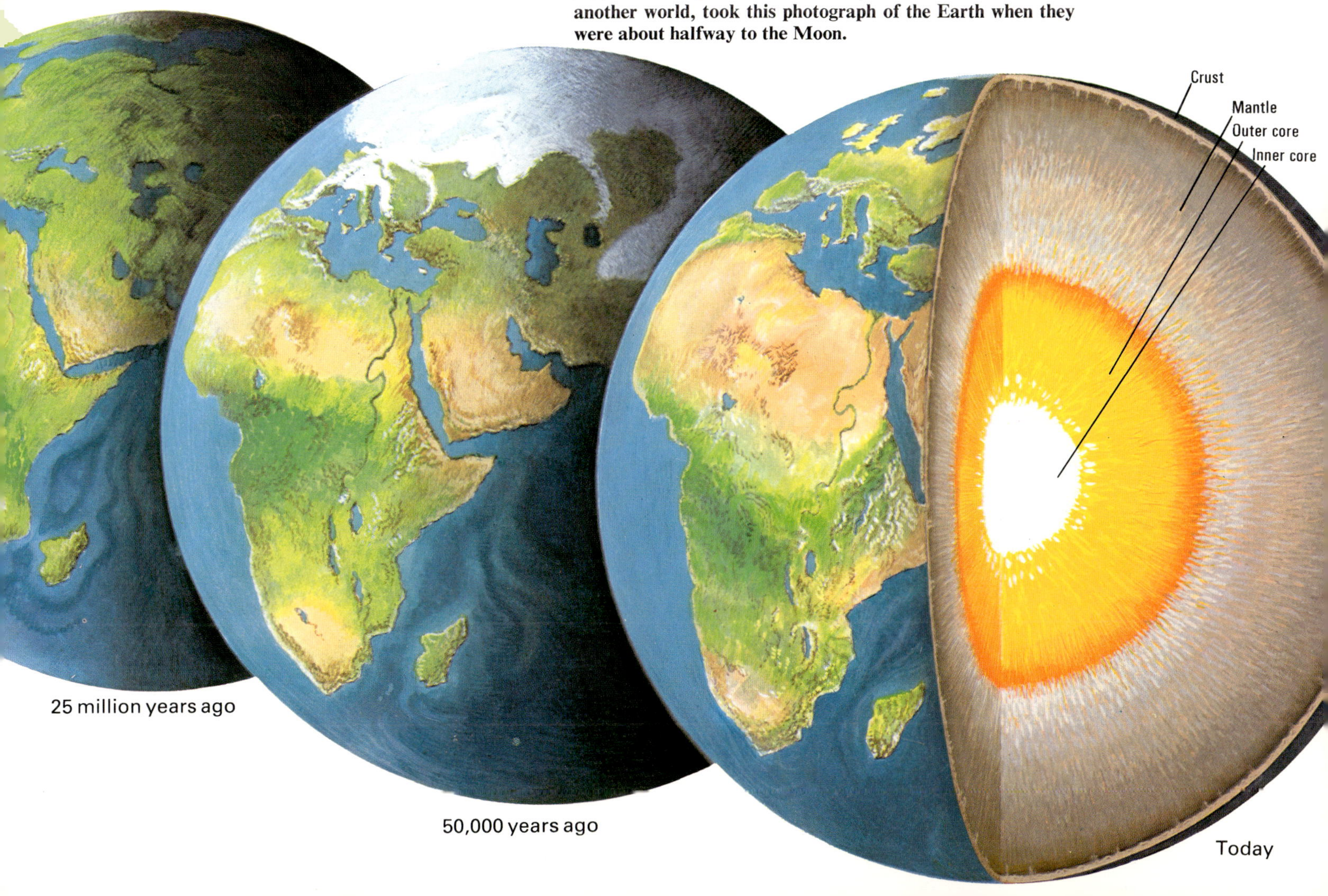

The Earth's tilted axis always points in the same direction—to the right in this drawing. As the Earth goes round the Sun, each hemisphere in turn is tilted towards the Sun. So we have summers and winters. In the picture, the northern hemisphere is having summer at the left; the southern hemisphere is having summer at the right.

Below, right: The Earth's axis is not perfectly upright to the plane of its orbit around the Sun. It is tilted at an angle of $23\frac{1}{2}°$.

Below: The Sun's rays shine steadily from one direction. So each 24-hour spin of the Earth gives night and day on opposite sides of the globe.

The Earth in Space

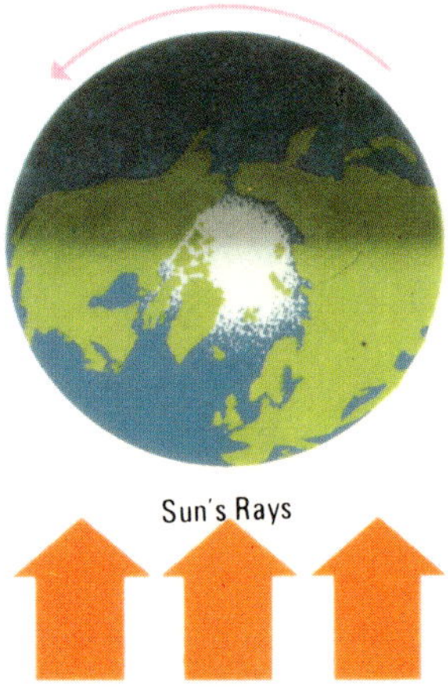

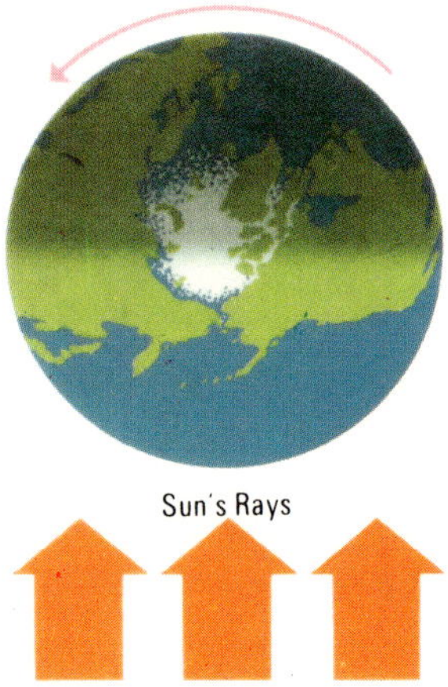

Earth Time

The Earth is the third planet from the Sun in the Solar System. The Earth completes one revolution around the Sun in a *solar year*, which takes 365 days, 5 hours, 48 minutes and 46 seconds. Our calendar, however, contains 365 days. The time difference, about a quarter of a day, is made up by having leap years of 366 days every four years. This stops our calendar year getting out of step with the solar year.

Besides travelling around the Sun, the Earth also spins on its axis, an imaginary line joining the poles and the centre of the Earth. One complete revolution of the Earth on its axis takes 24 hours, or one day. When a place on Earth points towards the Sun, it has daylight. When it points away from the Sun, it is dark.

Months were once measured by the movements of the Moon. But the time between one new moon and the next is $29\frac{1}{2}$ days. This bears no relationship to the movement of the Earth around the Sun. So, calendar months are adjusted in length so that 12 months equal one year.

Seasons

Seasons are caused because the Earth's axis is tilted by $23\frac{1}{2}°$. This means that, as the Earth rotates around the Sun, the northern hemisphere is sometimes tilted towards the Sun and sometimes away from it. On about March 21, the Sun is overhead at the equator. This is called the *vernal* or *spring equinox*. After March 21, the northern hemisphere starts to tilt towards the Sun. On June 21, the *summer solstice*, it is overhead at the Tropic of Cancer ($23\frac{1}{2}°$ North latitude). The overhead Sun then moves southwards until, on September 23, the *autumn equinox*, it is overhead at the equator. The southern hemisphere then tilts towards the Sun until, on December 21, the *winter solstice*, the Sun is overhead at the Tropic of Capricorn ($23\frac{1}{2}°$ South latitude). After December 21, the overhead Sun moves northwards and the cycle of seasons starts all over again.

The Moon and Tides

The Moon causes rises and falls in sea level, called tides. As the Moon rotates around the Earth every 24 hours and 50 minutes, there are two high and two low tides. Tides occur because, when the Moon is overhead at any place, it exerts a gravitational pull on the waters beneath it, causing a high tide. This pull is balanced by a second high tide on the far side of the Earth. The highest, *spring*, tides occur when the Moon, Earth and Sun are in a straight line. The gravitational pull of the Moon and Sun is then combined. The lowest, *neap*, tides occur when the Moon, Earth and Sun form a right angle, so that the pull of the Sun and Moon are opposed.

Below: As the Moon goes round the Earth, its gravity pulls the oceans directly underneath it. This causes the tides. The Sun has a smaller pulling effect too, so the biggest tides happen when the Sun and Moon are in line.

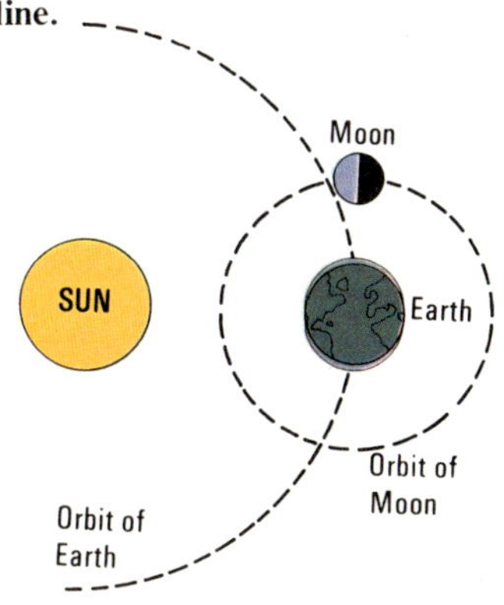

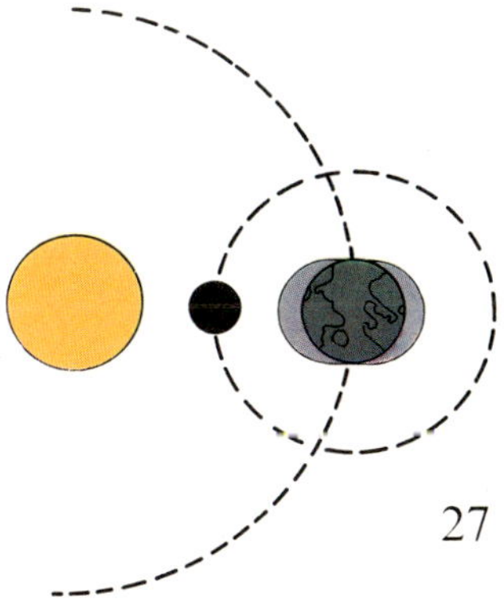

The Atmosphere

There are four main layers defined in the atmosphere. They are defined according to their distance above the Earth and their particular properties.

The exosphere is the highest layer of our atmosphere. UHF (ultra-high frequency) radio waves pass right through it into space.

The ionosphere is between 80 and 500 kilometres (50 and 300 miles) above the ground. Particles from the Sun disturb the ionosphere and make the glowing curtains of light called auroras. Air resistance makes meteors begin to burn. Artificial satellites orbit the Earth at this level. Short, medium and long radio waves are bounced back to Earth from the ionosphere.

The stratosphere is over 60 kilometres (37 miles) thick. Cosmic rays hit atoms in the stratosphere and make weaker cosmic rays that bombard the Earth. Cirrus clouds made of ice crystals reach 12,000 metres. Jet airliners fly in the lower stratosphere.

The troposphere is between 16 and 8 kilometres thick. Nine-tenths of all the air is in the troposphere. As you rise through the troposphere the temperature drops 7°C for every 1,000 metres.

CLOUDS

There are, broadly, two kinds of clouds. *Cumuliform* or 'heap' clouds rise upwards from a flat base. *Stratiform* or 'layer' clouds form thin blankets across the sky. Meteorologists classify 10 main cloud types, grouped according to their height. Five are low clouds – that is, they usually occur up to 2500 metres. They are *stratus*, a uniform grey cloud; *cumulus*, a white heap cloud; *cumulonimbus*, or thundercloud, the upper part of which often resembles an anvil; *nimbostratus*, a grey or dark layer, often blurred by falling rain and snow; and *stratocumulus*, a greyish-white, shaded sheet of cloud. Medium clouds occur between about 2500 and 6100 metres above the ground. Medium clouds are *altocumulus*, a greyish-white cloud composed of rounded masses which often merge; and *altostratus*, a greyish sheet of cloud often seen as depressions approach. High clouds, above 6100 metres, include *cirrocumulus*, a thin patch of cloud, showing ripples or rounded masses; *cirrostratus*, a fibrous, transparent, whitish cloud, which may cause a 'halo' around the Sun or Moon; and *cirrus*, a delicate white, fibrous cloud.

The Air Around Us

The atmosphere is an envelope of gases surrounding the Earth. The main gases are nitrogen (78.09 per cent), life-giving oxygen (20.95 per cent) and argon (0.93 per cent). The lowest layer of the atmosphere, the *troposphere*, contains about 90 per cent of all the air in the atmosphere. The troposphere on average is about 18 km thick over the equator and 8 km over the poles. Above the troposphere are other zones where the air gets thinner and thinner, until the atmosphere finally merges into space.

An invisible substance, called *water vapour*, is present in the air. It is mostly water evaporated from the oceans. Water vapour condenses (liquefies) around specks of dust and salt in the air. These tiny, visible water droplets form clouds, from which we get a regular supply of fresh water, in the form of rain or snow.

Winds are air currents which ensure that the atmosphere is always on the move. The main cause of winds is heat from the Sun. This makes air rise in the tropics. Currents of air from north and south flow in to replace it.

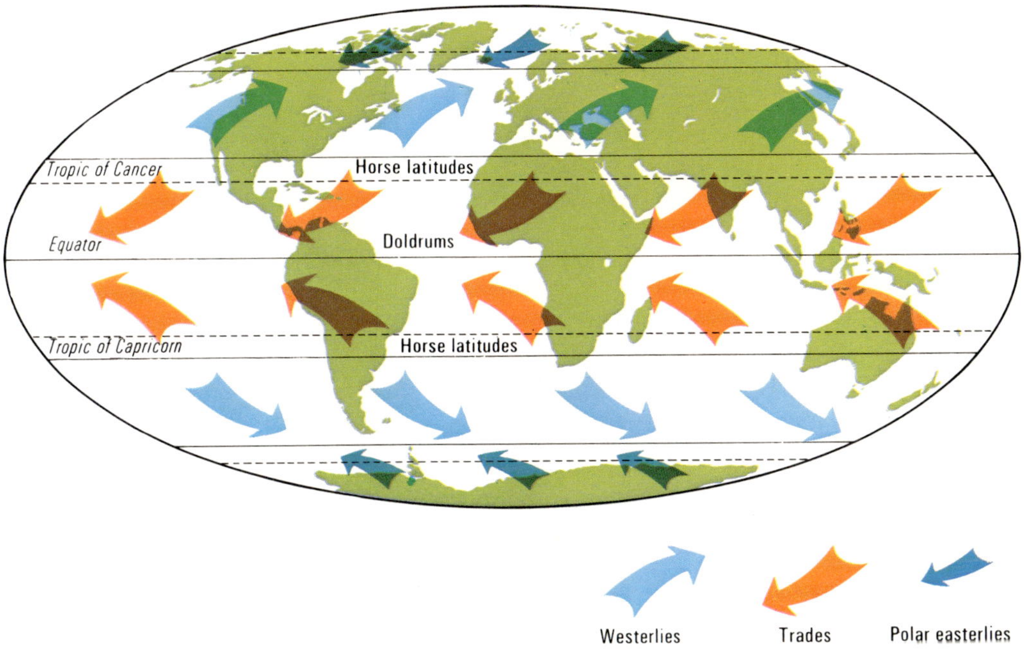

Right: This map shows the world's main wind belts. Winds are named after the areas they blow from. Knowledge of these winds was very important to sailors in the days of sailing ships.

World Climates

When we talk of the climate of a place, we mean the typical, or average, weather of the place. For example, the Mediterranean climate has hot, dry summers and mild, moist winters. This does not mean that no rain ever falls in summer. But it does mean that, on average, summers are dry and most rain falls in winter.

Factors Which Affect Climate

One factor which affects climate is latitude, because the Sun's heat is most intense at the equator. At the poles, more of the Sun's heat is absorbed by the atmosphere and the Sun's rays are spread over a large land area. Hence, climates are generally hottest near the equator and get cooler towards the poles.

Some other factors, however, complicate this simple pattern. For example, temperatures fall as one climbs above sea-level by about 7°C for every 1000 metres. Even near the equator, the highest mountains have snow at the top all the year round. Mountains also affect rainfall. Warm winds from the oceans rise when they meet mountain ranges. As they rise, the air cools and cannot hold its water vapour which, finally, falls as rain. But, when the winds descend on the far side of the mountains, the air becomes warmer. It tends to pick up moisture and so there is little rain.

Another factor is the nearness of a place to the sea, because water heats up more slowly than land and also cools more slowly. For example, coastal lands heat up quickly in summer. The warm air rises, creating low air pressures. Cooler air from the sea is sucked into the low pressure area, cooling the land. In winter, the opposite occurs. Warm winds from the sea blow on to the cold land, making the climate milder.

Far from the seas, however, large air masses form. In summer, warm, low pressure air masses

Right: A map of the world's climates. Tropical climates have average temperatures of more than 18°C in every month of the year. They have heavy rainfall and no winter season. Cold moist climates cover a broad belt in northern America, Europe and Siberia in Russia. These regions have evergreen forests of conifers which can stand up to the cold, snowy winters and short, cool summers. Dry climates have less than 250 millimetres of rain in a year. They include deserts and steppelands.

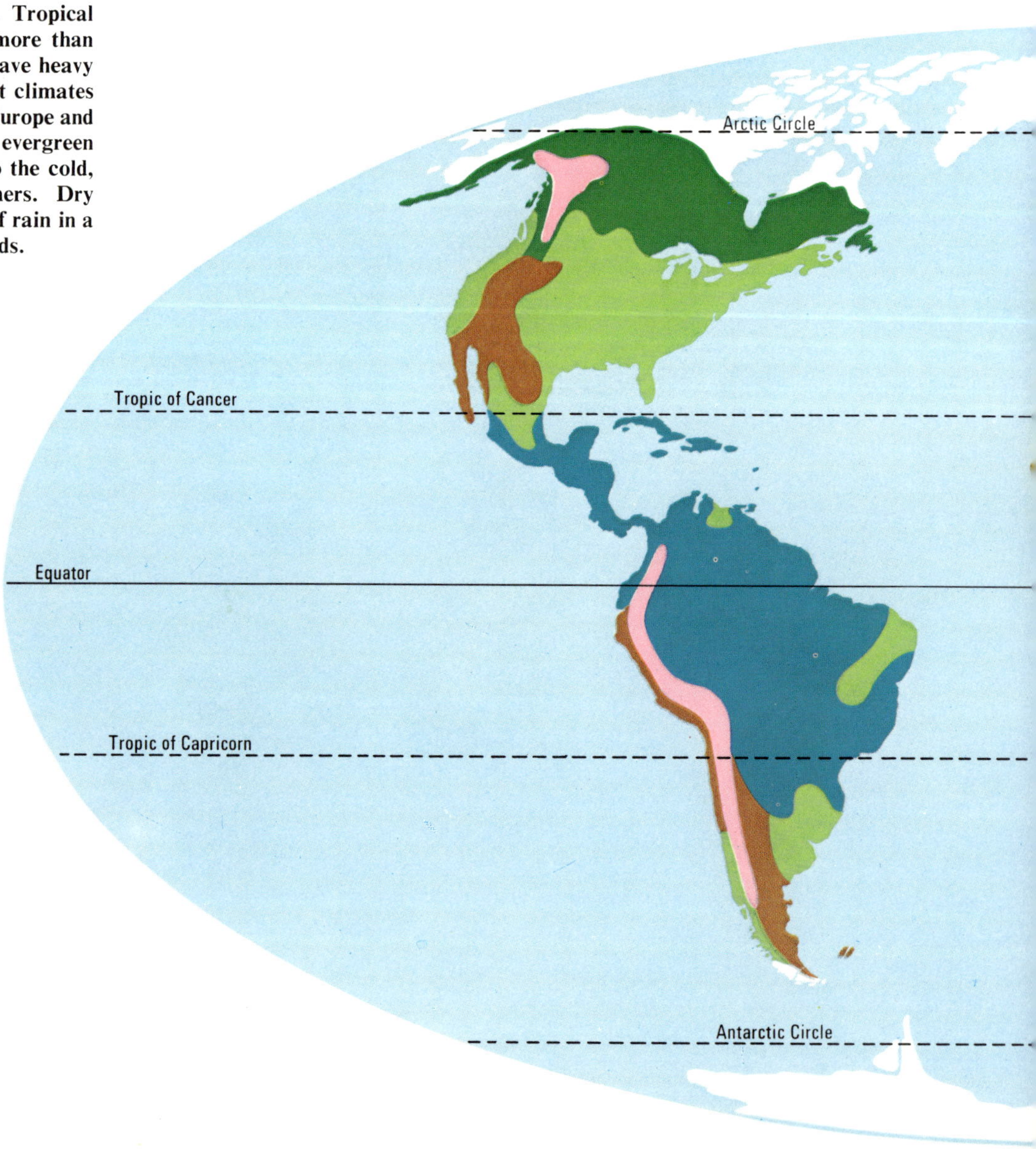

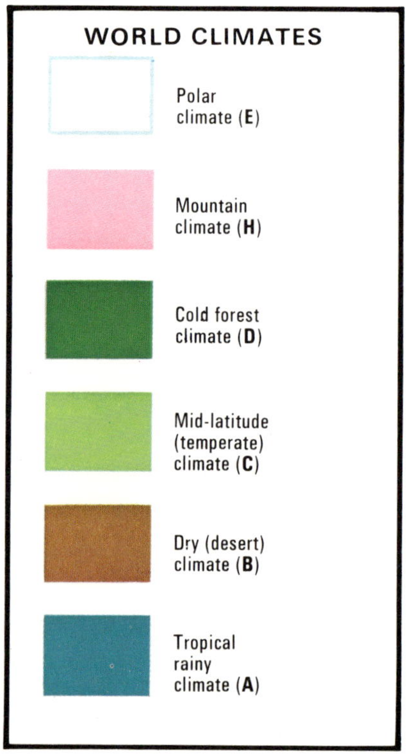

The main vegetation regions depend not only on their location, but also on their height above sea level.

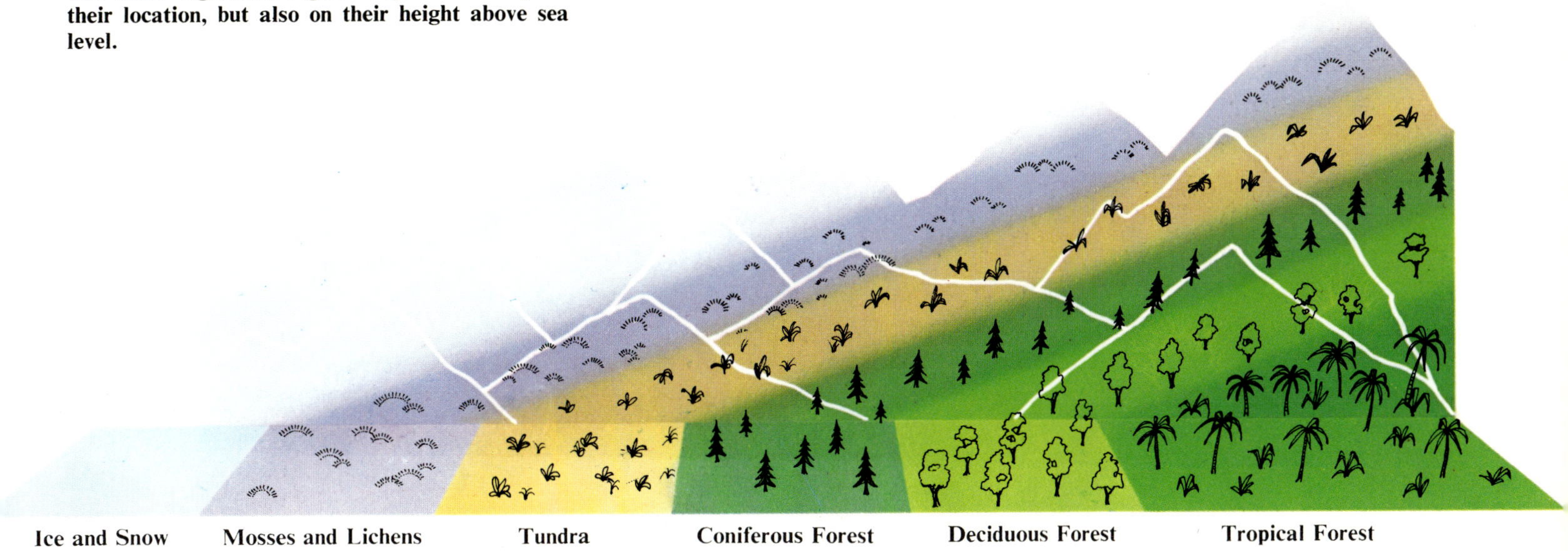

develop, while, in winter, cold, high pressure air masses form. They affect the climate of nearby lands. For example, icy winds blow out from the cold air masses which cover the hearts of North America, Europe and Asia in winter.

Climatic Regions

In climate, the chief weather features are temperature and rainfall. The world's main climatic regions are based on average temperatures and rainfall figures measured over many years.

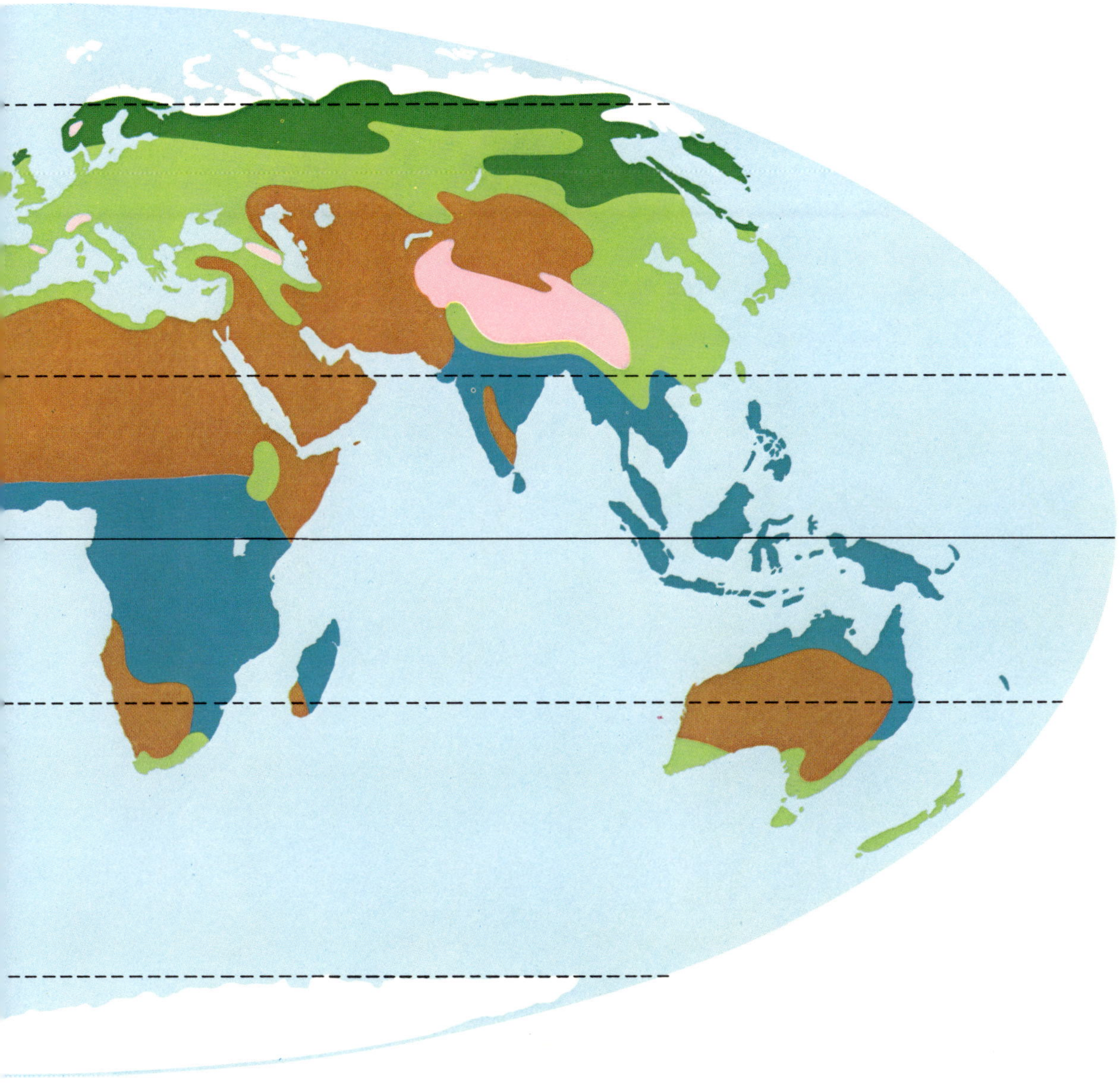

Below: Two views of the world as seen from space. They help us to realize that the oceans cover nearly three-quarters of the Earth's surface.

Water and Weather

Without a regular supply of fresh water, there would be no life on land. The fresh water reaches the land via the *water cycle*. The first stage of the cycle occurs when the Sun evaporates water from the oceans. Water vapour is swept upwards into the air, where clouds form. The clouds bring rain and snow to land areas.

The water returns to the oceans through rivers or by seeping through rocks. Rivers shape the land. They wear it away, transport the worn material, and deposit it along coasts or on the sea bed.

(1) A glacier of snow and ice melts into (2) a lake. (3) Water runs from the lake, on its way dropping down a waterfall (4) and cutting a steep gorge (5). It slows down as the land flattens and meanders across the lowland (6). Sometimes the river changes direction, leaving an isolated ox-bow lake (7). Eventually the river flows across the flood plain (8) and out into the sea (9).

MAKING WEATHER INSTRUMENTS

You can set up a simple weather station in the garden using home-made instruments. Take your instrument readings at the same times each day. Note down the general condition of the atmosphere—cloudy, sunny, rainy and so on.

A weather vane. Fix a piece of plywood to the end of a wooden rod. With a nail, fix the rod to the baseboard. Mark the compass points on the board. Mount it on top of a pole.

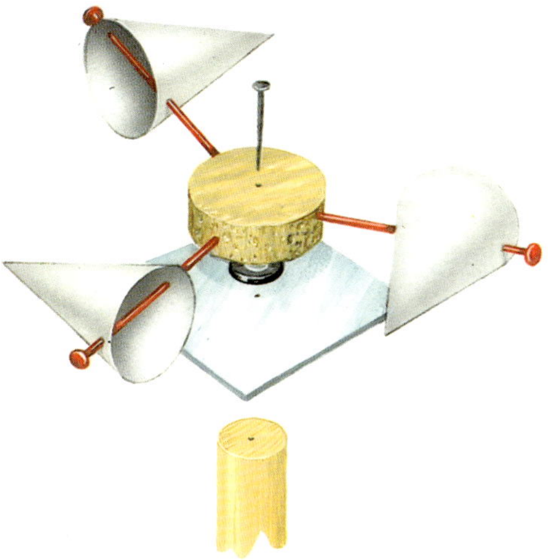

An anemometer (above) measures wind speed. Roll sheets of paper into cones, or use yoghurt cartons. Stick knitting needles through the cups and into a cork. Drill a hole in the middle of the cork so that it can rotate freely on a nail. Nail it to a board, with a washer or bead beneath it to reduce friction. Mount the board on a tall pole. The speed at which the anemometer spins gives an idea of the wind speed.

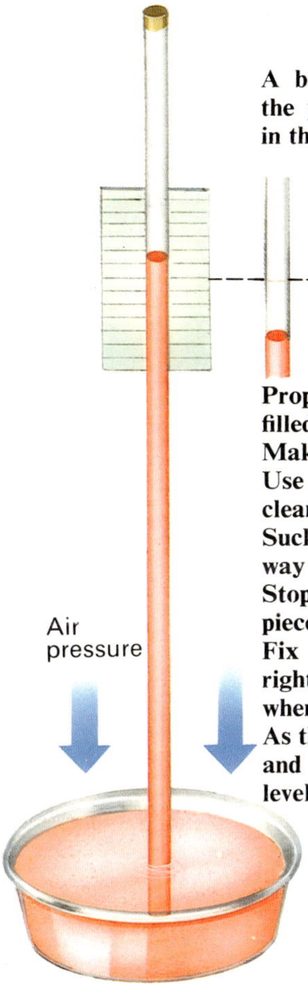

A barometer measures the pressure of the air in the atmosphere.

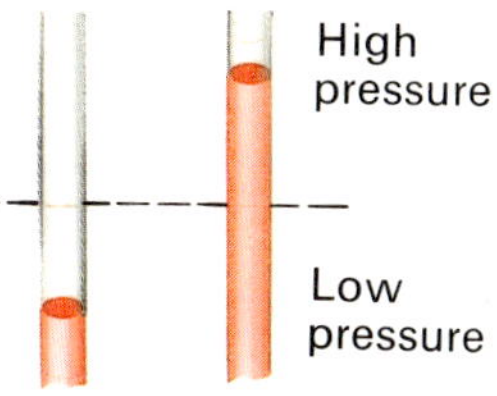

Proper barometers are filled with mercury. Make one using water. Use a long piece of clear plastic tubing. Suck water part of the way up it from a bowl. Stop up the top with a piece of plasticine. Fix the tube to an upright. Place a scale where the water level is. As the air pressure rises and falls, so the water level will rise and fall.

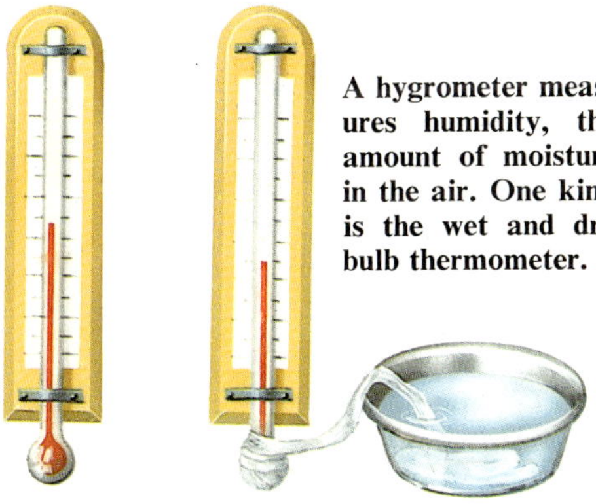

A hygrometer measures humidity, the amount of moisture in the air. One kind is the wet and dry bulb thermometer.

Take two thermometers. Wrap damp cloth around the bulb of one. The cooling effect of evaporation causes this thermometer to read lower than the other.

The humidity can be worked out from the difference between the two.

When humidity is low, water from the damp cloth evaporates quickly and cools the thermometer. When the humidity is high, evaporation is slower; the difference between the two thermometers is smaller.

A rain gauge to measure rainfall. Place a funnel in a tin can, making sure it fits securely. If the can is exactly the same diameter as the funnel mouth, measure the rainfall with a ruler. If not, put a collecting jar inside the can and make a scale for it.

Weather Forecasting

Weather stations around the world make regular measurements of weather conditions. They measure temperatures, rainfall, wind speeds and directions, air pressures, humidity, and so on with various instruments. The information is sent to local weather forecasting stations.

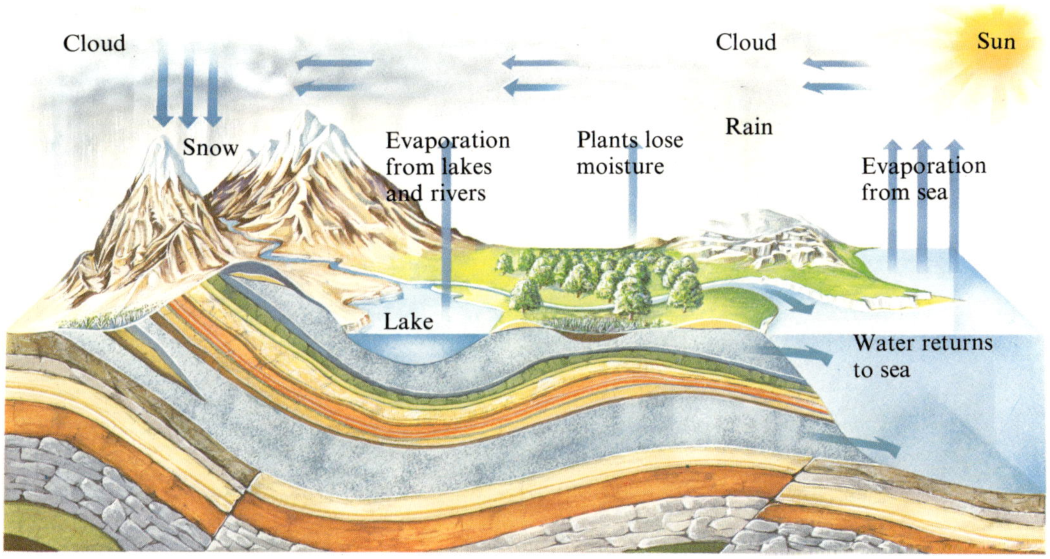

The Sun's heat draws up water vapour from the sea and land. The rising vapour turns into droplets that become clouds. Clouds drop their moisture as rain, hail or snow. The water runs into rivers or seeps into the ground. All this water in time finds its way to the sea. This process is called the water cycle.

Drifting Continents

In the early 1900s, some scientists noticed that the shapes of the edges of the Americas resembled those of Europe and Africa. They suggested that the continents had once been linked, but they could not prove this theory.

Evidence from the Oceans

In the 1940s and 1950s, studies were made of the ocean floor. Mapping of the oceans showed the true edges of the continents, which extend under the sea to the edges of the shallow continental shelves. The edges of the shelves on both sides of the Atlantic Oceans fitted together even better than the coastlines.

Rocks taken from the ocean floor were found to be no more than 200 million years old. They are, therefore, quite young rocks compared with many in the continents. The youngest rocks are around huge, underwater mountain ranges, called ocean ridges. These ridges are the centres of earthquake and volcanic activity.

Plate Tectonics

In the late 1960s, scientists produced the theory of plate tectonics. They showed that the Earth's crust is split into huge blocks, called *plates*, and that these plates are moving. The centres of the ocean ridges are plate edges, where new rock is being formed as molten material wells up from the mantle. The addition of this new rock is pushing the plates apart, widening the oceans. Also, some rocks in the upper mantle are liquid. They move in currents and, as they move, they carry the plates with them.

In other parts of the oceans, plates are being destroyed. These parts of the oceans are the deep ocean *trenches*, where one plate is being pushed down beneath another. As it descends, it is melted. The ocean trenches, therefore, are a second kind of plate edge.

The third kind of plate edge is a long *fault* (crack) in the Earth's crust, where two plates are sliding alongside each other. When the plates move, the ground shakes.

Effects of Plate Movements

The plate theory has helped us to understand how earthquakes and volcanic eruptions occur. It also explains how high mountain ranges are squeezed up from rocks on the sea floor when plates collide and push against each other. Also, evidence suggests that, 200 million years ago, all the continents were joined together in a super-continent, called *Pangaea*. Pangaea then split up and the continents drifted slowly to their present positions.

The biggest changes in the face of the Earth are caused by powerful slow-moving currents within the mantle. They split the crust, shuffle continents around, and build great mountain ranges.

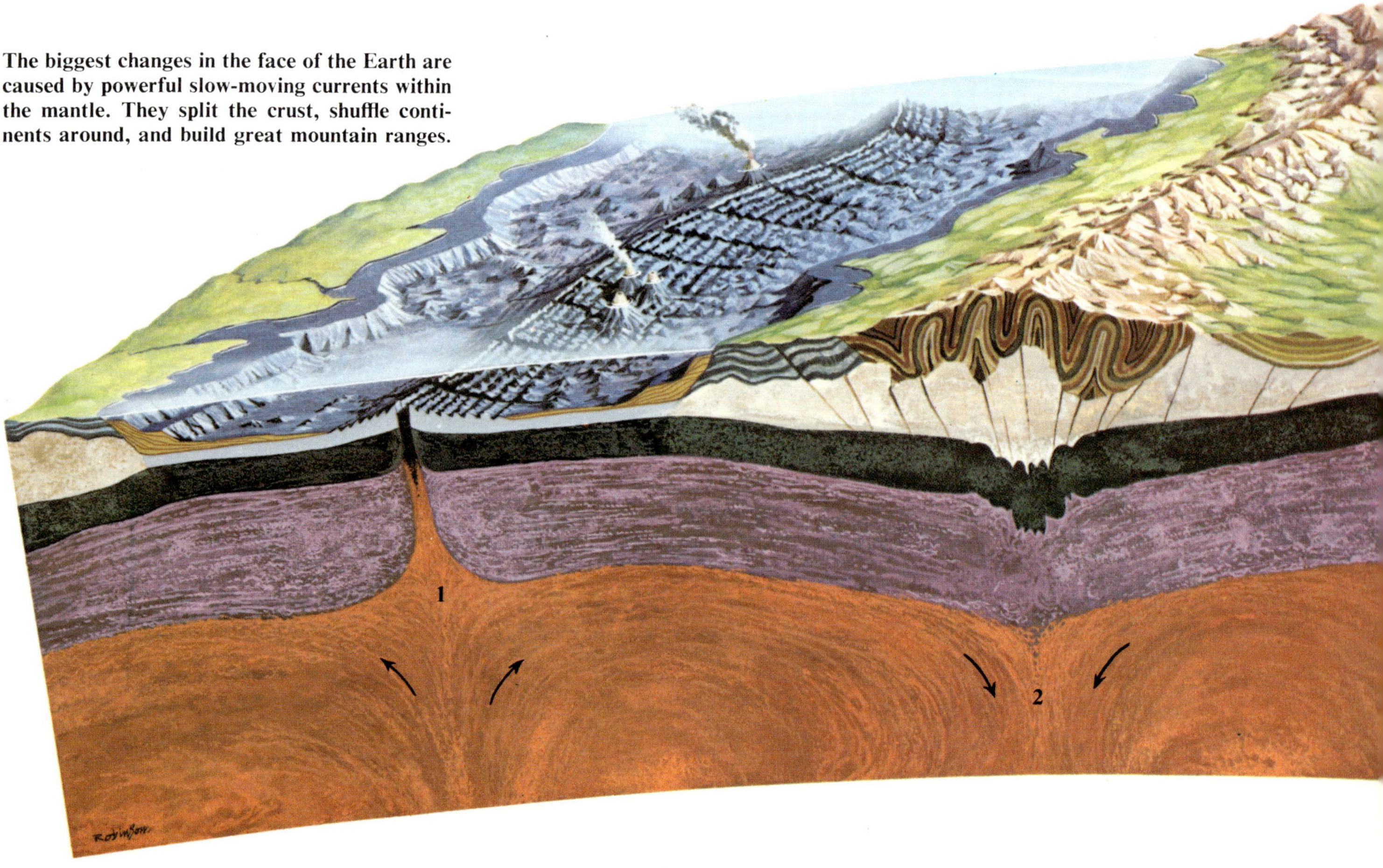

Below: Where a 'hot spot' of upwelling mantle occurs, the earth's crust is driven apart (1). Where two plates collide (2), mountain ranges are formed. If the collision is rapid (3), one plate may be driven deep into the Earth. The plate on top may be lifted and crumpled to form mountains with volcanoes and earthquakes. Sideways plate movements (4) cause pieces of the crust to slide past each other and trigger off earthquakes. Above: The ocean floor is also covered with mountains and ridges. Around each continent is a shelf of shallow water.

Volcanoes

Volcanoes are evidence of the turbulent forces at work inside the Earth. When volcanoes erupt, they eject molten rock, called *magma*, which is formed at great depths. At the surface, the molten magma may be exploded into the air in broken fragments, ranging from fine hot dust to large lumps called volcanic bombs, or it may spill out in runny streams of lava.

Quiet volcanoes, such as those on Hawaii, discharge little gas, so there are no explosive eruptions.

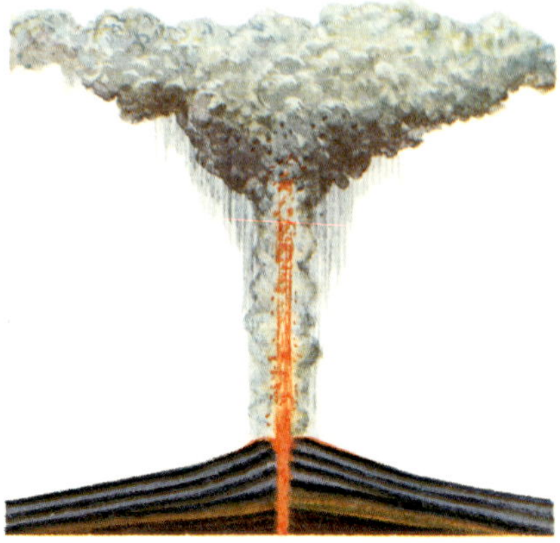

Explosive volcanoes erupt dramatically, shooting clouds of hot ash and rock into the air.

Many volcanoes are made up of layers of ash, dust and lava (1). The volcano's vent (2) goes down to molten rock called magma (3). Other vents cut through the volcano (4). Sheets of magma squeeze through the rock to form dykes (5). Horizontal sheets of magma (6) are called sills. Magma is sometimes forced up but does not reach the surface. It forms dome-shaped mounds (7). Extinct volcanoes (8) often have craters, sometimes filled with water. Lava sometimes streams out of cracks in the ground (9). In some volcanic regions there are geysers (10).

When Mt Pelée erupted in 1902, a *nuée ardente* (glowing cloud) of hot gas and dust rolled downhill.

Vesuvius, an intermediate volcano, exploded in AD 79. The violent eruption expelled great clouds of ashes which were distributed over a wide area.

Above: In Rotorua, New Zealand, huge mudpools have formed in waterlogged ground. Heat from deep inside the Earth makes them boil and bubble.

Most volcanoes are near plate edges. Some lie on the ocean ridges, while others are alongside the ocean trenches, where one plate is forced beneath another. The descending plate is melted and the resulting magma may rise to the surface under pressure. Some volcanoes, however, are far from plate edges. The magma for these volcanoes is probably caused by radioactive heat in the mantle.

There are about 450 active volcanoes on land and 80 or so on the ocean floor. The exact number is unknown, because, in the past, volcanoes thought to be extinct have erupted. Eruptions can cause enormous damage. Many active volcanoes in populated areas are now closely watched by scientists, who look out for any changes on the surface caused by pressure from below.

Atoms and Molecules

Atoms are tiny particles of matter that make up all the solids, liquids and gases in the universe. There are only just over a hundred basic kinds of atoms. But these can combine in many ways to form thousands of different substances.

Atoms are not the smallest particles of matter. For they are composed of even smaller particles called protons, neutrons and electrons. At the centre, or nucleus, of an atom the heavier protons and neutrons are formed. The protons have a positive charge, while the neutrons have no charge. Orbiting around the nucleus are the much-lighter electrons. Normally, an atom has the same number of electrons as protons. Each electron has a negative charge as strong as the positive charge of a proton. As a result, the charges cancel each other out.

Above: Atoms are so small that if an atom were the size of your little finger nail, then your hand would be large enough to grasp the Earth!

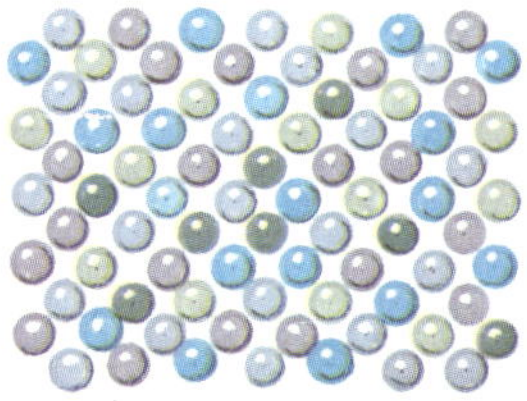

Solid

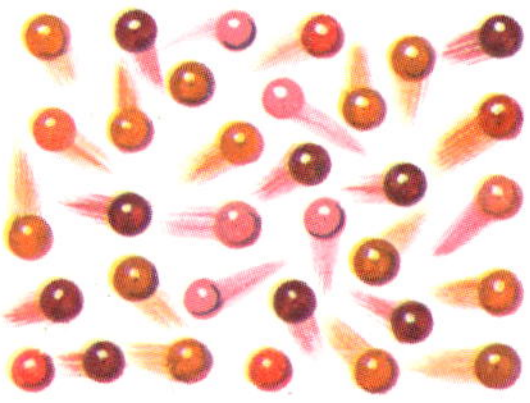

Liquid

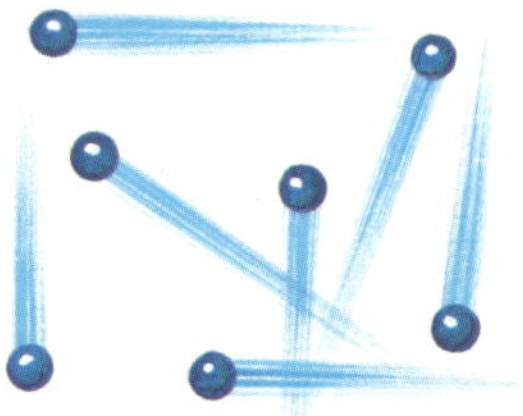

Gas

Left: In a solid, the atoms or molecules that make it up are packed tightly together. So solids are strong enough to support themselves, and sometimes other objects too. In a liquid the atoms or molecules have a looser arrangement. The liquid can flow. In gases the atoms or molecules are not arranged in any way. They can move apart until the gas fills its container.

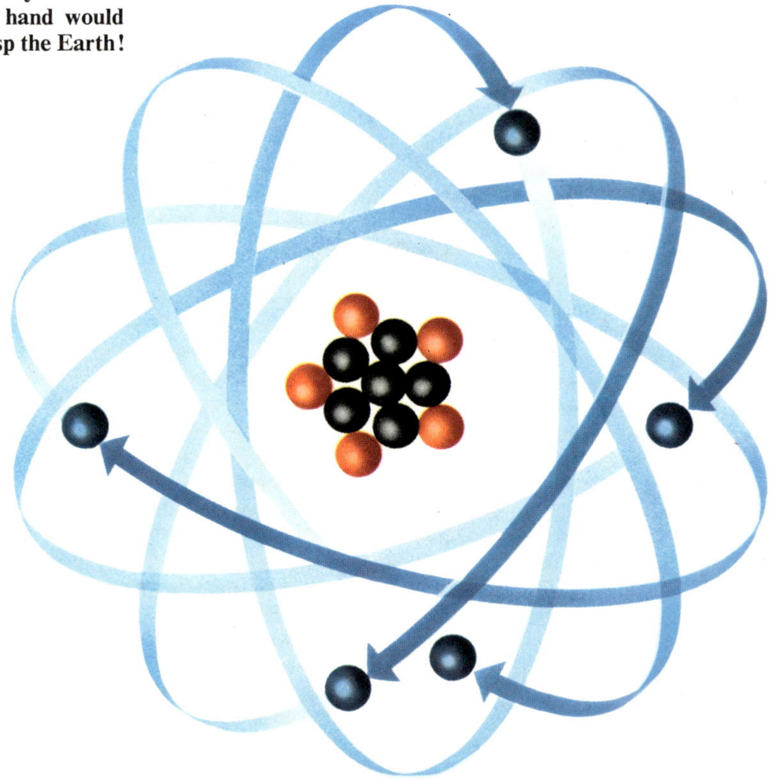

Right: An atom is made up of a positively charged centre or nucleus, made up of protons and neutrons, surrounded by whizzing negatively charged particles called electrons. The atom of boron shown here has five protons, six neutrons and five electrons.

An atom has a tiny central nucleus surrounded by electrons. If the nucleus were the size of a lift button, the whole atom would be as big as a skyscraper.

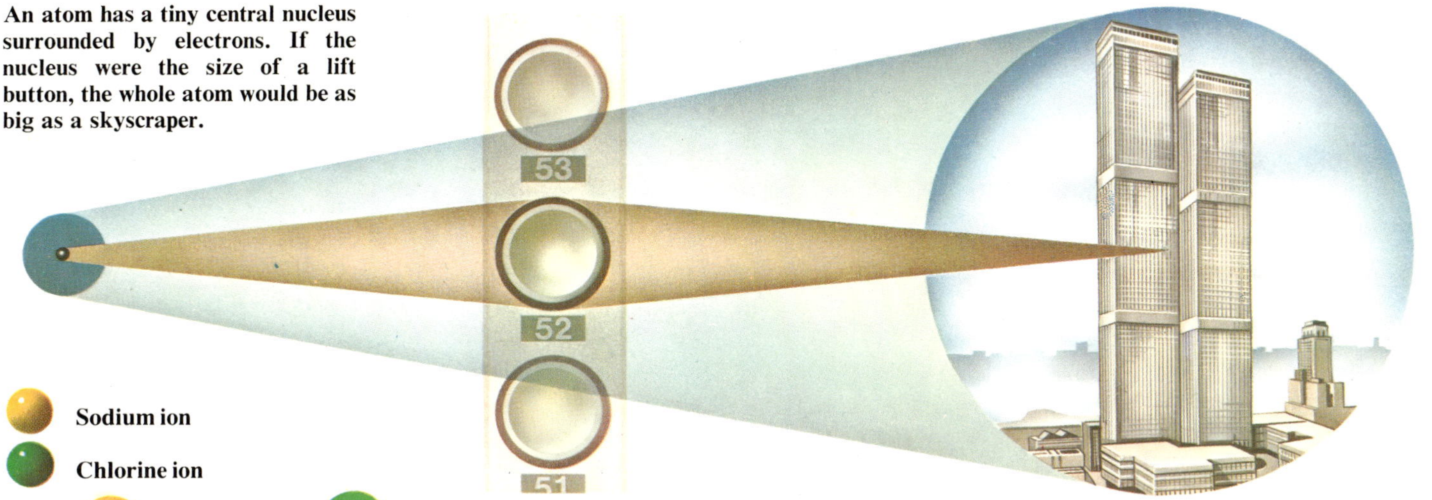

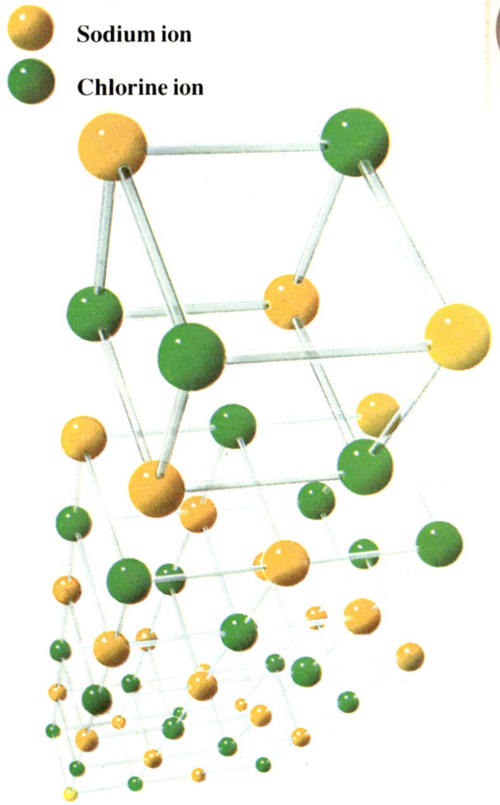

Because the charges inside the atom balance, there is no overall charge. However, it is quite easy to upset this balance by altering the number of electrons. If the atom gains electrons, it will have an overall negative charge. If it loses electrons it becomes positively charged. When an atom, or group of atoms, becomes charged in this way, it is called an ion.

Elements are substances made up from atoms which contain the same number of protons. This number, called the atomic number, is how we tell one element from another. Common elements include carbon (atomic number 6), oxygen (8) and iron (26).

Groups of atoms joined together are called molecules. An oxygen molecule, for example, consists of two oxygen atoms. A substance whose molecules contain more than one kind of atom is called a compound. For example, in the compound carbon dioxide, each molecule contains one carbon atom and two oxygen atoms.

In any element, although each atom has the same number of protons, the number of neutrons usually varies. Atoms of the same element which contain different numbers of neutrons, are called isotopes of that element.

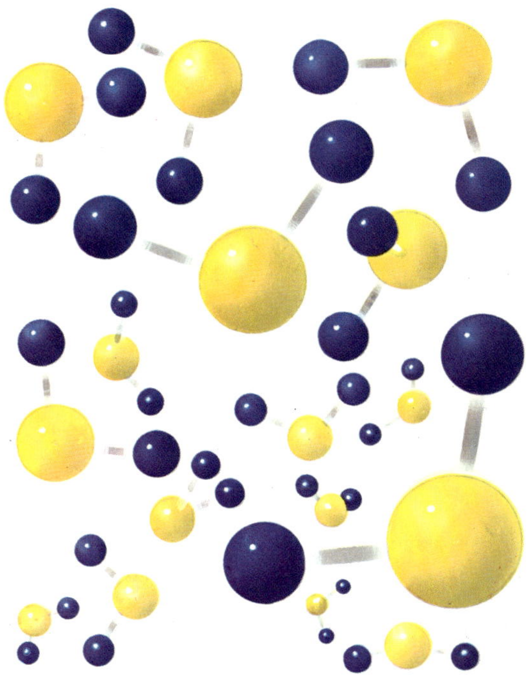

Left, above: Common salt or sodium chloride is made up of sodium and chlorine atoms joined together in a cube-shaped network.

Left, below: Water consists of many separate molecules of water. Each one is made up of two hydrogen atoms and one oxygen atom joined together by bonds.

Right: Comb your hair strongly and some of the hairs will stick to the comb. As you move the comb in your hair electrons are rubbed from the atoms in your hair to the atoms in the comb. The comb gains a negative charge and the hair a positive charge. Unlike charges attract, so the charged hairs are attracted to the comb. The hair then regains its lost electrons, the difference in charge disappears, and the hair drops back towards your head.

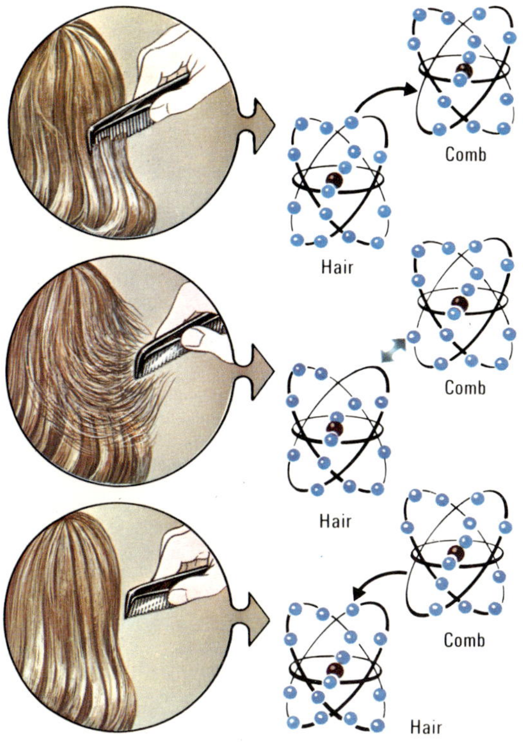

Power from the Atom

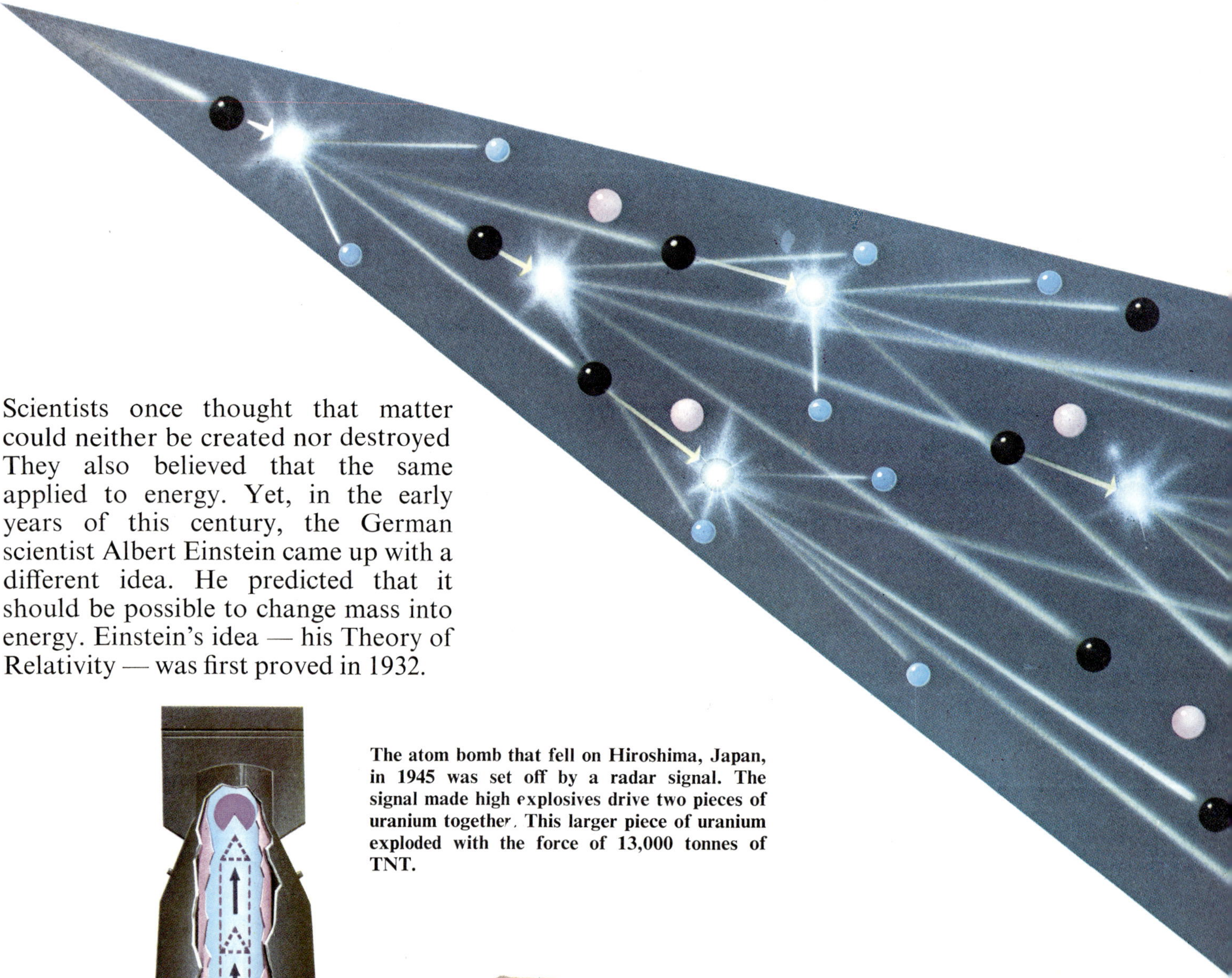

Scientists once thought that matter could neither be created nor destroyed They also believed that the same applied to energy. Yet, in the early years of this century, the German scientist Albert Einstein came up with a different idea. He predicted that it should be possible to change mass into energy. Einstein's idea — his Theory of Relativity — was first proved in 1932.

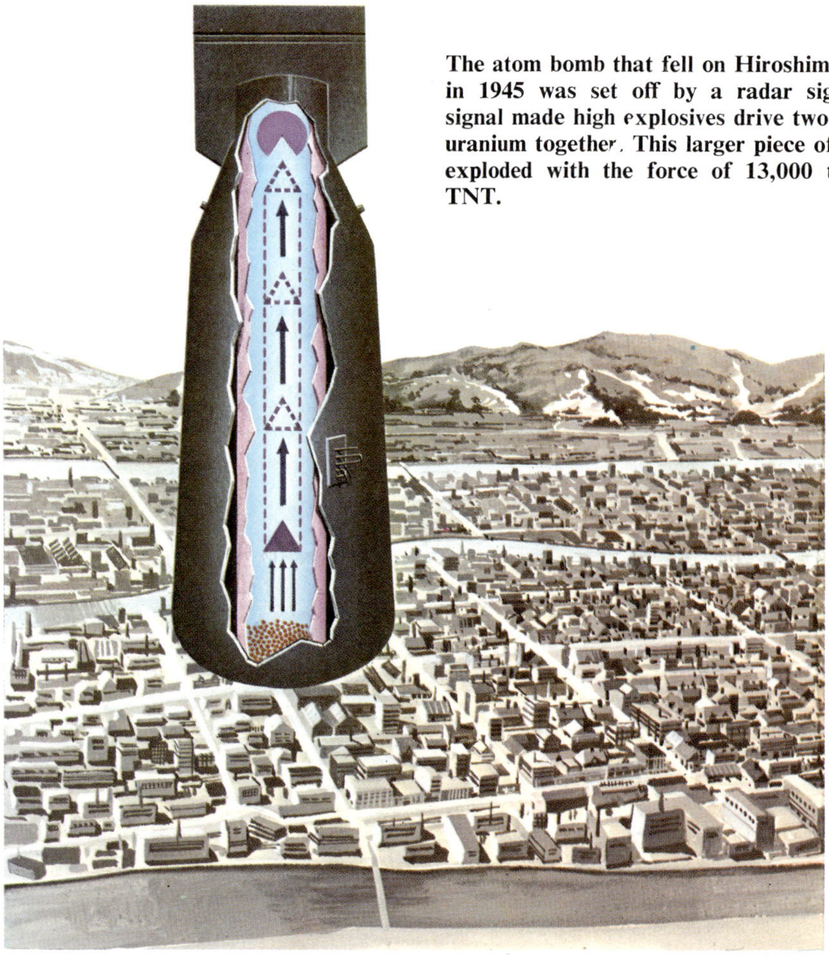

The atom bomb that fell on Hiroshima, Japan, in 1945 was set off by a radar signal. The signal made high explosives drive two pieces of uranium together. This larger piece of uranium exploded with the force of 13,000 tonnes of TNT.

Einstein's theory was proved by British scientists Sir John Cockcroft and Ernest Walton of Ireland who were investigating the nature of the atom. They had built the world's first particle accelerator. This was a long, straight, empty tube, in which protons were passed through a series of cylindrical electrodes. Negative charges on the electrodes attracted the positively charged protons, making them speed up. As the protons left each electrode, they would be given a positive charge. This pushed them away making them speed up still more. By the time the protons reached the far end of the tube, they were travelling extremely fast.

Cockcroft and Walton used the fast-moving protons to bombard atoms of the metal lithium. When one of the atoms was struck by a proton, the nucleus split in two and released a large amount of energy. This energy had been produced by the destruction of matter. The mass of the two parts together was less than that of the original nucleus. The energy released was exactly as predicted by Einstein in his famous mass-energy equation: $E=mc^2$. In this equation, E is energy in joules, m is mass in kilograms and c represents the speed of light in metres per second. The value of c is about 300 million metres per second, making c^2 about 90 thousand million million. So, even a very small mass will release an enormous amount of energy.

In the atomic bomb, this energy is released suddenly in a violent explosion. In a nuclear power station, the nuclear fission (splitting) process is controlled at a certain rate to produce useful heat energy.

Below: A chain reaction starts as a neutron strikes a nucleus of uranium-235. The nucleus breaks apart into two smaller nuclei, and three more neutrons are shot out. These neutrons strike more uranium nuclei, and so on. Little explosions spread rapidly through all the uranium, producing great heat. The whole process takes place in the fraction of a second. This is called nuclear fission.

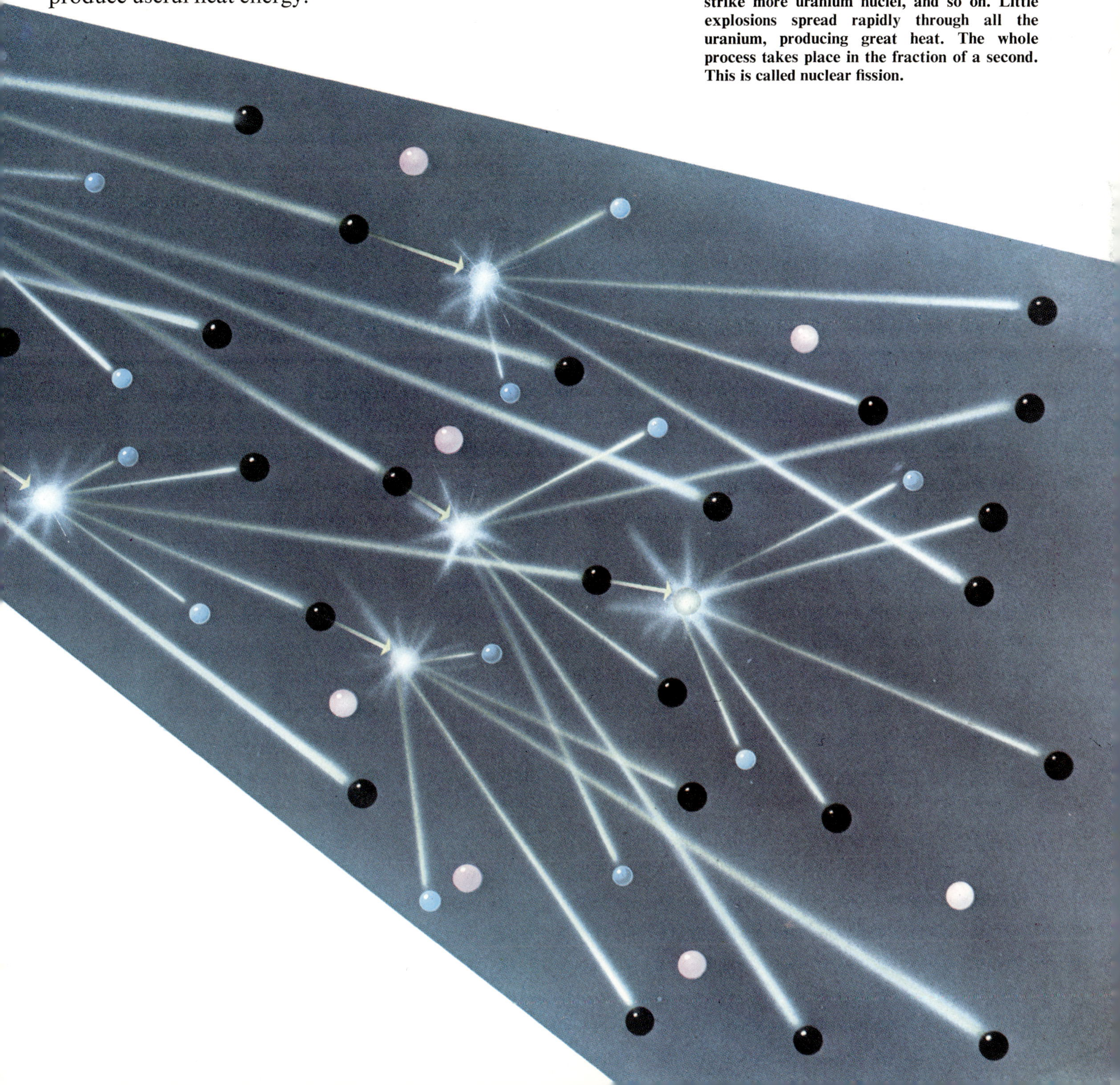

The Nuclear Reactor

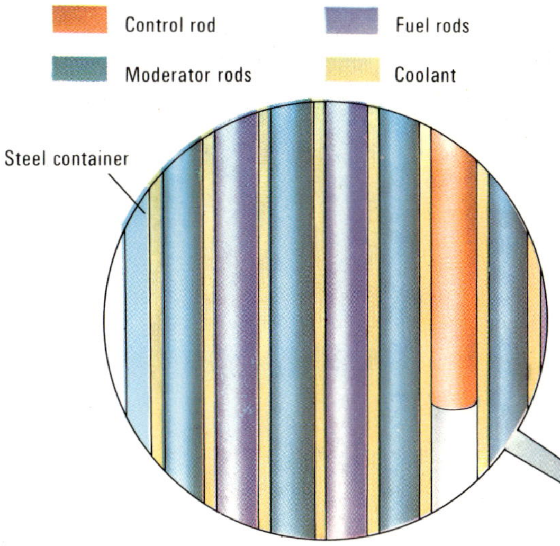

Below: The core of the reactor is built inside a strong steel container. It has fuel rods made of uranium, housed inside tubes. The fuel rods make heat. Control rods can be moved in or out of the reactor to vary the heat produced. The rods are surrounded by moderator rods which slow down the neutrons produced by the fuel. This makes the chain reaction run steadily. Through the core runs a coolant, liquid or gas, to remove heat from the core. It is this hot coolant that supplies the energy to make electricity.

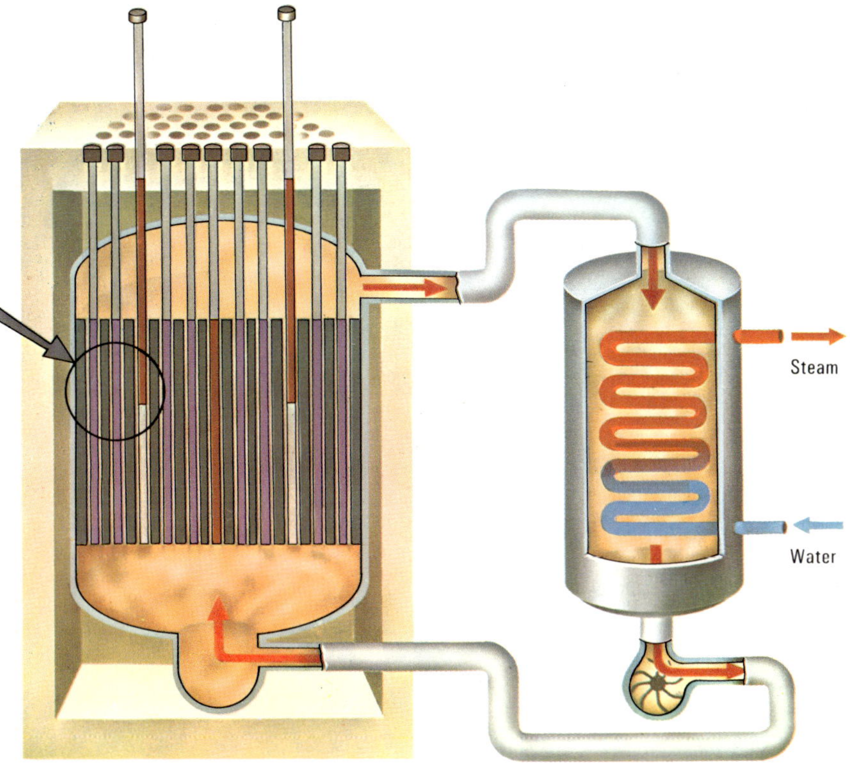

USING NUCLEAR POWER

A reactor is at the centre of every nuclear power system. It can produce plutonium or radioisotopes directly. Otherwise, the reactor's heat is used via a heat exchanger.

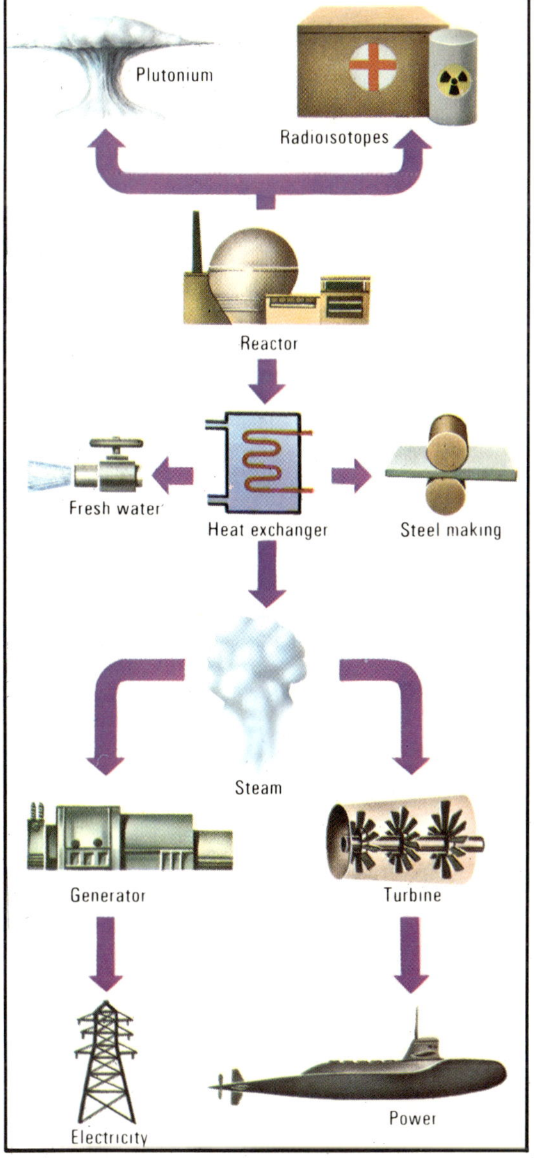

Atomic Power Stations

In atomic power stations, controlled nuclear reactions produce energy in the form of heat. The equipment in which the process takes place is called a nuclear reactor. A suitable fuel, such as uranium-235, is bombarded with a stream of neutrons. These strike some of the uranium atoms, causing fission (splitting) of their nuclei. Energy is released, and more neutrons produced. These collide with other uranium nuclei, and so the reaction continues, releasing energy all the time. Scientists call this self-sustaining process a chain reaction.

The main part of a reactor is called the core. This is a strong steel container in which the chain reaction takes place. The heat produced is extracted by pumping a liquid or gas coolant through the core. Water or carbon dioxide are often used for this purpose. After passing through the core and absorbing heat, the coolant flows through a heat exchanger. Here it passes around a pipe through which water is pumped. The water absorbs heat from the coolant and turns to steam. Then the coolant is pumped back to the core to absorb more heat. The steam produced is used to turn turbines, as in a conventional power station burning oil, coal or gas. The turbines are coupled to generators, which produce electricity.

Future power stations may use fusion reactions, in which atomic nuclei join together with the release of energy. Such reactions produce the devastating power of the hydrogen bomb.

Magnetism

Magnets occur naturally as a mineral called lodestone. This is a magnetic type of black iron oxide, also known as magnetite. Throughout the ages, many people must have noticed the curious way in which this ore attracted pieces of iron. The Greek philosopher Thales of Miletus studied magnetism around 600 BC.

Any magnet, whether natural or man-made, has two regions where its magnetism is strongest. These are known as the magnet's north and south poles. A magnet's north pole should really be called its north-seeking pole. For the magnet tends to swing towards the Earth's North Pole if it is free to move. This is how the magnetic compass works. The Chinese may have used the compass first, but European sailors were using it by the twelfth century.

Right: This series of photographs and diagrams shows how the magnetic field of a magnet changes.

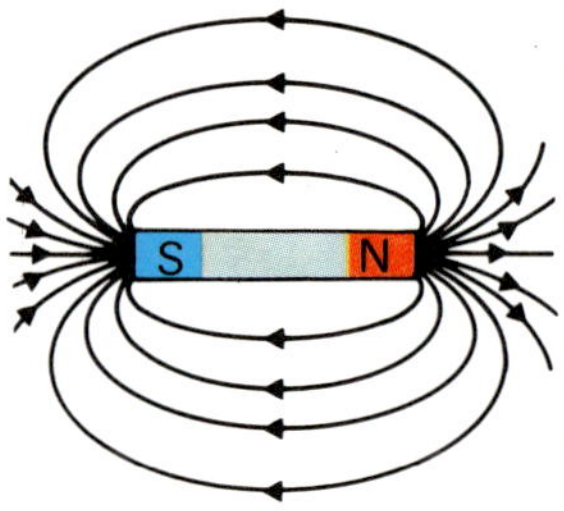

The shape of the magnetic field of force around a magnet can be shown with the help of iron filings. When they are sprinkled around a magnet, they form into loops between the ends, or poles, of the magnet.

The mineral called magnetite is a natural magnet. It is an ore of iron, and will attract iron objects to it.

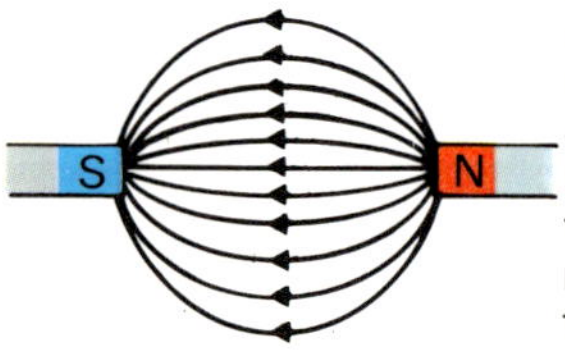

When the pole of one magnet is brought near the pole of another, the magnetic fields affect one another. When one is a north pole and the other a south pole, lines of force link the two magnets. The magnets are drawn together.

MAKE A MAGNET

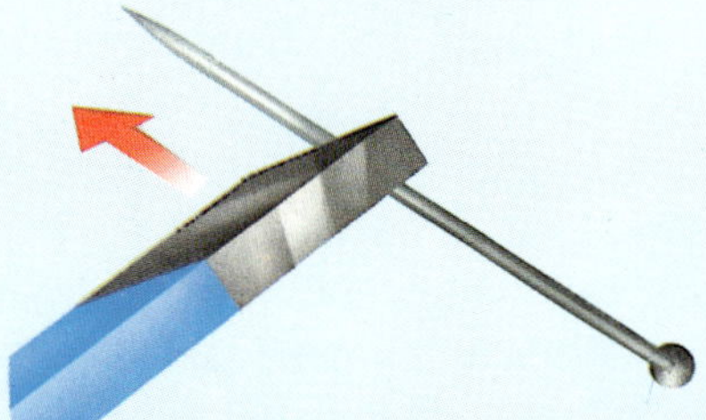

Once you have one magnet, you can easily make others – from steel knitting needles for example. All you do is hold the needle in one hand and stroke it a number of times with one end of your magnet, always in the same direction. Lift the magnet high in the air after each stroke. If you use the north pole of the magnet to stroke the needle, the end of the needle farthest away from you will be a south pole.

If the same poles of two magnets are placed close together, they repel (push away) each other. But the north pole of one magnet will attract the south pole of the other. In other words, like (same) poles repel, and opposite poles attract. You may wonder, therefore, why a magnet's north pole tends to point to the North Pole of the Earth. This is because the Earth's Magnetic North Pole, which is situated near the Geographical North Pole, is really a magnetic south pole.

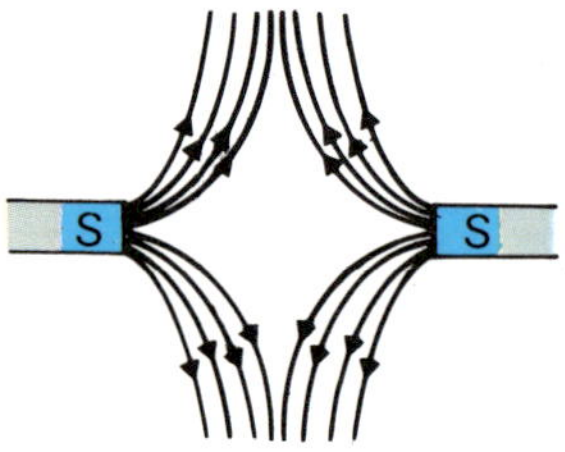

When, however, a north pole is brought near another north pole, the magnetic lines of force loop away from each other. The same thing happens when two south poles are brought together. The magnets push each other away.

Electromagnetism

A Danish physics professor called Hans Christian Oersted found in 1819 that electricity had a magnetic effect. While passing a strong current through a wire, he noticed that a nearby compass needle no longer pointed to the north. But, when he switched off the current, the needle went back to its normal position. This soon led to the production of powerful electromagnets.

A coil was found to give much stronger magnetism than a straight wire, and putting an iron core inside the coil increased the effect still further. Coils used to produce magnetism became known as electromagnets.

When an electric current passed through a straight electromagnet, the iron core behaves like a bar magnet. A north pole is formed at one end, and a south pole at the other. Reversing the direction of the current through the coil makes the north and south poles change ends.

Like ordinary magnets, electromagnets can cause movement. In 1821, Michael Faraday became the first person to use electromagnetism to produce continuous movement. He had invented a form of electric motor. Later, he reversed the process, and found that movement could produce electricity. This is how generators work. Movement between a magnet and coil produces a voltage across the coil.

ELECTRICITY WITH A KICK

You can use the simple apparatus pictured below to show the principle on which the electric motor works. Position the wire loop between the poles of a horseshoe magnet, and make sure that the loop can swing freely in its supports. Make a circuit by connecting the supports through a simple switch to a battery. Press the switch and you will see the loop give a sharp kick.

Turn the magnet over and try again. The loop kicks, but in the opposite direction. Reverse the battery terminals and repeat. The loop kicks in the original direction once more, for you have reversed both the direction of the magnetic field and the electric current.

Remove the magnet and repeat the experiment. Nothing happens, you can now state your conclusions. To obtain a motor effect – a kick – you need both a magnetic field and an electric current. The direction of movement depends on the direction of the field and the current. A practical motor has many loops, or coils, of wire and an iron core to intensify the magnetic field.

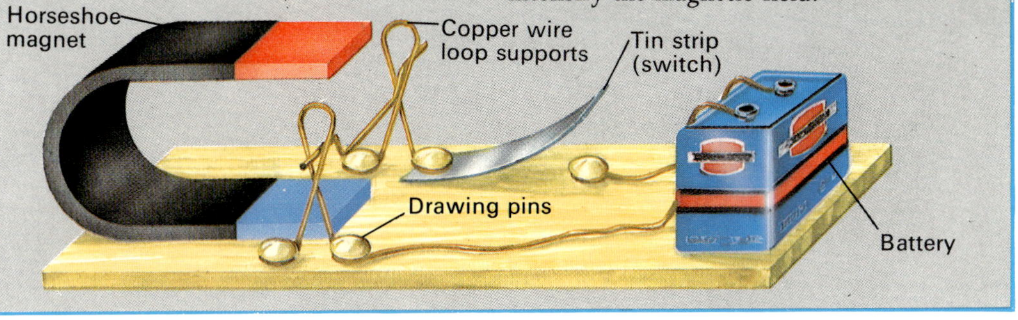

When an electric current flows through a wire, a magnetic field is set up at right angles to it.

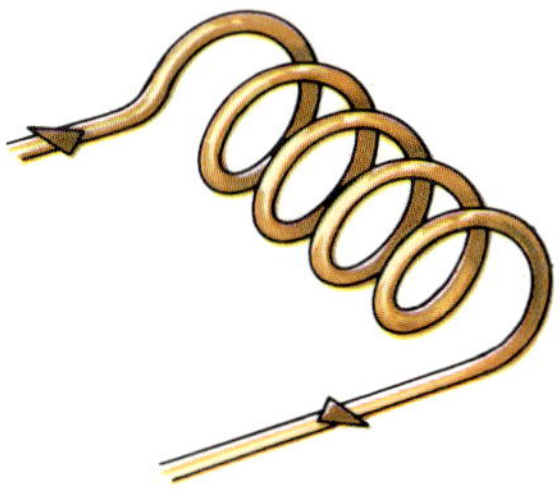

When the wire is coiled, a much stronger field is set up. The coil becomes a magnet while the current flows.

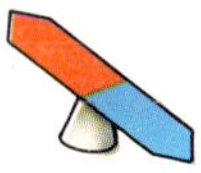

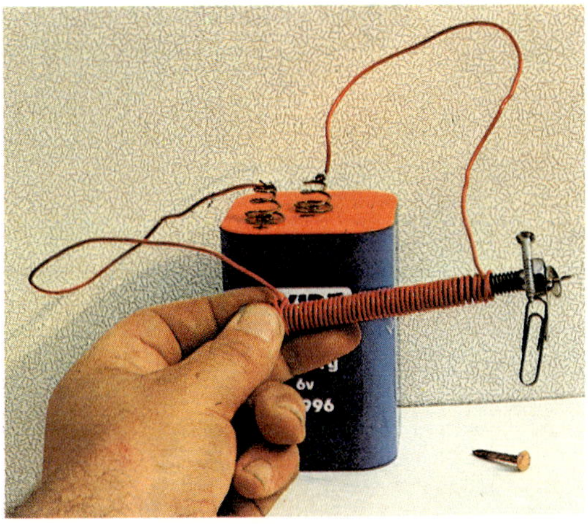

Above: An iron bolt with a coil of insulated wire wound around it acts as an electromagnet. When the ends of the coil are connected to a battery, the bolt becomes magnetized. It attracts small iron or steel objects.

Below right: Transformers can be used to change the strength of an alternating voltage. The step-up transformer, with more turns on the output coil, gives an increase in voltage. The step-down transformer has less turns on the output coil and decreases the voltage.

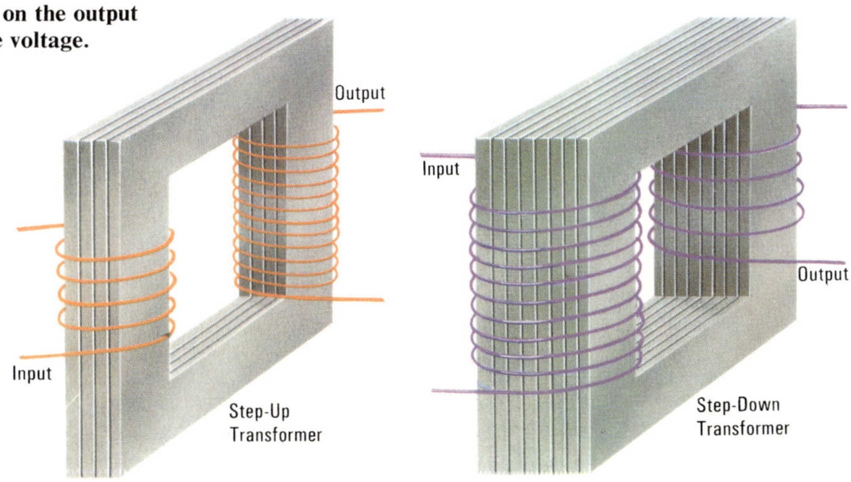

Electricity

Below: These balloons cling to the beam in the ceiling. The attraction is caused by electrical charges, given to the balloons by rubbing them with a woollen cloth.

The word electricity comes from the Greek *elektron*, which means amber. If you rub amber with a cloth it will attract light objects. This fact was discovered in Greece around 600 BC. But the Greeks did not know they were experimenting with static electricity — that is electricity at rest.

Try an experiment. You can charge a toy balloon with electricity by rubbing it with a woollen cloth. It will then attract small pieces of paper or another, uncharged balloon. The cloth, too, will become charged and will attract things to it.

Uncharged objects contain equal numbers of positive and negative charges. But friction between two objects may upset this balance by passing on charges from one object to the other. Here, the balloon ends up with more negative charges than positive, and the cloth has a surplus of positive ones. Charged objects attract uncharged objects, or those of opposite charge. But two objects with similar charges repel each other.

An electric current is a flow of electric charge. Cells, batteries and generators supply current for numerous appliances.

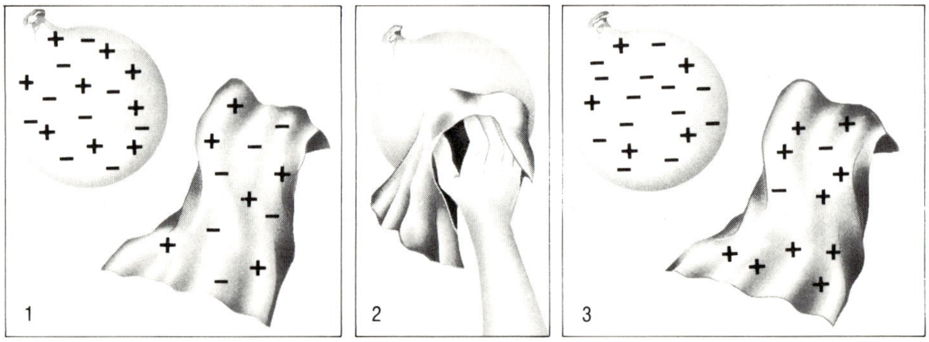

Above: A balloon can be charged by rubbing with a woollen cloth. Initially (1), both have a balanced number of positive and negative charges. Rubbing the balloon (2), causes negative charges to transfer to it. So the balloon becomes negatively charged and the cloth becomes positively charged (3).

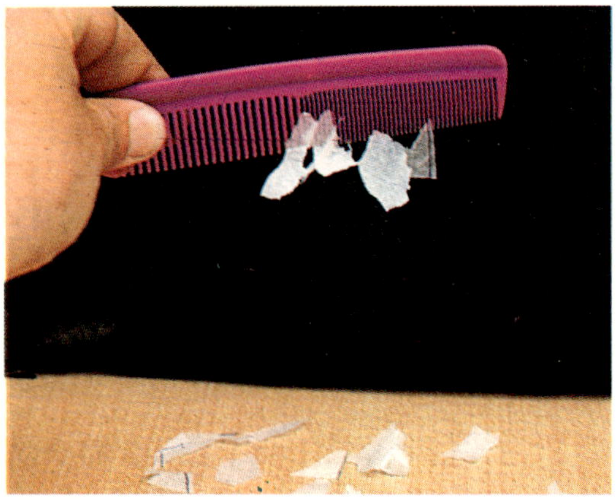

Below left: A plastic comb will become charged with electricity if you run it through your hair a few times. You can see the presence of this charge by holding the comb near some small pieces of tissue paper. They will be attracted to the comb until its charge leaks away.

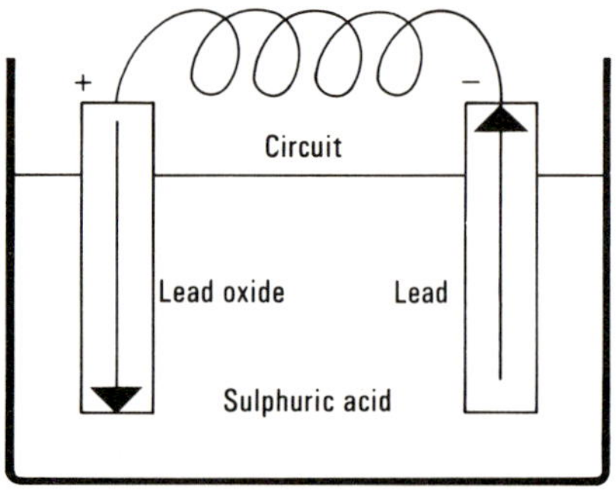

Right: A simplified diagram showing the operation of a lead-acid cell. This type of cell is used in most car batteries. Plates of lead and lead oxide are immersed in dilute sulphuric acid. The wire joining the plates represents a circuit to which the cell is supplying an electric current. Reactions at the lead plate cause the acid to give up electrons. These flow through the wire as a current.

Electricity at Home

Electricity is a form of energy. It has a great advantage over other forms of energy for it is so easy to transfer from place to place by means of wires. We use electricity by changing it into other forms of energy. For example, in an electric fire, the current passes through a wire element, making it glow red hot. An electric light bulb works in the same way, but here the fine wire filament glows brightly as it gets white hot.

Many devices depend on the magnetic effect of an electric current. A coil of wire, wound on an iron former (core), acts as a magnet when a current is passed through it. This device is an electromagnet. In a typical electric bell, two electromagnets attract a metal strip — the armature. At the end of the armature is a striker, which hits the bell gong. But movement of the armature cuts off the electric current. So the coils no longer act as magnets, and the armature springs back to its original position. This reconnects the circuit, letting the current flow and, the armature is again attracted to the coils. As a result, the armature goes to and fro, striking the gong continually.

In the telephone, signals pass through an electromagnet in the earpiece. The varying magnetism produced makes a metal disc vibrate. It reproduces the voice of the person at the other end of the line.

Our homes are full of devices and machines that run on electricity. Light bulbs, irons, electric fires, and hair dryers use the heating effect of an electric current. Electric bells and telephones work because of the magnetic effect of an electric current. So do the electric motors which power vacuum cleaners and washing machines.

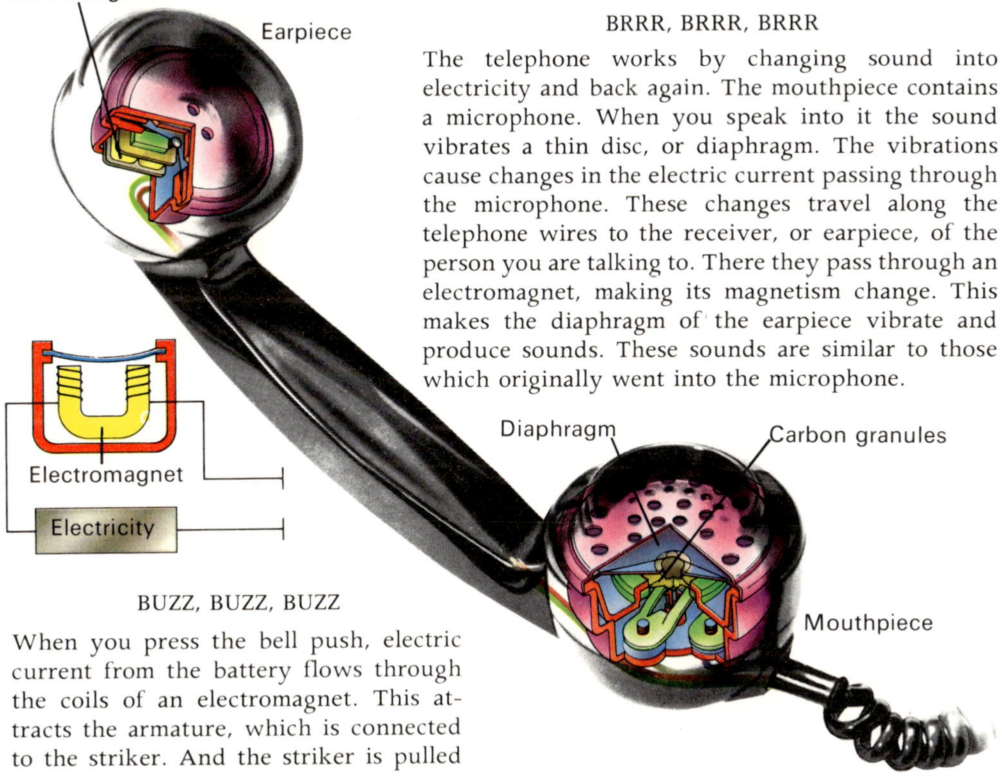

BRRR, BRRR, BRRR

The telephone works by changing sound into electricity and back again. The mouthpiece contains a microphone. When you speak into it the sound vibrates a thin disc, or diaphragm. The vibrations cause changes in the electric current passing through the microphone. These changes travel along the telephone wires to the receiver, or earpiece, of the person you are talking to. There they pass through an electromagnet, making its magnetism change. This makes the diaphragm of the earpiece vibrate and produce sounds. These sounds are similar to those which originally went into the microphone.

BUZZ, BUZZ, BUZZ

When you press the bell push, electric current from the battery flows through the coils of an electromagnet. This attracts the armature, which is connected to the striker. And the striker is pulled on to the bell, which rings.

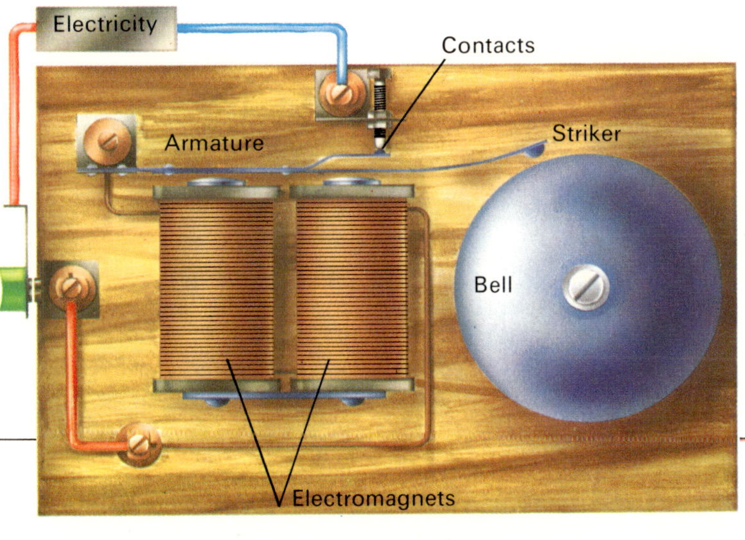

The Force of Gravity

Gravity is a force of attraction that exists between any two bodies. The Earth's gravity acts like a magnet, pulling objects towards it. It gives them weight, and makes them fall to the ground. Astronauts orbiting the Earth experience weightlessness. They are so far from the Earth that they cannot feel the force of its gravity.

The Earth's gravity keeps the Moon in orbit around it. The Moon's gravity has a marked effect on the Earth. Its pull on our oceans is the main cause of the tides.

Gravity causes acceleration. An object dropped on Earth accelerates or goes faster at a rate of about 9.8 metres per second.

The gravity of a planet attracts bodies to its surface; the more massive the planet, the greater its force of gravity. A person weighing 65 kg on the Earth's surface would weigh 11 kg on the much smaller Moon, 172 kg on the giant planet Jupiter, and 1800 kg at the surface of the Sun. Jumping performance is also affected by gravity. The effort required to jump one metre clear of the Earth's surface would take the athlete to a height of $4\frac{1}{2}$ metres on the Moon, 28 cm on Jupiter, and less than 3 cm on the Sun.

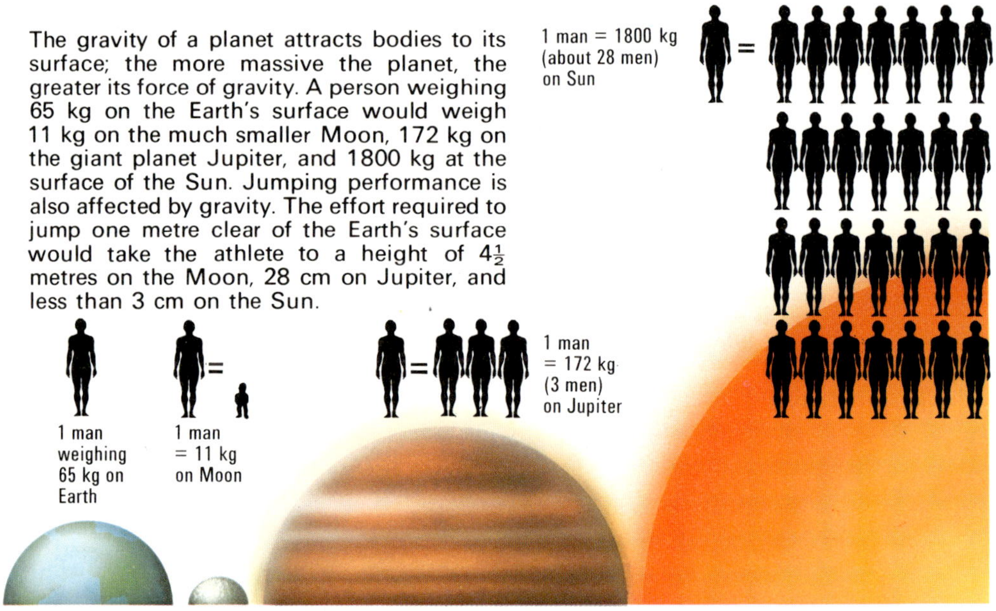

Below left: The Italian Galileo Galilei (1564-1642) made important discoveries in many branches of science. He often performed experiments to test his theories. Here, Galileo is seen at the top of the leaning tower in his home town of Pisa. He released two different weights at the same time to show that they would fall at the same rate and reach the ground together.

Below: During a training session in an aircraft, astronauts practise drinking under weightless conditions. In order to simulate the weightless conditions of space, the aircraft is put into a steep dive. It falls towards the Earth so fast that its floor no longer gives any support for the occupants. So they float around, just as if they were in an orbiting spacecraft.

Above: A powerful cannon fires a ball which, eventually, falls to the ground (1). If the power of the cannon is further increased, the rate at which the ball falls to the ground is equal to the rate at which the surface curves away from it (2). So the ball continues to follow a path, or orbit, around the Earth. If fired at an even greater speed (3), the ball escapes into space.

Light and Colour

In the middle of the day, sunlight generally appears colourless. But this is misleading, for it contains many colours. We get proof of this when the Sun comes out during a shower of rain. The raindrops split up the white light into a rainbow of colours. Many shades are present, but seven main bands can be identified — red, orange, yellow, green, blue, indigo and violet. A similar effect can be produced by sunlight passing through a triangular glass prism. If you let the emerging rays fall on a screen, you will see a band of colours, called a spectrum. (If a glass prism is not available, you can use a mirror and a bowl of water.) A second prism, in the right place, can produce a single, white beam again.

THE PRIMARY COLOURS

Everyone knows that green paint can be made by mixing equal quantities of blue and yellow paint together. If you wanted to, you could make paint of any colour, except white, by mixing together different amounts of blue, yellow and red. They are called the primary colours.

Any coloured light can be produced by mixing together different amounts of blue, green and red. These are the primary light colours. When all three are mixed together, white light is produced.

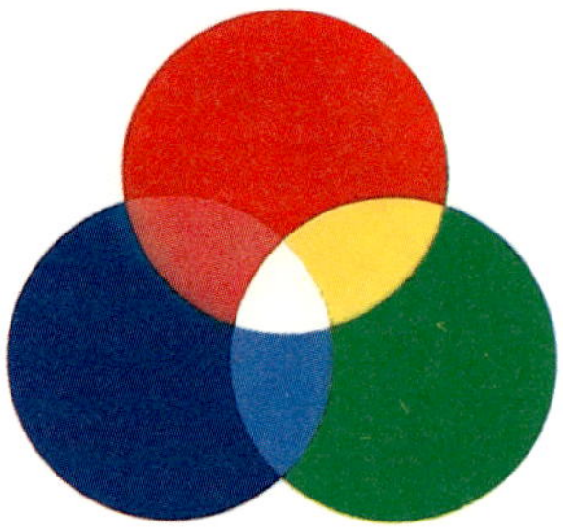

Light can produce a rainbow or spectrum because it bends when it passes from one substance to another. Each section of colour bends by a different amount. Red bends the least, while violet bends the most. Often the effect is too small to notice, but when it does happen it is usually undesirable. In cheap telescopes and other optical instruments, unwanted fringes of colour may form around the images in this way. This defect (fault) is known as chromatic (colour) aberration. In high quality instruments, the problem is overcome by using lenses made of two different types of glass. As in the experiment with the prism, light may be split up by one lens, but the other one will recombine the rays to form a single beam again. Lenses made in this way are said to be achromatic (without colour).

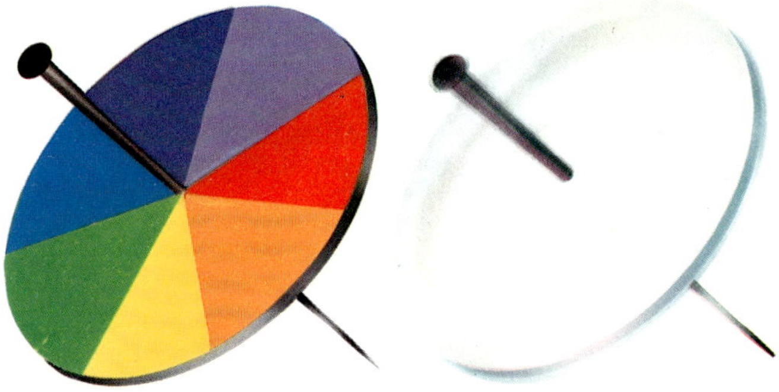

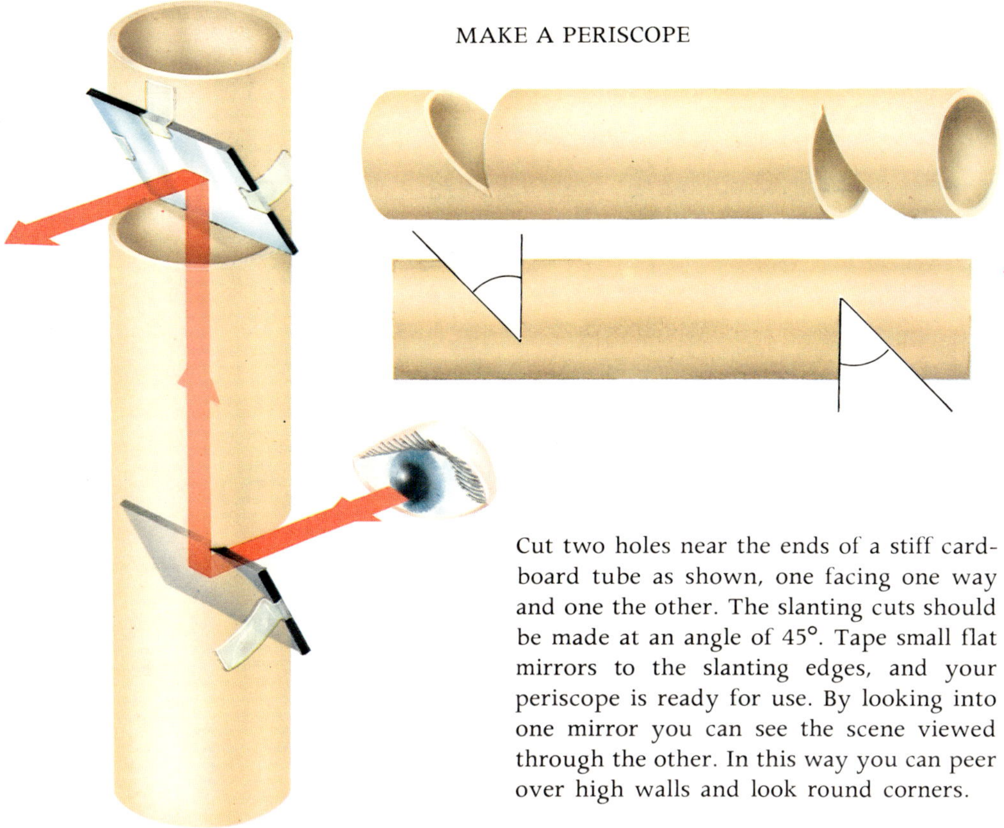

Cut two holes near the ends of a stiff cardboard tube as shown, one facing one way and one the other. The slanting cuts should be made at an angle of 45°. Tape small flat mirrors to the slanting edges, and your periscope is ready for use. By looking into one mirror you can see the scene viewed through the other. In this way you can peer over high walls and look round corners.

Below: The upper lens is described as bi-concave because it has two concave (hollowed) surfaces. It is one type of diverging lens. This means that it makes a parallel beam of light passing through it diverge, or spread out. The lower lens is bi-convex—it has two convex (bulging) surfaces. It is a type of converging lens. It makes parallel rays converge, or come together, to focus at a point on the other side of the lens. If the lens is at right angles to the incoming rays, as shown in the diagram, then the point at which the rays come together is called the principle focus. And the distance between the lens and the principle focus is called the focal length of the lens. It is very easy to find the focal length of a converging lens. Simply use it to focus the rays of the sun onto a piece of white card. Adjust the distance between the lens and card until a sharp spot of light appears on the card. Then measure this distance to obtain the focal length.

Left: Straight rods appear to be bent when placed in a glass of water. This effect occurs because light is refracted (bent) on passing from water to air. In fact, light is refracted at the junction of any two substances in which it travels at different speeds. Besides making the rods appear bent, refraction also makes them look bigger. The curved glass has shaped the water so that it magnifies.

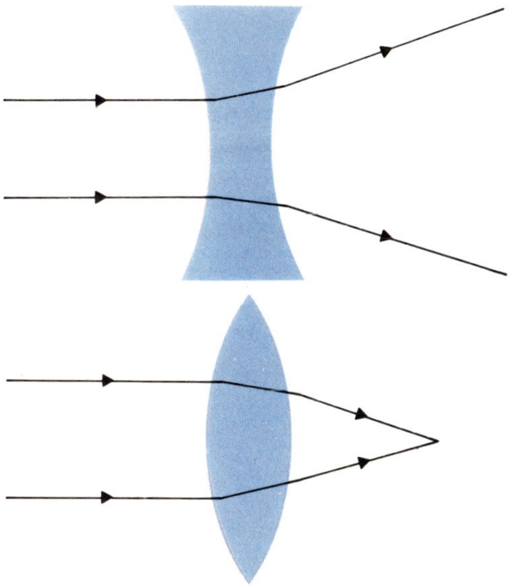

The Nature of Light

Like radio waves, infra-red (heat) rays and ultra-violet rays, light is a form of electromagnetic radiation. They travel through space at nearly 300,000 kilometres per second. The main difference between these various forms of radiation is their frequency — the rate at which the waves of energy are produced. Our eyes can only see waves within certain frequency limits, and this is the range we know as light. Different frequences, or mixtures of frequences, in this range give rise to different colour sensations.

Left: White light appears to be pure. But nothing could be further from the truth. For, in fact, white light is a mixture of colours. This is why sunlight can be split up by raindrops to form a rainbow of colours. If these colours are recombined, white light is formed once more. You can demonstrate this by painting the colours of the rainbow on a cardboard disc, as shown in the left-hand diagram. Then push a large pin through the disc and make it spin, like a top. This will cause the colours to appear to merge together so the spinning disc will look almost white.

On a sunny day, fill a bowl with water and rest a flat mirror against the side. Draw the curtains of the room so that only a thin shaft of sunlight falls on the mirror. By adjusting the angle of the mirror you will be able to project a rainbow, or spectrum, on to a card or wall nearby. The 'wedge' of water between the mirror and the surface acts like a prism, and splits the incoming sunlight into its component colours.

Heat

Heat is a form of energy. Scientists used to think heat was a weightless, invisible fluid that could flow from a hot body to a cooler one. But we now know that the heat in a body is due to the motion of its molecules. In a hot body, the molecules vibrate quickly. In a cool body, they move more slowly. If a body could be cooled down to −273.15°C, its molecules would stop moving altogether, and it would contain no heat at all. This temperature, called absolute zero, can be closely approached, but never reached.

Temperature is a measure of hotness, not of heat. A match flame has a higher temperature than a heating radiator, but does not give out so much heat.

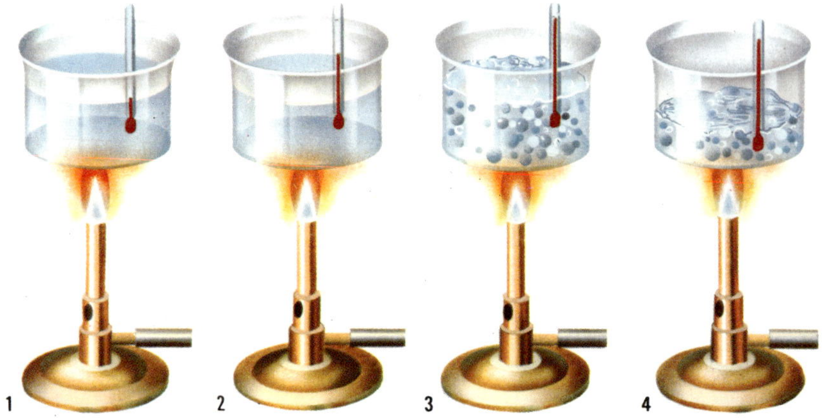

Above: As a beaker of water is heated, it takes in heat and its temperature rises (1 and 2). When it reaches boiling point, it begins to boil (3). More heat is needed to keep it boiling, but the temperature of the water does not increase (4). A lot of heat is needed just to change water into steam.

Left: A fire fighter wears a special suit so that he can walk through flames. The silvery surface of the suit reflects away heat. And it is woven from fibres of asbestos, which is a very poor conductor of heat.

Below: A vacuum flask is made to keep in as much heat as possible. There is a vacuum between the double glass walls of the container to prevent heat loss. And the container is silvered to stop heat radiating away.

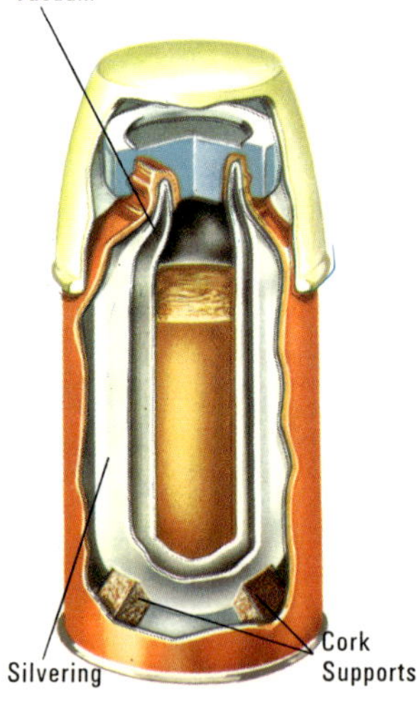

A thing may be heated in one of three ways — by convection, conduction or radiation. When water is heated convection currents circulate in it. They occur when the warm water, being lighter, rises, and cooler water sinks to take its place. Convection also occurs in other liquids and in gases. If one end of a metal bar is heated, the other end gradually becomes hot too. We say that the heat is carried along the bar by conduction. Heat radiation is the pushing out of heat as a form of waves. Also known as infra-red radiation, it is given off by all hot objects. Black surfaces are better as heat radiators than are white surfaces.

Above: The fennec fox lives in hot desert regions. Its huge ears allow heat to be given out over a wide area. They act like the cooling fins on an engine.

Right: This engineer is cooling piston linings before inserting them in an engine block. When the linings warm up and expand, they will fit tightly in place.

Below: At the seaside we often have on-shore breezes by day and off-shore breezes at night. During the day the land takes in more of the Sun's heat than the sea. Warm air rises over the land and cooler air blows in from the sea to replace it. At night the land cools more quickly than the sea. Air rises over the sea and winds blow from the land towards the sea.

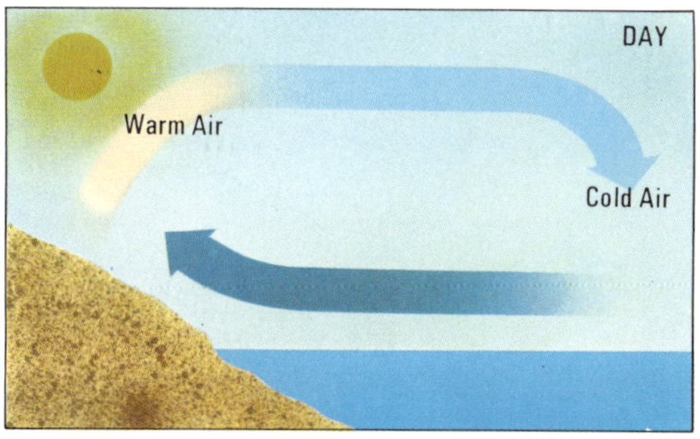

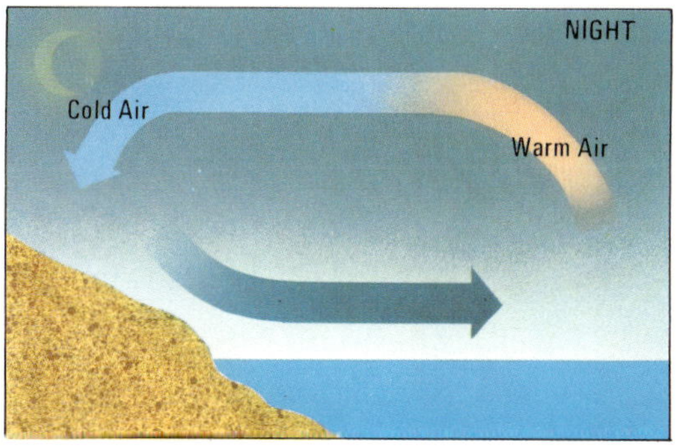

Sound

Noise is caused by vibrations. These pass through the air to our ears, and are interpreted as sound by the brain. Unlike electromagnetic radiation, such as radio, heat and light waves, sound needs a medium (substance) through which to travel. This can be demonstrated by placing an electric bell inside a sealed container from which the air is slowly drawn out. The ringing, clearly heard at first, gradually becomes fainter. However, even if all the air could be removed, the sound would never become completely inaudible. For some vibrations would pass directly through the base of the container and reach the outside. Substances carry sound by passing on the vibrations from one molecule to the next. In air at a temperature of 0°C, this process takes place at a speed of about 332 metres per second.

When an explosion occurs, the blast pushes against nearby air molecules, pressing them closer together. The force of the compression travels like a ripple through the air. At each point along the sound path, the molecules experience this sudden disturbance and then return to their normal positions. Sound vibrations are described as longitudinal, because the molecules of the medium vibrate along the direction in which the sound travels.

Above: The player makes the air in the coiled tube of the trumpet vibrate. The frequency of the sound produced can be varied by changing the tension of the lips and by pressing the valves.

Below: The size of an object affects the rate at which it vibrates. Plucking a long, flexible rod produces a low-frequency note (top). A short rod gives a high-frequency note when plucked (bottom).

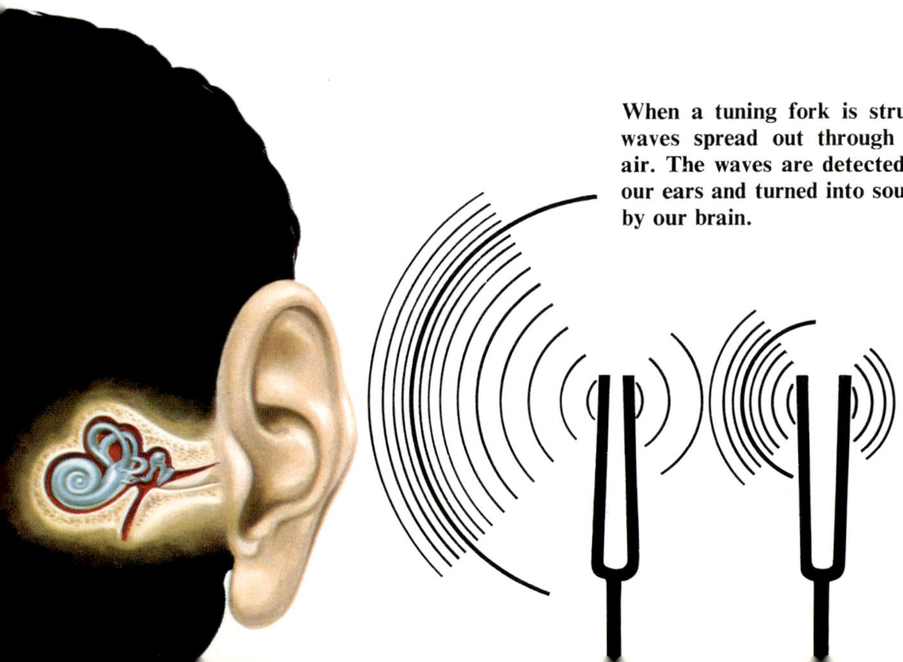

When a tuning fork is struck, waves spread out through the air. The waves are detected by our ears and turned into sounds by our brain.

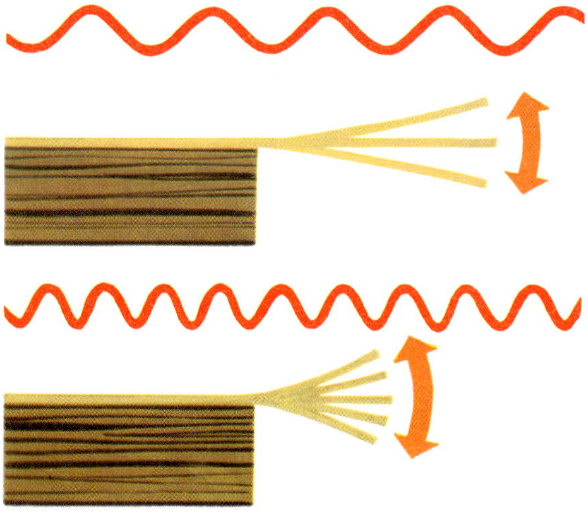

Left: A recorder player closes different holes to change the length of the vibrating column of air. In this way she makes different notes.

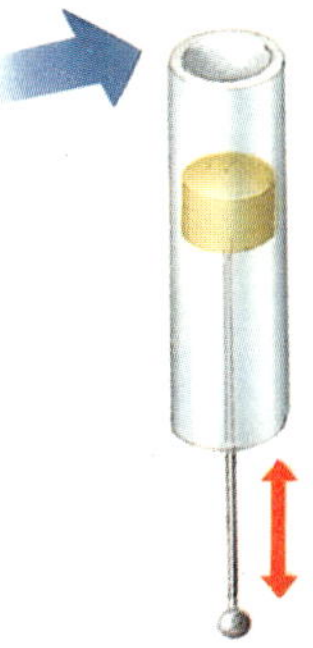

When a column of air vibrates, it gives out a musical note. As its length changes, so does the note. Prove it with this simple musical instrument (right). Blow across the open top, and move the knitting needle and cork up and down. The note changes as the cork rises and falls.

You can make a simple guitar from a cardboard shoebox (right) and some elastic bands. Cut a hole in the lid of the box and tack lengths of elastic of different thicknesses to it. Fit a wedge of wood beneath the bands and they will give out different notes when plucked.

By rubbing the rim of a partly filled wine glass with a wet finger (below), you can produce beautiful sounds. You can make a glass harmonica using several glasses filled to different levels.

A source of prolonged sound, such as a vibrating guitar string, alternately compresses and stretches the surrounding air, so that a regular series of vibrations travels along. These are called sound waves.

Frequency and Wavelength

The *frequency* of a sound is the rate at which the waves are produced. This used to be expressed as a number of cycles (complete waves) per second. But, by international agreement, we now express frequency in units called hertz. One hertz (Hz) is equal to one cycle per second. A person with extremely good hearing can detect sounds ranging from about 20 hertz to 20,000 hertz. This is referred to as the audio (sound) frequency range. Medium and high audio frequencies are often quoted in kilohertz (kHz), one kilohertz equals 1,000 hertz.

A body or instrument vibrating at a high frequency produces waves that follow closely one behind the other. In other words, their *wavelength* — the distance between the start of one wave and the next — is relatively small. Low-frequency vibrations, on the other hand, produce relatively long waves.

Below: Ultrasonic (higher-than-sound) waves sent from the bottom of a ship are reflected by the sea bed. The depth can be found from the time delay.

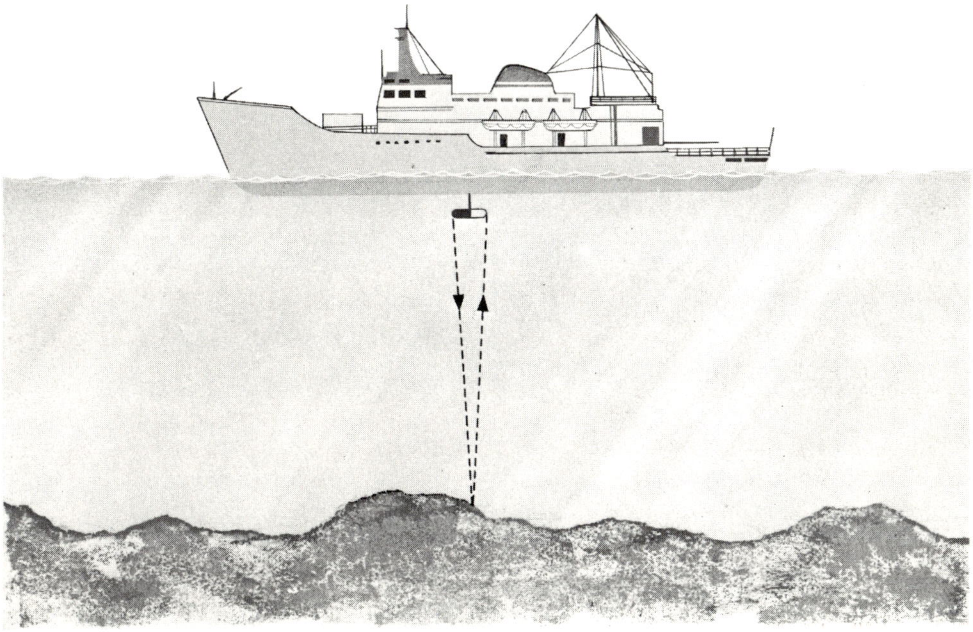

Differences in the frequencies of sounds are interpreted by the brain as *pitch*. A piccolo, for example, giving high-frequency vibrations, sounds high pitched. But the low-frequency vibrations of a tuba give a deep, low-pitched sound.

Harmonics

The main, or *fundamental frequency* of a note determines its pitch. But other, higher-frequency vibrations, called *harmonics*, are usually present too. These vary, but help to give each individual instrument its own sound.

The Air Around Us

PUT OUT THE LIGHT

Nothing can burn without oxygen. That is why the quickest way to put out a fire is to cover it and exclude the air. A simple experiment enables you to find out roughly how much oxygen there is in the air. Light a candle and stand it in a shallow bowl of water. Quickly place over it a bottle or jar, with the mouth of the bottle below the surface of the water. As the candle burns, the oxygen in the bottle will be used up, and the water will gradually rise in the neck of the bottle to take its place. Soon the candle will go out, showing that all the oxygen has gone. Note the level of the water in the bottle and on the candle, and then remove the bottle.

You can now find out what volume of water was sucked into the bottle. Remember to allow for the volume of the candle. To find the volume of the bottle minus the candle, fill it with water and stick in the candle to the level it was during the experiment. Some water will spill over. Pour the rest into a measuring jug and note its volume. Now, keeping the candle in position, pour water in the bottle until it reaches the level reached (the other way up) in the experiment. Measure that volume. The difference in volume will give you the volume of oxygen in the bottle. It should be about one fifth of the total volume. Is it?

We are normally unaware of the air around us. Yet it exerts great pressure on our bodies. Pressing down on our head and shoulders is a column of air weighing about one tonne. The reason that this is no burden is that the downward pressure is balanced by a similar pressure inside our body. The fact that air has weight can be shown by first pumping some of the air out of a strong container before sealing it. The container is then placed on one pan of a pair of sensitive laboratory scales. Weights are added to the other pan until the pans are balanced. When the seal is undone, air rushes into the container, adding extra weight and upsetting the balance.

It is easy to demonstrate what air pressure actually does. When you suck a drink up through a straw, you first have to take in some air from it. This reduces the amount of air pressure in the straw with the result that the normal air pressure on the surrounding liquid is no longer balanced. So, it is able to push the liquid in the container down and force it out up the straw.

Air pressure can be made to crush a large tin can. First a little water is boiled in the open can. The steam produced drives out all the air. After carefully removing the can from the heat, it is tightly sealed with its lid or cap. As the can cools, the steam inside condenses to form a few drops of water. With no steam or air pressing on the inside of the can, there is nothing to resist the external air pressure. So the can gradually buckles under the strain.

Above, right: The gases of the air move over the surface of the Earth as wind. They are strong enough to move a yacht across water.

Right: Joseph Priestley discovered the gas oxygen. When the candle had used up all the oxygen in the glass, it went out.

Left: Fill a glass with water and place a flat card over it. Hold the card in place and turn the glass upside down. Take your hand away. The air presses against the card, keeping the water in the glass.

The Versatile Atmosphere

We make use of the air around us in many ways. When we breathe in, we absorb some of the oxygen present in the air. This gas is essential for life processes in man and other animals. When we breathe out, we expel some waste carbon dioxide, which is used by plants. Thus both plants and animals depend on the air for their survival. The atmosphere of air surrounding the Earth is very thin, but it provides us with vital protection, by filtering out harmful rays from the Sun. It also tends to even out temperature variations on the Earth. This stops us from being roasted by the daytime heat and frozen at night.

Various instruments, tools and machines make use of air pressure. Barometers measure the air pressure so that we can forecast changes in the weather. Aircraft pilots measure air pressure using an instrument called an altimeter. This gives them an indication of how high the aircraft is, for the pressure decreases with altitude. Machines called compressors provide high-pressure air to operate pneumatic drills and other tools.

Hovercraft skim across the land or sea, supported by the pressure of their air cushion. Aircraft have specially shaped wings that cause a greater air pressure underneath than above. This results in an upward force, called lift, which keeps the aircraft in the sky.

How Chemistry Helps Us

Chemistry is the branch of science that deals with the composition of substances and the ways in which they split up or combine with other substances. The term chemicals is usually applied when speaking of substances used in various processes. Dyes, for example, are chemicals used to colour cloth and other materials. Bleaching agents are chemicals that change dyes into other, colourless substances. However, everything around us could be described as a chemical, or a mixture of chemicals. Water is a chemical compound called hydrogen oxide. The air is a mixture of chemicals in the form of gases.

Chemistry is now divided into many specialized branches. Organic chemistry is the study of the organic compounds found in living things. Even our bodies are made up of extremely complex chemicals containing carbon. Biochemistry deals with the chemical changes that occur within the organisms. Physical chemistry is the study of physical changes that occur when chemical reactions take place. Such changes include the emission or absorption of energy, and changes in the structure of atoms and molecules. Processes developed in the laboratory are put into full-scale industrial operation by chemical engineers.

Above: Some of the more common items found in a chemistry laboratory are shown here. They are: 1. Chemical balance; 2. Bottles with ground glass stoppers; 3. Centrifuge; 4. Microscope; 5. Burette; 6. Conical flask; 7. Filter funnel; 8. Measuring cylinder; 9. Long-necked flask; 10. Pipette; 11. Flat-bottomed flask; 12. Beaker; 13. Test tube and holder; 14. Bunsen burner; 15. Mortar and pestle; 16. Condenser; 17. Tripod stand.

CHEMICALS IN THE HOME

We use an enormous variety of chemicals in our everyday lives. We eat them, cook with them, wash with them, and rely on them to cure our aches and pains.

1 We use table salt as a flavouring and preserving agent. Its chemical name is sodium chloride. It is one of many chemicals called salts.

2 Vinegar contains acetic acid. Its sharp flavour makes salads more appetizing and it helps preserve foods.

3 Lemon juice is citric acid.

4 Aspirin is the most common pain-killer that we use as medicine. It is an acid called acetyl salicylic acid. When you have an upset stomach you need, not an acid, but an antacid. This contains an alkali, which fights the acidity.

5 Some fabrics shrink or lose their colour in soap and water, so they must

Above: In a laboratory, chemicals and equipment are arranged in an orderly fashion. The flasks in the foreground contain a chemical indicator that changes colour to show when the liquid is acidic. Each flask has been marked to identify the sample under test.

be dry cleaned with chemicals which dissolve grease and stains and evaporate quickly.

6 Soaps are made from strong alkalis called caustic soda and caustic potash. Detergents are more powerful cleansing agents. They are made from chemicals obtained from petroleum, or crude oil.

7 To make cakes rise, you must add baking powder to the cake mixture (unless it is already in the flour). Baking powder contains a chemical called bicarbonate of soda. When this is heated, it gives off carbon dioxide gas. As the gas tries to escape, it makes the mixture rise, and you get a light cake.

Water

About 70 per cent of the Earth is covered with water. Heat makes it evaporate into the air. There the invisible steam often condenses to form clouds of tiny water drops. When these become large, they fall on the Earth as rain, snow or hail. We use this water for drinking, and for watering our crops. We can also make use of the energy of moving water to generate electricity.

We are all about three-quarters water. If we don't have any of it in food or drink for a week, we die.

Ripe watermelons are about 97 per cent water.

A tomato is 95 per cent water.

Even an egg is 74 percent water.

Right: The waterwheel was first used in Roman times. Its invention enabled man to use the energy of moving water to grind corn and do other useful tasks. At last, man was learning to harness the forces of nature. The waterwheel shown here is a breast wheel. It is turned by water falling behind it and flowing beneath it. An overshot wheel is powered only by falling water, and an undershot wheel by flowing water.

Frozen Water Floats

Water is also a strange liquid. It is one of the very few things that grows bigger (expands) when it freezes. That is why huge icebergs float. Icebergs are frozen fresh water.

The Strength of Water

What happens if we fill a bottle with water, stopper it tightly and put it in a freezer? The bottle burts. This is because the water has grown bigger when it turned into ice. Water is very powerful stuff when it freezes. It can burst pipes. If it freezes in cracks in rocks it can split the rocks asunder.

The enormous power of waterfalls can be used to drive water turbines. Turbines turn electricity generators.

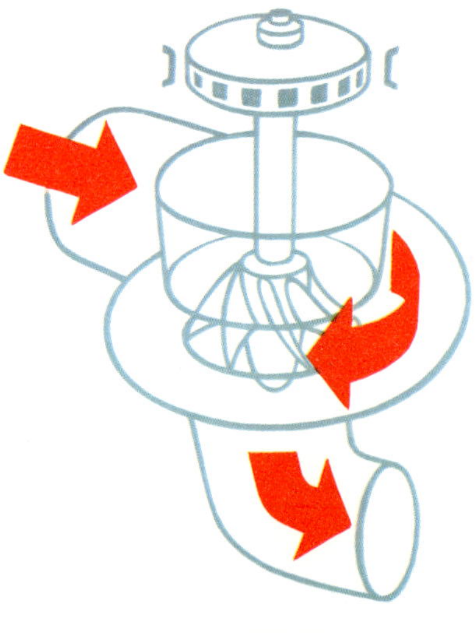

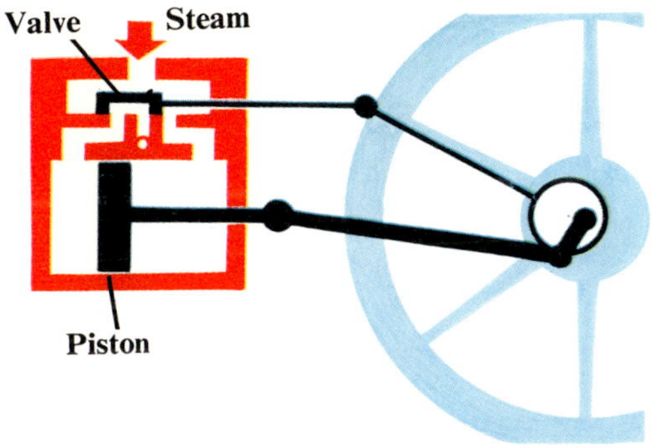

This is *Puffing Billy*, one of the oldest steam engines. It was built in 1813 and can still be seen in the Science Museum in London. The invention of the steam engine started the modern Machine Age. Men could get all the power they wanted, just by heating water.

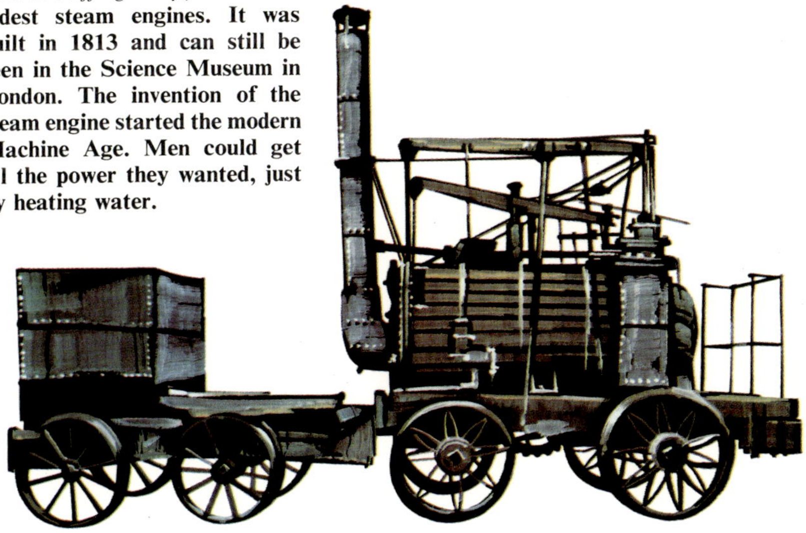

Steam Power

Water is also very powerful when it is heated and becomes a gas—steam. When water becomes steam it expands to about 1700 times its size. Steam engines use the energy of expanding steam to drive wheels or do other work. The diagram above shows how a simple steam engine works. A valve slides back and forward. It lets steam into the cylinder at one end, then at the other end. So the steam pushes the piston one way, then the other. The piston turns the wheel.

Below: Water from the ground can rise up the walls of houses. We call this effect 'rising damp'. A similar effect occurs when a fine glass tube is dipped in water. An attraction between the glass and water causes the water to rise up the tube. In a wall, the water rises up thousands of tiny pores in the brickwork.

Water Facts

The oceans hold 96 per cent of all the Earth's water.

In one cubic kilometre of sea water there are 28,000,000 tonnes of table salt. In all the oceans there is enough salt to cover the continents with a layer 150 metres thick.

The jellyfish holds the animal record for the water inside it. This slithery creature is 95 per cent water, almost the same as the sea water in which it lives.

Sea water is heavier than fresh water because of the salts dissolved in it.

An ordinary loaf, even after baking in a hot oven, is still about one-third water.

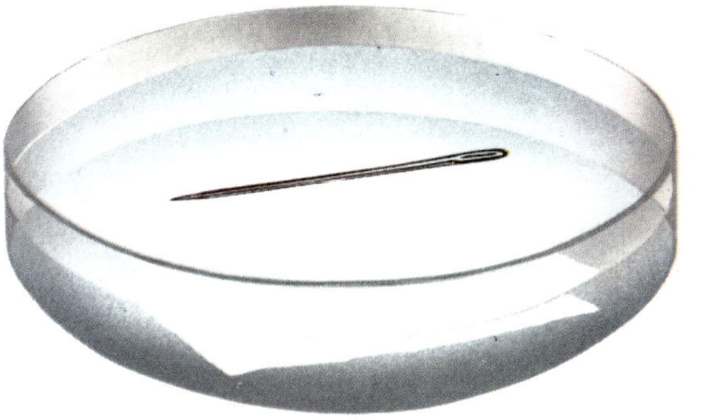

Above: An effect called surface tension makes water act as if it is covered with a skin. This will enable a steel needle to float. Put a dry needle on some tissue paper, and place it gently on the water. The paper will sink, leaving the needle on the surface.

Below: The water skater can walk on the surface of a pond, even though its body is more dense than water. It is supported by surface tension—an attraction between water molecules on the surface. The insect's weight dents the surface as if it were made of thin rubber.

Below: In the Earth's rivers and oceans live more than 20,000 kinds of fish. These need oxygen to live, just like land animals. But, instead of taking in oxygen from the air, as we do, fish get their oxygen from the water. They take in water through the mouth. The water then passes through the gills. These organs, on either side of the head, contain many tiny blood vessels. As the water passes over the blood vessels, some of the oxygen it contains is taken into the fish's blood.

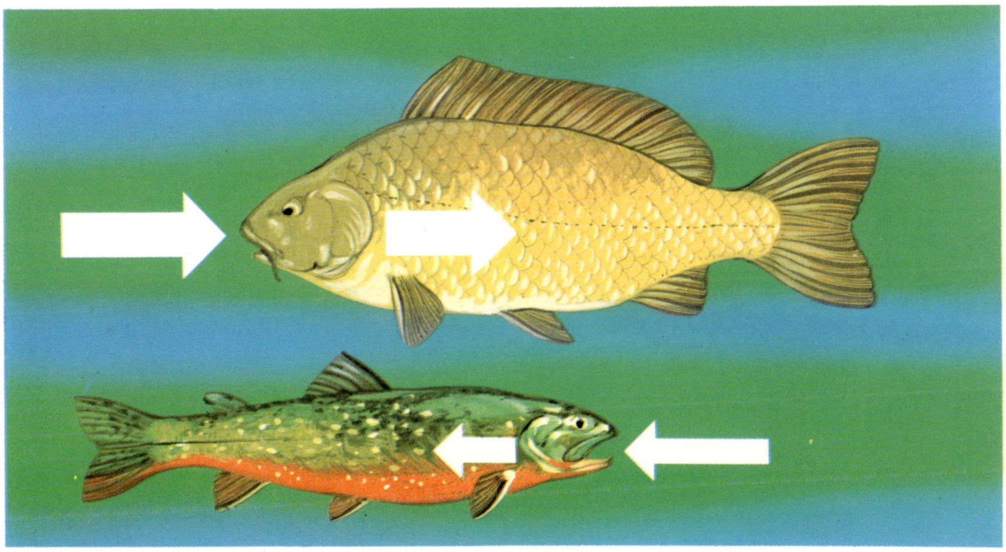

Glass

Ordinary glass is made by melting a mixture of sand, soda and lime. It has many uses. For glass is transparent, easy to shape and is unaffected by most chemicals. So it is a suitable material for making apparatus used in chemistry laboratories. Glass is also a good electrical and heat insulator.

Various substances can be added to ordinary glass to give it special properties. The addition of lead oxide produces lead glass. This is used to make optical lenses and high quality decorative glassware. Lead glass is also called crystal glass, or flint glass. Other special forms of glass include the toughened and heatproof types.

This English glass was made in the 18th century. The pattern in its stem is made by bubbles of air trapped in the glass.

This beautiful wine glass was made in Venice. From the 13th century, Venice was the glass-making city of the world.

Above: The red-hot lava that flows down the sides of an erupting volcano consists of molten rock. If the right ingredients are present, the lava forms glass when it cools and hardens. At the Yellowstone National Park in Wyoming, USA, there is a whole mountain of volcanic glass.

How Glass is Made
The right amounts of sand, lime and soda are mixed. Some broken glass, called 'cullet', is added to speed up the melting. The mixture is heated in a huge furnace.

Old Window Glass
Until the 1800s, flat sheets of glass for windows were made by the *crown* process. A round bubble of glass was blown. The end was cut off and it was spun until it was a flat sheet. The sheet was cut into small window panes.

Blowing Glass
The glassblower takes a blob of molten glass on the end of the blowpipe (1). As he blows through the tube, the glass inflates (2). He turns the pipe and shapes the glass by rolling it (3 and 4). Another rod is attached to the other end of the glass, and the blowpipe is cut off (5). The glass is cut and shaped (6).

Above: Glassblower's equipment. The blowpipe is rolled across the chair to keep glass in shape.

For about 1500 years men have shaped glass by blowing through tubes. This is a Medieval glass blower.

Modern Window Glass

Molten glass, like thick, sticky toffee, flows between rollers (left). The flat sheet of glass is carried along on other rollers. The glass is slowly cooled. When it is hard it is ground smooth and polished. This sort of glass is called *plate glass.*

Float Glass

Window glass can also be made by what is called the *float process.* Red hot molten glass is floated on a bath of liquid tin (below). As the glass flows along it becomes very flat and smooth. It does not need to be ground and polished.

Keeping Warm with Glass

Glass can be made into very fine threads. It is then called *fibre-glass.* Fibre-glass can be pressed into thick rolls of material. This is used in the roofs of houses to keep the warm air in (below).

Keeping Heat In and Out

A vacuum flask keeps things hot or cold. It has inside it a glass bottle with double walls. The space between the walls has had all the air pumped out of it. There is no air, so heat has difficulty crossing the space between the glass walls.

Double Glazing

In double glazing, a layer of air is trapped between two panes of glass. Air is a bad conductor of heat. So little heat can pass from the inner pane to the outer one. This is why a house with double glazing loses less heat than one with ordinary windows.

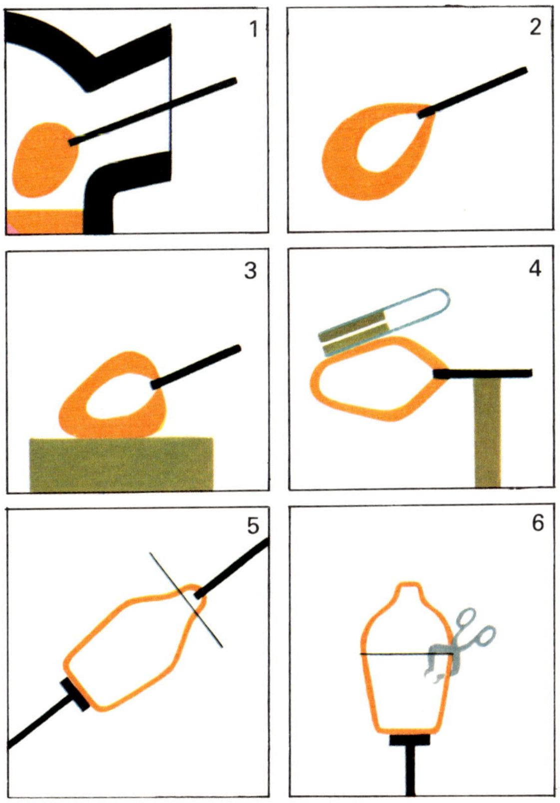

Stained Glass

When a stained glass window is being made, small pieces of glass are fitted together like a jigsaw puzzle. The artist paints on the glass with coloured enamel paints. Then the glass is fired in an oven and the enamel becomes part of the glass. The glass jigsaw is held together by lead strips.

Making Electric Light Bulbs

The electric lamp below was invented by Thomas Alva Edison in 1879. The glass bulbs for Edison's lamps were blown, one at a time, by men with blowpipes. Today, electric light bulbs are mass produced by machines. One machine can make 2,000 bulbs each minute. As shown below, air jets blast a ribbon of hot, soft glass into a series of moulds. The moulds then separate so that the bulbs can be removed. After fitting the other parts, the bulbs are filled with gas and then sealed.

Metals

Real progress in technology began when man learnt to use metals to make tools and machines. Most of the elements are metals, although many are very rare. Copper, gold and a few other metals occur naturally. But most metals are found in combination with other elements as chemical compounds. Any compound used as a source of metal is called an ore. Bauxite, for example, is the main aluminium ore. It consists of the metal oxide in combination with water. While free copper is found in some places, most of the metal is obtained from various ores. Usually these are quite unlike the metals in appearance, and have entirely different properties. Sodium chloride, for example, is the main ore from which sodium is obtained. Sodium is a metal that reacts violently with water, giving out much heat. And yet sodium chloride is the salt we sprinkle on our food.

Various methods are used to extract metals from their ores. Processes involving heat are called smelting. Sodium is obtained by passing an electric current through the molten ore. Metals vary in their properties, such as hardness, melting point and strength. Metals are often mixed when molten to make alloys. These have properties that are different from those of the original metals.

There are nearly 3000 minerals in the Earth's crust. A few are pure, or nearly pure, elements. For example, gold and silver are sometimes found in a pure state. These minerals are called *native elements*. But most minerals are combinations of two or more of the 92 elements which occur naturally in the crust. For example, quartz is a combination of the two commonest elements, silicon and oxygen.

Over the centuries, men have shaped metals into beautiful objects. Gold has always been a favourite because of its shiny yellow colour. It is easy to beat into shape like the ancient Greek mask in the picture (1). The shiny gold mask of Tutankhamen, an ancient Egyptian pharaoh, is over 3,000 years old (2). The statue of Buddha is made of bronze coated with gold (3). Arms and armour have always been an important use for metals—especially iron. The beautifully decorated breastplate (4) was made in the 16th century. The swords (5) come from Japan.

Making Iron and Steel

Steel can be made in different ways to do different jobs. It is really a mixture (an alloy) of iron and carbon. On the left is a huge ladle of molten steel. Iron ore that comes from the ground is melted in a huge blast furnace. To the ore are added coke and limestone. The limestone helps to remove impurities from the ore. These impurities, called slag, run off near the bottom of the furnace. The molten iron runs out right at the bottom.

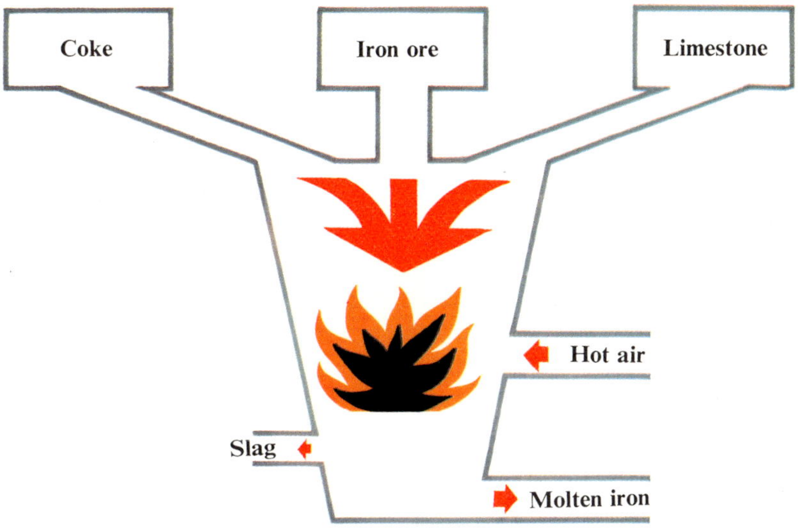

Joining Metals

Two ways of joining metals together are riveting and welding. In riveting, one end of a red-hot rivet is hammered until it has a head which holds the two pieces together. In welding, the two pieces of metal are heated until they melt together.

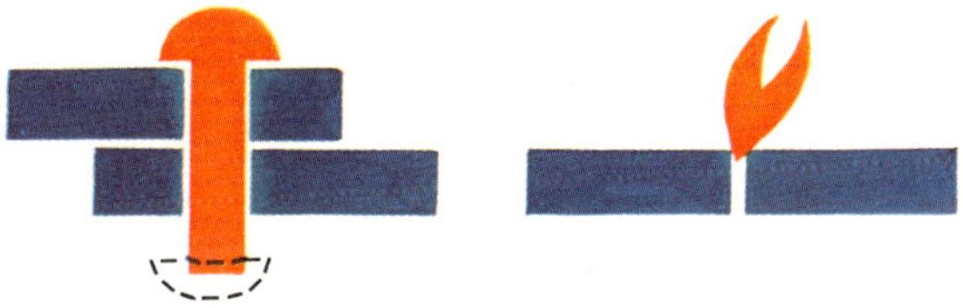

Soldering Metals Together

In soldering, an alloy, often a mixture of lead and tin, is melted between the two pieces to be joined. When the solder cools it makes a firm joint. A paste called flux is put in to make a better joint.

Some Common Alloys

Brass is a mixture of copper and zinc. The more zinc, the harder the brass. Bronze is a mixture of copper and tin. Statues are often made of it. Pewter is a mixture of lead and tin. It was once used for making tablewear.

Unusual Metals

All metals are not hard. Mercury (below left) is a silvery liquid. It is used in thermometers and barometers. Some metals are so light they float on water.

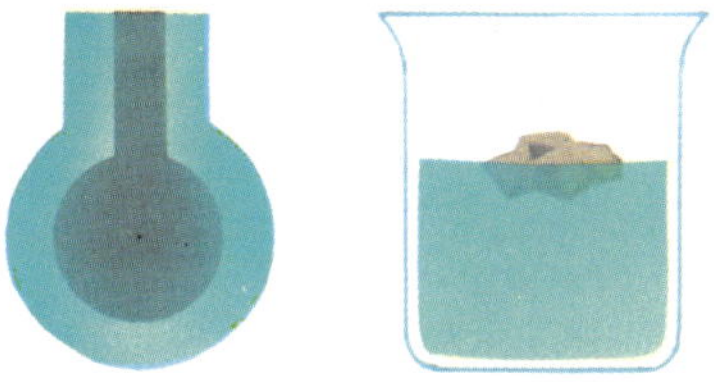

Cutting Metals

Metals can be cut by using an oxyacetylene burner. This kind of burner makes a very hot flame by burning acetylene gas in oxygen.

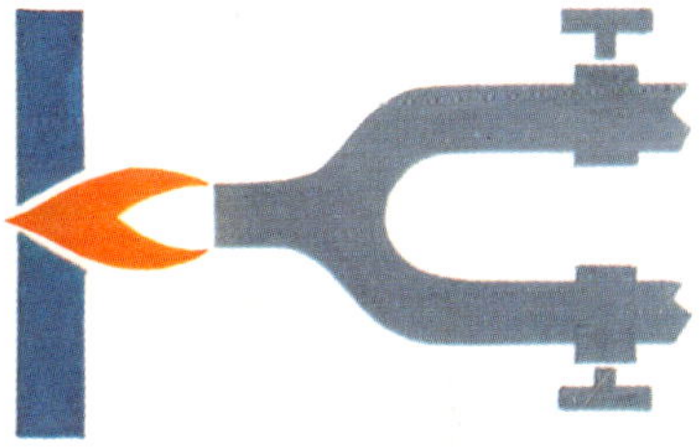

Shaping Metals

There are many ways to shape metals. In casting (1) metal is poured into a mould. Pressing (2) is used to shape sheets of steel. Forging (3) has long been used by blacksmiths. The red-hot metal is shaped on an anvil. In rolling (4) a white-hot piece of metal is squeezed between rollers until it is a thin sheet. In drawing (5) thin rods are made by pulling metal through small holes.

Crystals

Every mineral has a definite chemical composition (of atoms, ions and particles), although the formulae of many minerals are very complicated. Because they have a definite composition, they also have special properties.

Mineral Crystals

One special property is the crystal form taken by minerals. These forms occur because the components are arranged in a particular way.

Most minerals have crystals, but there are exceptions. Among these exceptions are opal, an *amorphous* mineral. This means that it is shapeless, with no regular internal arrangement. Some minerals look shapeless, but are *cryptocrystalline*. This means that they contain tiny crystals which can be seen only under a microscope.

Crystals often grow in large clumps like the calcite crystals above.

Snow crystals are all different, but they all have six sides or points.

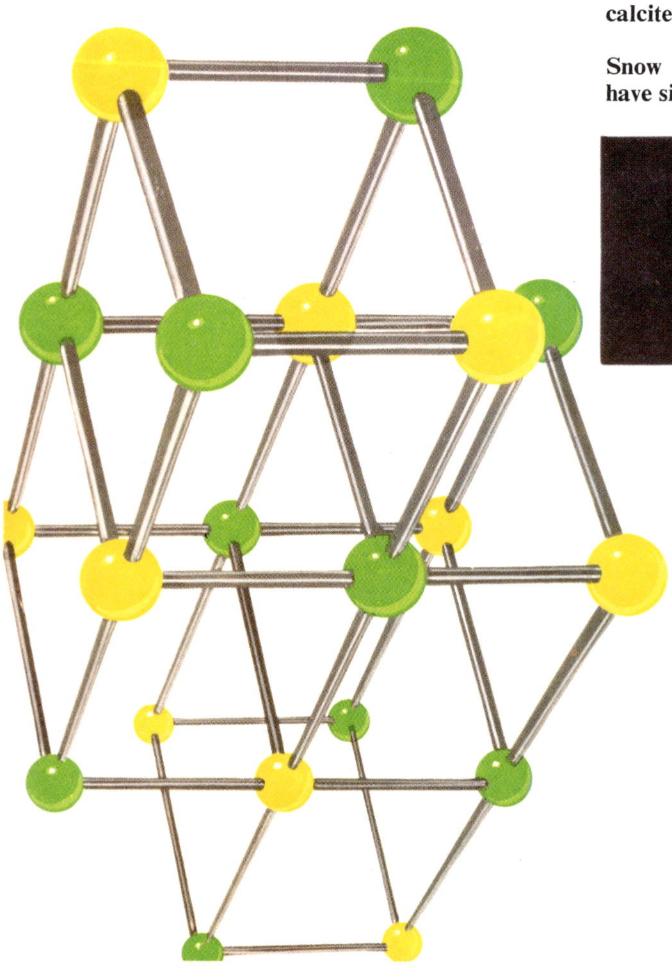

The salt you put on your food is called sodium chloride by chemists. It is made up of two different kinds of atoms — sodium atoms and chlorine atoms. These tiny atoms are arranged in cube patterns as you can see in the picture on the left. Thousands and thousands of these tiny cubes join together to make one grain of salt. And each grain of salt also wants to be a cube. If you look at some grains of salt through a magnifying glass, you will see that they are all little cubes.

Crystal Systems

Crystals may occur in a wide variety of forms. But they can all be divided into seven main systems, according to their symmetry.

On the next page you can see a diagram of these seven systems. They range through a hexahedron (with six faces), various rhomboids and an octahedron. How many faces does this have?

If you look at grains of salt through a magnifying glass, you will see that they are all little cubes (hexahedrons).

Diamonds are crystals. They are the hardest substance that we know of.

A sugar cube has three *axes of symmetry*. These axes are imaginary lines, joining the centre points of the opposite sides. The axes are equal in length and they meet, at right angles, in the centre of the cube. If you rotate the cube round any of these axes, it will show the same appearance four times. We say that it has three four-fold axes of symmetry. This defines the *cubic crystal system*. The other main crystal systems are similarly defined by symmetry, the lengths of the axes, and the angles between them.

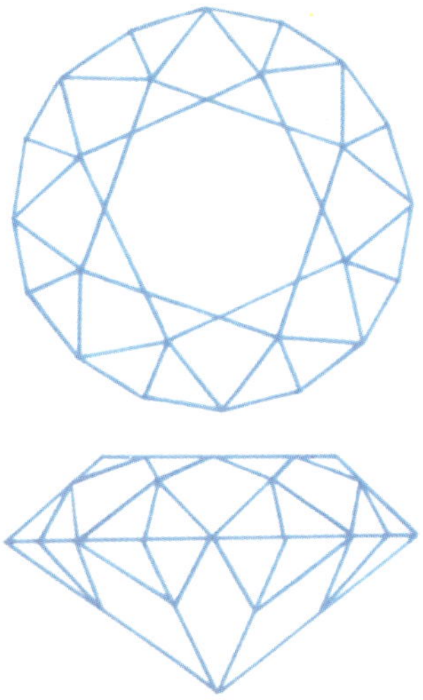

There are several different ways of cutting diamonds to make them sparkle. One of the most popular (shown above, from the top and from the side) is called the brilliant cut. In this cut there are 58 faces, each of which has to be cut and polished.

Right: Much more common than diamonds are stones like agate. Agates are a kind of quartz, one of the commonest minerals on Earth. Their beautiful coloured bands are arranged in many different ways.

Below: Some of the shapes of natural crystals.

When a ray of light goes into a diamond, it hits one of the faces and is reflected to another face. It is reflected again and comes out showing all the colours of the rainbow.

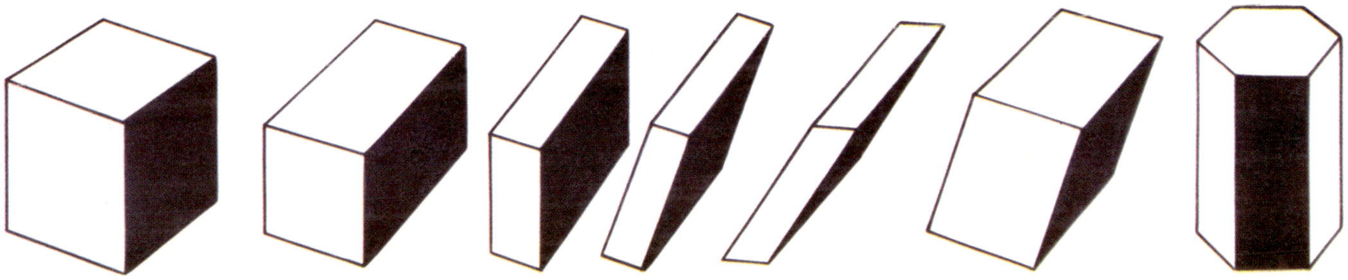

Making Crystals
Stir sugar into a little water until no more sugar will dissolve. Pour the sugary water into a saucer and leave it. As the water evaporates, crystals will form. But these crystals will be very small and not perfect in shape. To grow a perfect crystal, take some table salt or sugar or borax or alum. Stir your substance into hot water until no more will dissolve. Pour the liquid into a jar and leave it. Crystals will form. Pick out one of the best crystals and hang it on a thread in a new saturated solution. Watch it grow.

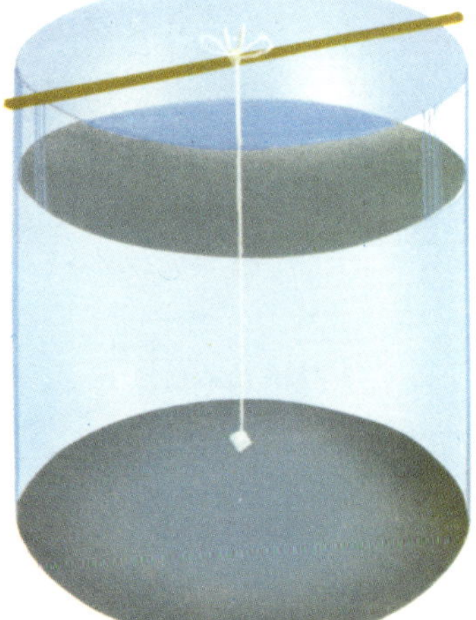

Where Crystals Form

As magma cools, the minerals in the magma start to crystallize. But there is usually too little space for well-developed crystals to grow. As a result, igneous rocks, formed from magma, consist of a mass of tiny, irregularly shaped grains.

Well-formed crystals are often formed in rock cavities from mineral-rich fluids. Some, called *nodules*, are rounded. Nodules may contain inward-growing crystals. Other crystals form in long cracks, called fissures.

Food Preservation

Most foods go bad quickly unless we take precautions to preserve them. The main cause of decay is the presence of germs in the air. Scientists call these tiny living cells micro-organisms. They include yeasts, moulds and bacteria, all so small that they cannot be seen with the naked eye. Germs may also reach food through handling, or may be deposited by insects or other creatures. Some insects may lay their eggs on the food, so that the larvae (maggots) can eat soon after hatching. Often, food is spoiled by staleness. It may loose its moisture to the air and become hard and dry. And reactions with oxygen in the air may spoil the flavour. For example, when butter is exposed to the air for a long time, the fat combines with oxygen and acquires a most unpleasant taste. Some foods decay through attack by natural chemicals, called enzymes, which they contain.

Many different techniques are used to preserve food. These include heat treatment, chilling, freezing, drying, curing and the use of chemicals. After these processes, packaging in airtight containers may be carried out so that the food can be kept for a long time. Sterilization is a form of heat treatment in which the food is raised to a high temperature to kill any germs present. Pasteurization is partial sterilization, using only a moderately high temperature to avoid spoiling the flavour of the food.

Left: Louis Pasteur showed that microbes could be killed by heat. He looked at a drop of milk through a microscope and found that it was full of microbes. He heated the milk and cooled it quickly. Most of the microbes were dead. Today, most of our milk is heated and cooled in this way—it is pasteurized. It is safe for us to drink.

Canning

Canning is the most important way of preserving food. Cans are made of thin steel. The steel is coated with tin. After the food is put in the can, the lid is sealed. A machine puts a sealing strip between the lid and the can. Then it presses them tightly together. No air can get into the can. The can is then heated to kill off any germs that would make the food go bad. As the can is airtight, no live germs can get at the food. So it stays fresh for years.

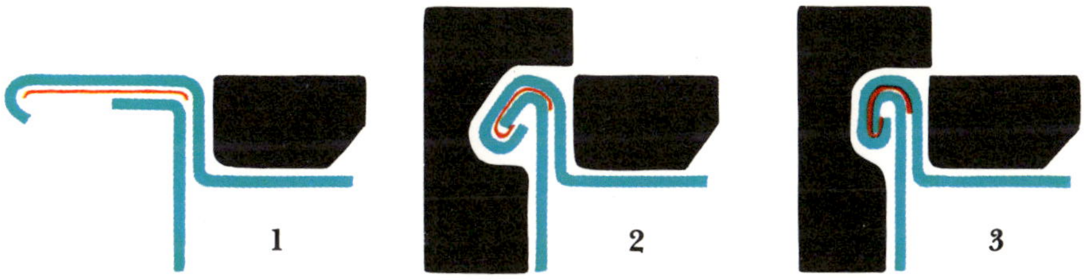

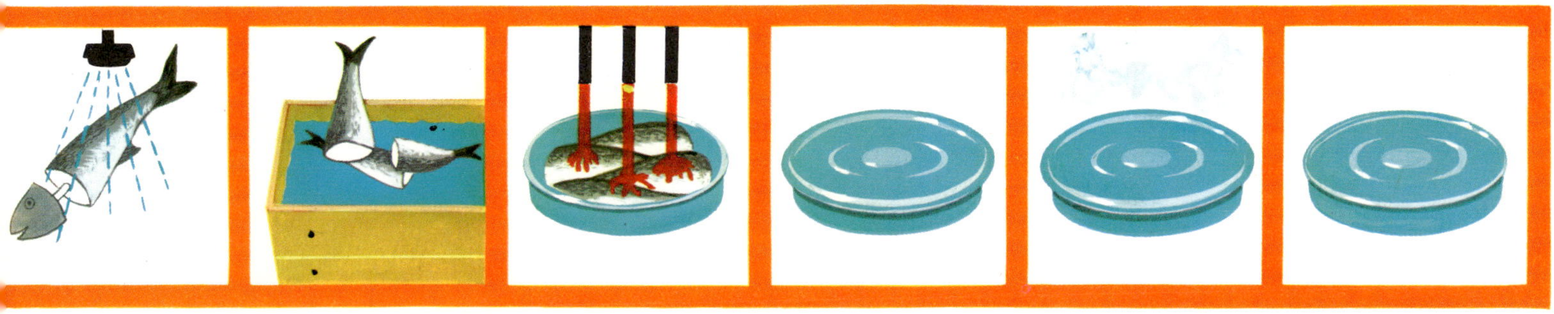

Sometimes sauce is added

Tin half sealed as 2 above

Air is driven out by heat

Can is sealed and heated

Pickling

For many years, fish has been preserved by pickling in brine (strong salty water). Food lasts for quite a long time after being pickled, but it changes its flavour. Most of the 'pickles' we eat have been pickled in vinegar. The picture below show how fish is pickled in barrels.

The fish is cleaned and cut up.

They are soaked in salt water.

They are packed in a barrel

Brine is poured into barrel

More fish are added to barrel

Lid of barrel is closed

Smoking

Fish and meat are preserved by smoking. Herring, salmon and haddock are hung over slow-burning wood fires. The heat of the fire and the chemicals in the wood smoke preserve the fish.

Freezing

Freezing keeps food from going bad. Most food that has to be kept for a while is now quick-frozen. The food is put in a special cold room. There fans blow a steady blast of very cold air over the food. It is frozen very quickly. Then it has to be kept frozen until it is to be used in your kitchen. If the food is not frozen very quickly its flavour and texture are harmed.

Textile Fibres

Most of our clothing is made by knitting or weaving threads of yarn. Through a magnifying glass, you can see that each thread consists of many strands. Each one is finer than a human hair. These strands are called fibres. Natural fibres are obtained from various plants and animals. The most common natural fibres are cotton and wool. Others include flax, silk and hair. Artificial fibres are man-made. These include nylon polyester and rayon. Some materials are made from a mixture of natural and artificial fibres.

Cotton fibres come from the bolls, or seed pods, of the cotton plant. This grows in hot regions, such as Egypt, and the southern United States. When the bolls ripen, they burst to expose a mass of fluffy fibres. The longer ones, called lint, are separated by machine for use in textiles.

Australia is the world's largest producer of wool. Much of it comes from the Merino sheep. This animal has been specially bred for its extremely thick fleece.

Wool from the Merino sheep (1) is cleaned and combed before it is spun into yarn. Linen is made from the flax plant (2). Silk comes from the cocoon (3) of the silkworm (4). Some of the finest cloth comes from the hair of the camel (5). Cotton comes from the seed pods of the cotton plant (6). These cotton *bolls* go into a machine called a gin (below). It separates the fibres from the seeds.

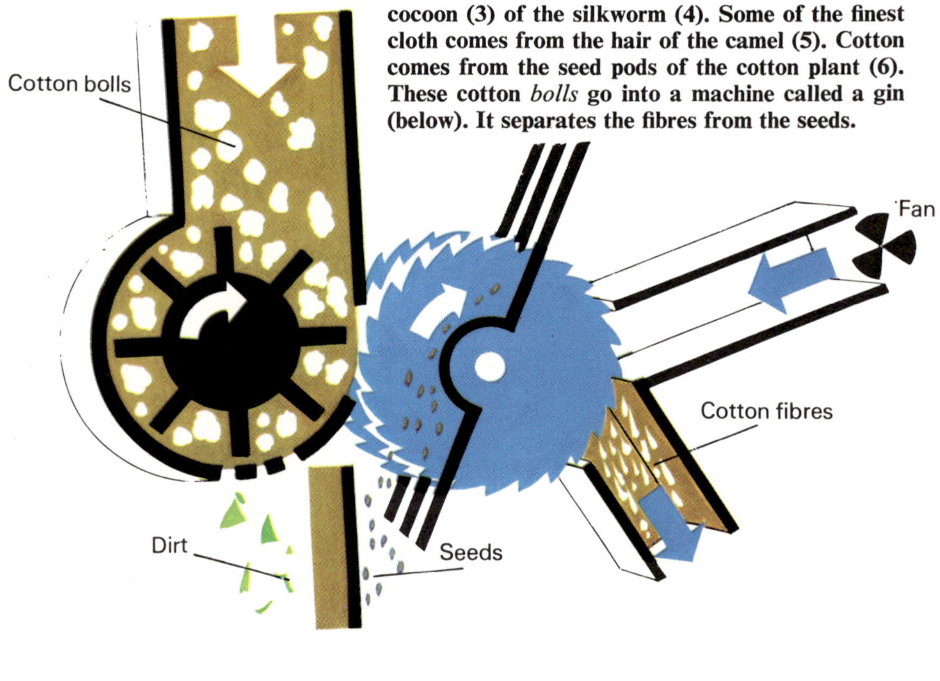

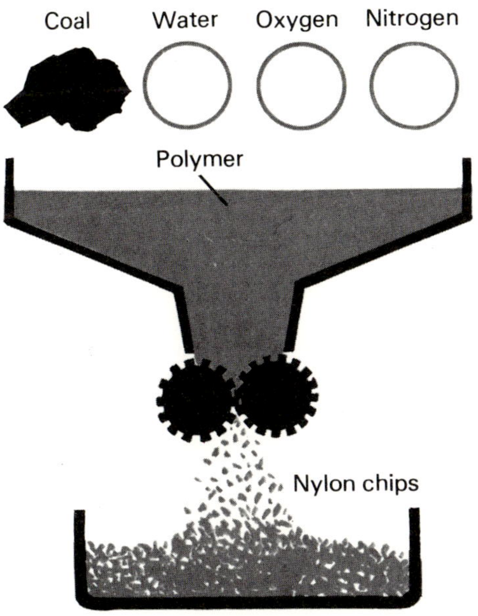

Cloth from Chemicals

Today, most of our clothes are made from chemicals. Fibres are made by mixing chemicals into plastics called polymers. Then the polymers are turned into long threads. Nylon is one of these *synthetic fibres*. It can be made from coal and other chemicals as you can see on the left and right. The chemicals are turned into nylon chips. These chips are melted and the liquid nylon is forced through very small holes. This makes long threads which are hardened by a blast of cool air. The threads are wound onto a reel. Then they can be made into cloth, just like cotton.

Synthetic fibres are stronger than natural fibres. They wear better, are waterproof and do not crease as easily. But they are difficult to dye.

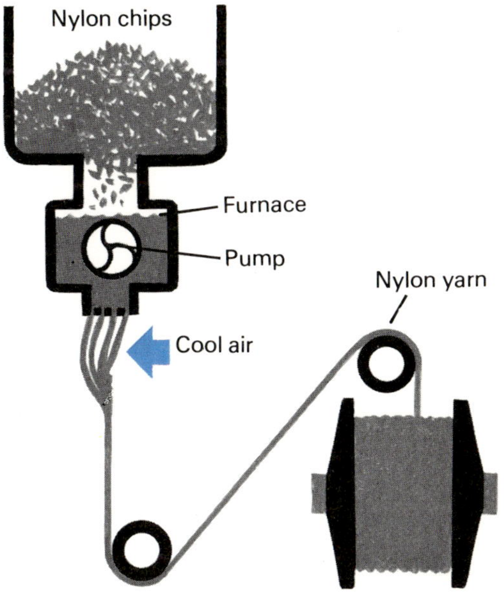

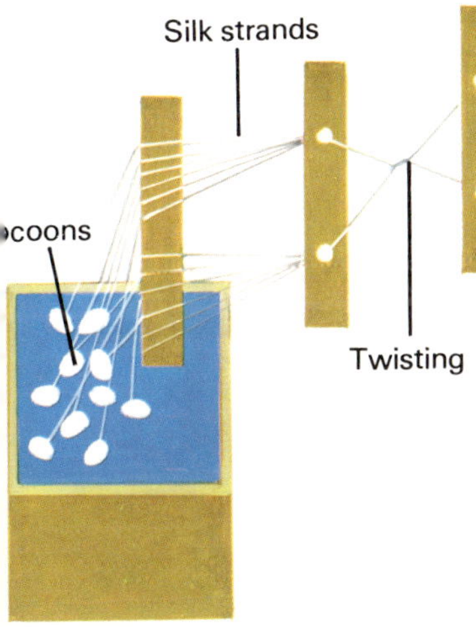

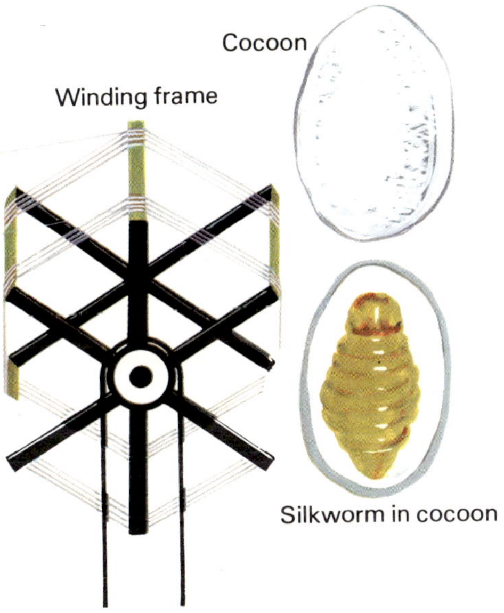

Unwinding the Silk Cocoon

We saw on the opposite page that silk comes from the cocoon of the silkworm. Unravelling this very fine thread from the cocoon is a delicate job. The cocoons are placed in hot water to melt the gum that holds the threads together. Then the threads from several cocoons are pulled out together and twisted. The silk is wound on a frame.

If we look at woollen yarn through a microscope, the fibres are all tangled up.

To make what is called *worsted* yarn, the wool fibres are combed and straightened.

Only man-made fibres and silk have long, continuous strands like those above.

Natural fibres like cotton and wool are made up of short, twisted strands.

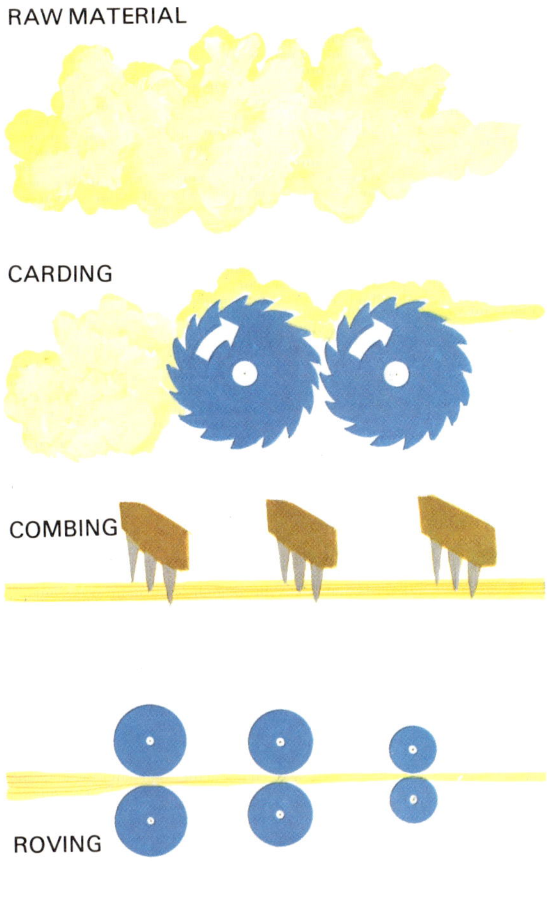

SPINNING

How a Fibre is Made into Strands

The rough cotton or wool has to be made ready for spinning. First it goes through a *carding machine*. This straightens the fibres out and gets rid of the shortest strands. The fibres are then combed by another machine before they go through a roving machine. It pulls the fibre through rollers into finer yarns. They are ready to be spun.

Spinning and Weaving

Fibres, such as wool and cotton, are made into cloth by spinning and weaving. In spinning, numerous fine fibres are twisted together to form a yarn, or thread. The yarn is then woven on looms to make cloth, carpets and other products. Alternatively, the yarn may be made into cloth by knitting.

The earliest examples of spinning and weaving must have perished long ago. But these techniques were certainly practised in western Asia over 8000 years ago. Weaving was probably first used to make mats and baskets from the dried stems of plants. Spinning developed later, and the thread produced was used for many purposes, including the manufacture of fishing nets. Materials woven from the thread proved ideal for clothing. And this eventually led to the production of a wide range of textiles, many with intricate patterns woven into them.

The spinning wheel was used to make yarn. The one shown here has a foot treadle to make it turn.

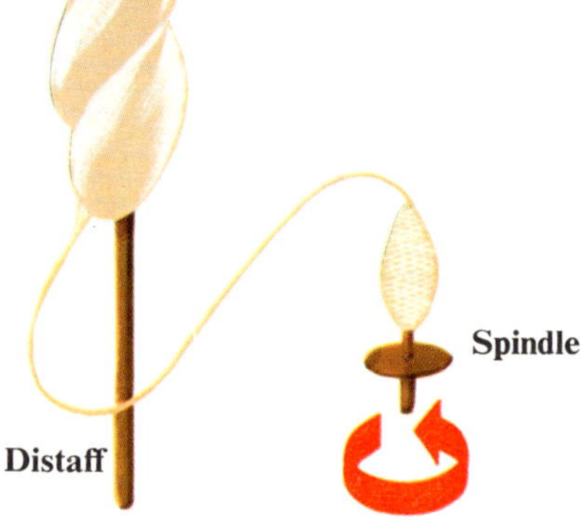

The distaff and spindle for spinning yarn from the rough wool, flax or cotton. Spinning was done in this way from about 1000 BC.

'Cheeses'

Treadle spinning wheel

Spinning

Early spinning was carried out by twisting the fibres by hand. It must have been an extremely slow process until the invention of the spindle, around 1000 BC. Rough wool or cotton was wrapped on a stick called a distaff. Some of the fibres were pulled away and attached to a small spindle. This was twirled in the hand, so that it pulled and twisted the fibres to form a continuous thread. Later, a large wheel, mounted on a stand, was used to turn the spindle. The spinning wheel was used for centuries.

Weaving

Weaving yarn into cloth is done on a loom. A loom threads one set of yarns across another set of yarns. Look closely at a handkerchief and you will see that it is made of very many fine threads going both ways. It has been woven on a loom.

Modern looms like the one below work very quickly and can weave complicated patterns in the cloth. You have heard names like *poplin*, *velvet*, *corduroy*, *gingham*, and *satin*. They are all different ways of weaving cloth.

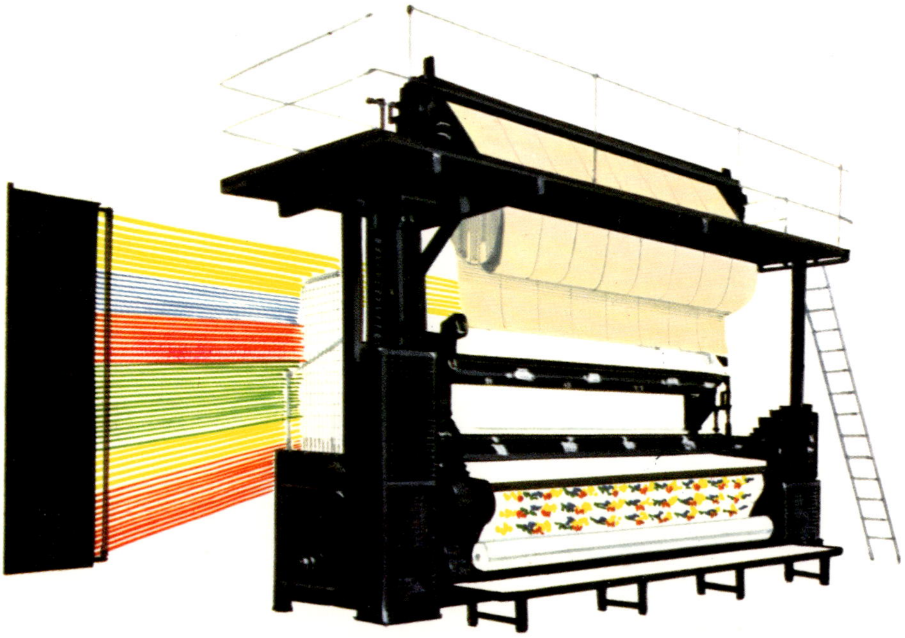

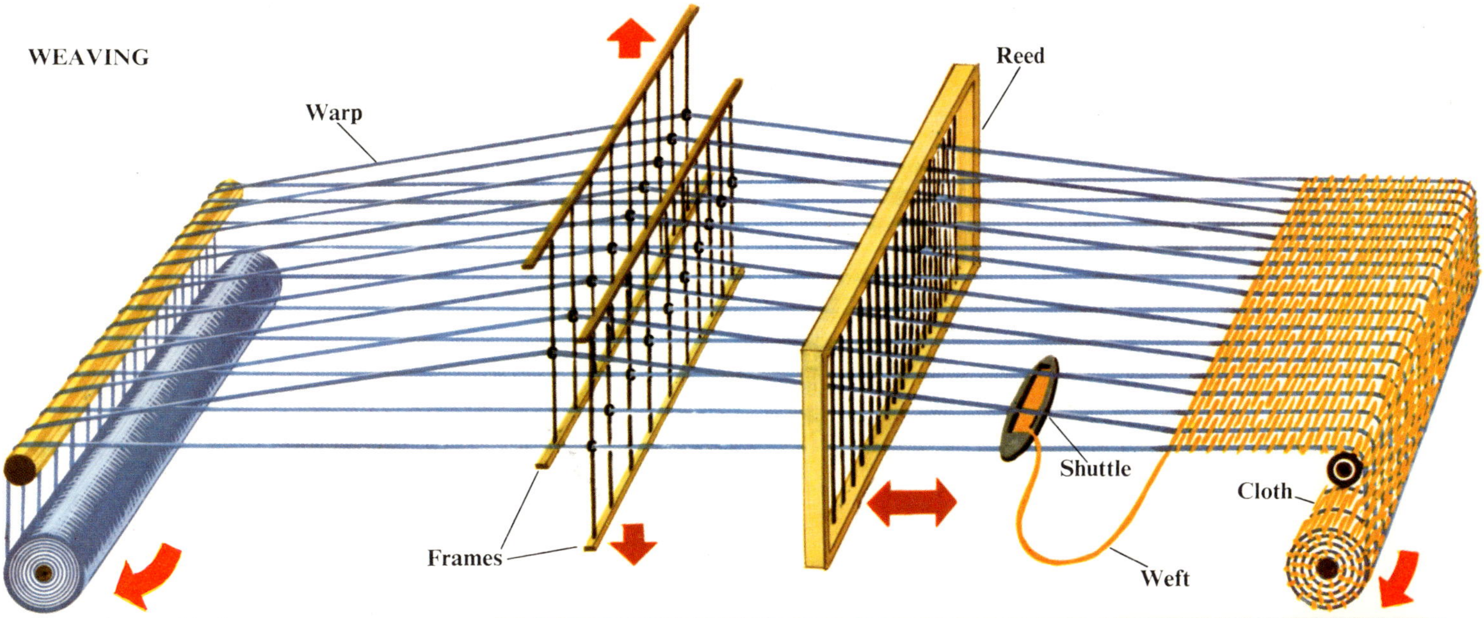

How a Loom Works
One set of yarns (the warp) is stretched over a frame. Then another yarn (the weft) is threaded back and forth over and under the warp. To make threading easier, the warp is raised and lowered by frames. The shuttle with the weft is thrown through between the up and down yarns. The reed is pulled up to the cloth to tighten the weave.

Machines for Materials

Weaving is carried out on frames called looms. Until the 1700s, the weaver had to pass a shuttle of thread by hand between other threads running along the loom. Then, in 1733, John Kay invented the flying shuttle. This moved across the loom on its own. The speed of weaving was increased so much that a yarn shortage followed. To increase yarn production, James Hargreaves invented the spinning jenny in the 1760s. This enabled one person to spin several threads at a time. Powered looms were introduced in the late 1700s. Today, computer-controlled looms can weave complex patterns at high speed.

Wilton carpet weave

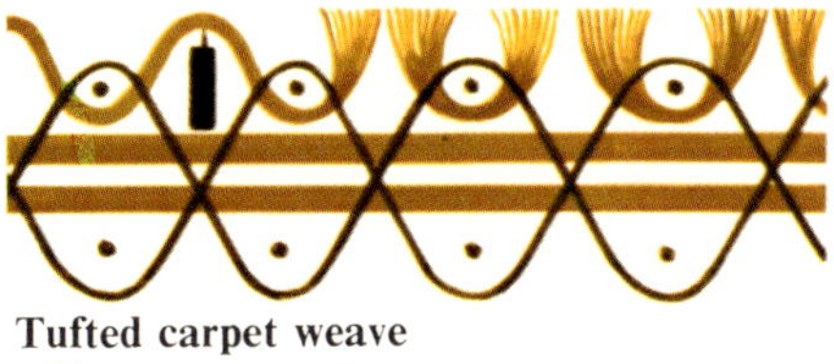

Tufted carpet weave

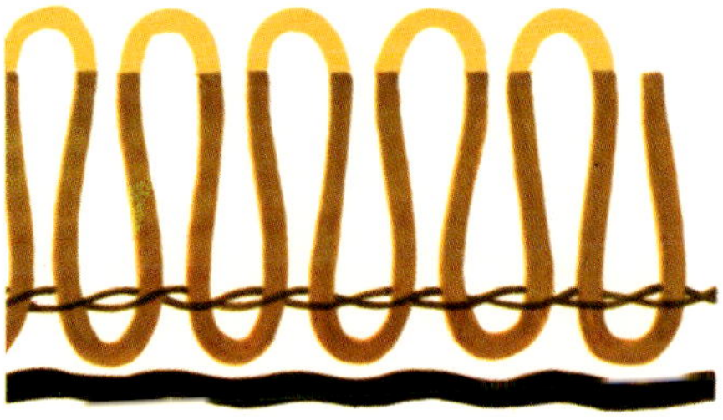

Different Weaves
Different patterns in the cloth can be made by different kinds of weaving. In the plain weave (top right) the weft yarn goes over one warp yarn and under the next. Twills (centre right) are made by passing two or more weft yarns over and under two or more warp yarns. This makes slanting lines in the cloth. Gabardines and denims are woven in this way. Satin weaves give a smooth surface to the cloth. Fine material is sometimes used for the weft yarn, and coarse material for the warp.

Knitting
Knitting is another important way of making yarn into cloth. In knitting, only one yarn is used. If you look closely at something made of very thick wool you will see how this yarn is in rows of loops. And each row of loops hangs on the row above it. Most knitting is now done by machines (below) that can have hundreds of needles working at high speed. They can complete millions of stitches every minute.

Knitting machine

PLAIN WEAVE

TWILL WEAVE

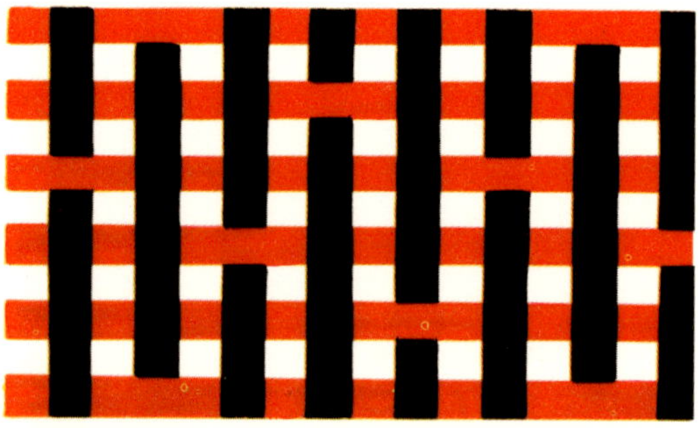

SATIN WEAVE

KNITTING

Digging Machines

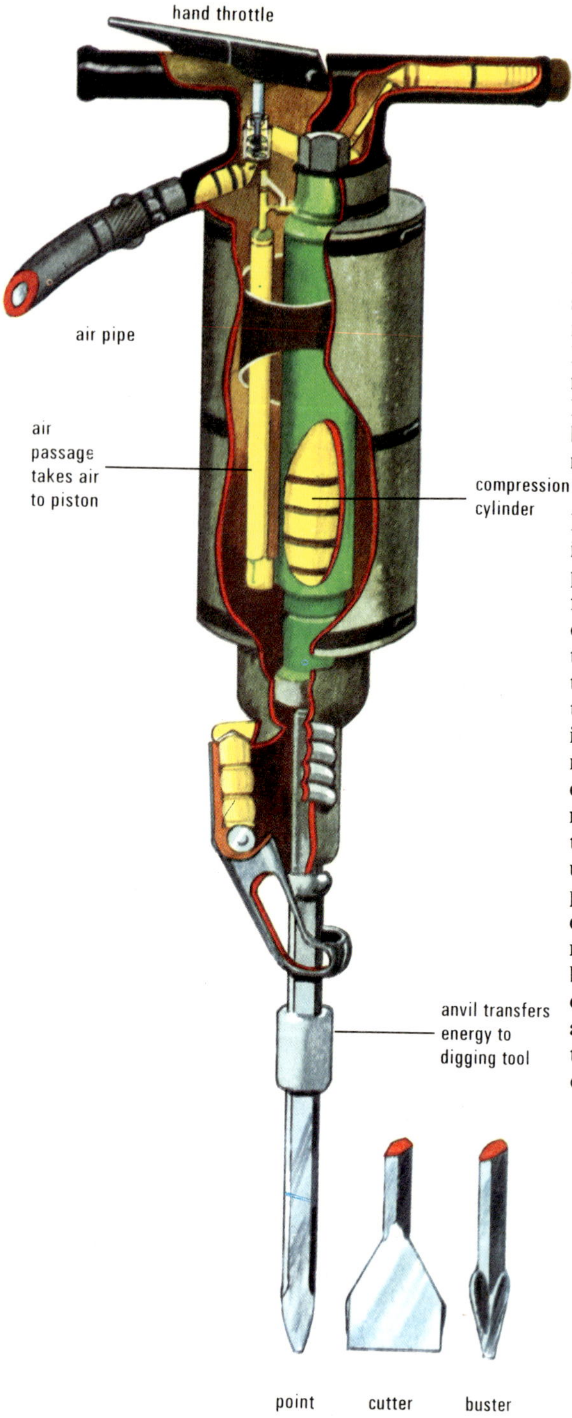

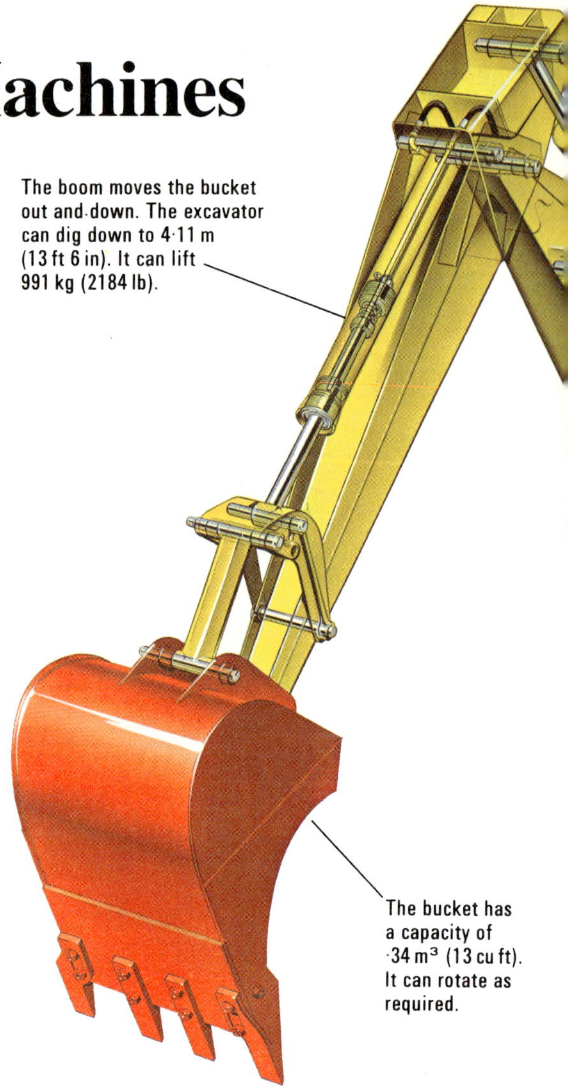

Right: This huge machine is a JCB crawler excavator. Many firms find it uneconomic to spend the large sum of money required for such equipment. Instead, they prefer to hire the machine when it is needed. Lights enable the excavator to be operated at night, so that maximum use can be made of it.

Left: the pneumatic road-breaking drill is powered by compressed air. The air is supplied from a compressor driven by an engine. A flexible pipe carries the air from the compressor to the top of the drill. A hand throttle controls the flow of air into the drill. The air is used to make a piston move inside a cylinder. Valves in the drill make the air push first on the top of the piston, then on the underside. As a result, the piston moves rapidly up and down. This motion is transmitted to a cutting tool at the bottom of the drill. Different cutting tools can be fitted according to the type of material to be broken up and the kind of cut required.

Excavation means digging out soil, rock or other material from the ground. This is done for various reasons. In strip mining, surface earth is excavated to reveal coal or other minerals. Civil engineers excavate surface material in order to lay down foundations for buildings.

Tunnelling often means excavating enormous amounts of rock, as well as earth. Dredging is the removal of silt and other deposits from waterways. Excavation equipment includes special machines and tools, and explosives.

Left: Many types of machine are used for digging underground. Some dig out shafts and tunnels for transport systems. Others are used to mine useful minerals, such as coal. The picture here shows a tunnelling machine at work near London Airport. The tunnel, now completed, is used by trains connecting the airport with central London.

RECORDS AT WORK

- Despite the huge excavating machines which are now in use, the record for the fastest excavation was set up by manual labourers. In 80 days Chinese workers excavated nearly 70 million cubic metres (91·5 million cubic yards) in the North Kiangsu Canal in 1969.
- Big Muskie (right) will move about 1000 million cubic metres (1350 million cubic yards) during a working life of 25 years.
- The record tunnelling distance was set up in 1967. 127·7 m (419 ft) of the Oso Tunnel in an irrigation scheme in Colorado, USA were dug in one day. The average weekly rate of progress was 580·6 m (1905 ft).
- The dredger, *Prins den Nederlanden*, is described as 'the world's most productive muck-shifting tool'. She can dredge 20,000 tonnes from the sea-bed and deposit it at the dumping-ground within an hour.

Right: Big Muskie is the largest mobile machine ever built. It measures nearly 125 metres in length, and 46 metres across. At a staggering 12,000 tonnes, the machine weighs more than 150 Boeing 727 aircraft. And about 1,100 people could be packed into the 167 cubic metre capacity of its bucket. Big Muskie is electrically operated. It consumes enough electricity to power over 27,000 average houses. From a fixed position, the machine can excavate earth from an area of 2.4 hectares (6 acres). It can be used to uncover coal seams.

Clocks and Watches

Methods of telling the time all depend on some regular event, either natural, or planned. The oldest form of clock is the sundial, which depends on the daily movement of the Sun across the sky. The position of the shadow thrown by a stick or rod indicates the time of day. Another ancient time-keeping device was the clepsydra or water clock. The simplest form of clepsydra was a large container from which water leaked slowly from the bottom. The level of the water left inside showed the time on a scale.

Another ancient clock was the sandglass. This was a sealed container with an extremely narrow waist. A quantity of fine sand took a known time to trickle through the waist. The modern egg-timers that many people have in their kitchens work in the same way as a sandglass or hourglass.

The period of time that sand took to trickle through a sand-glass was often a half-hour or an hour. As soon as all the sand was at the bottom, the glass was turned the other way to start timing again.

Candles with notches at regular intervals were not reliable timekeepers. They gave a rough idea of how much time had gone since being lit, but their rate of burning varied.

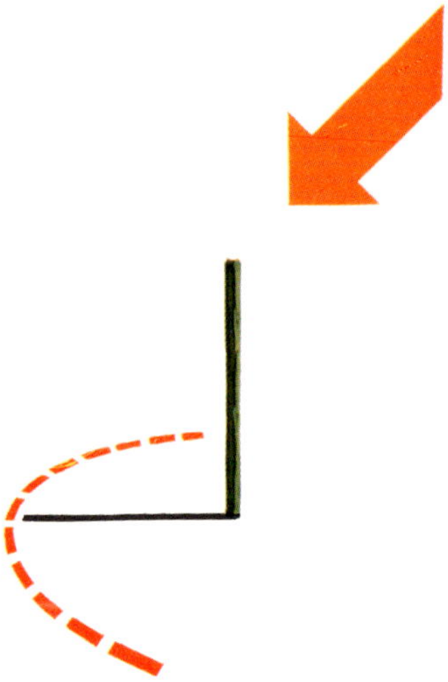

Long, long ago, people used the sun to tell the time. A stick in the ground threw a shadow. The shadow moved around the stick as the sun went across the sky. The shadow told the time of day.

Right: The most famous clock in the world is at the Houses of Parliament, in London. The clock's great bell is known as Big Ben and weighs 13½ tonnes. The pendulum is 4 metres long.

Below: Mechanical watches, and small mechanical clocks are regulated by a balance wheel and hairspring. The wheel spins first one way and then the other. It makes an arm rock to and fro. This allows an escape wheel to move round, one step at a time. The escape wheel is driven by the clock's mainspring, which slowly unwinds.

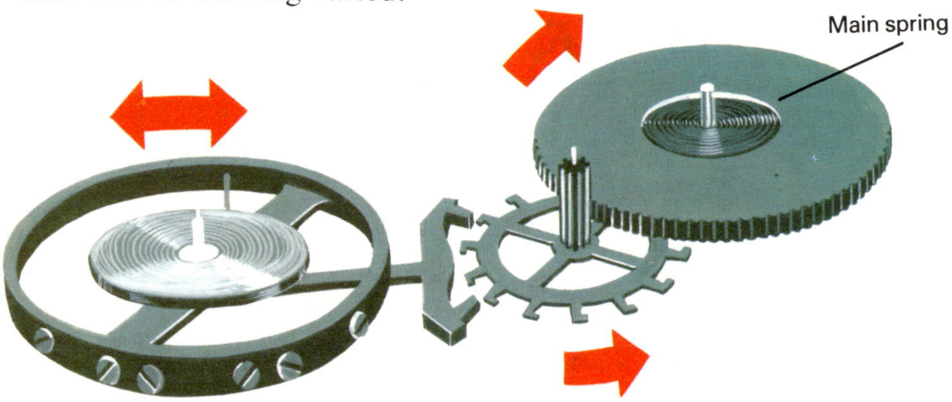

Mechanical clocks

Mechanical clocks appeared in Europe in the 1300s. A weight on a rope descended slowly to turn the mechanism, and a device called an escapement controlled the movement of a toothed escape wheel. The pendulum, introduced in the 1650s, improved accuracy. Today's highly accurate electronic clocks and watches are regulated by vibrating quartz crystals. Atomic clocks are even more accurate, and use vibrating caesium atoms.

Many modern clocks and watches do not have hands at all. The time is shown by numbers which change on the dial or face. These clocks are called digital clocks, because they show the time in digits, or numbers. They are often driven by mains electricity or batteries.

KEY
1. Sundial
2. Water clock
3. Sandglass
4. Notched candle
5. Pendulum
6. Escapement
7. Digital clock
8. Atomic clock
9. Quality wristwatch

Science Tricks

Today's research scientists carry out numerous experiments using complicated equipment which costs thousands of pounds. But important discoveries are sometimes made using very simple apparatus. For example, in 1955, inventor Christopher Cockerell experimented with two tin cans and an electric blower. These ordinary items showed him that an annular (ring-shaped) air jet could be used to lift a sea-going vessel above the waves — a discovery which led to the invention of the hovercraft.

The experiments shown here should help you to demonstrate many scientific principles using simple, everyday objects. The more experiments you try, the more you will understand science. You may also have ideas for devising your own experiments. Those shown here are safe. Make sure that yours are too.

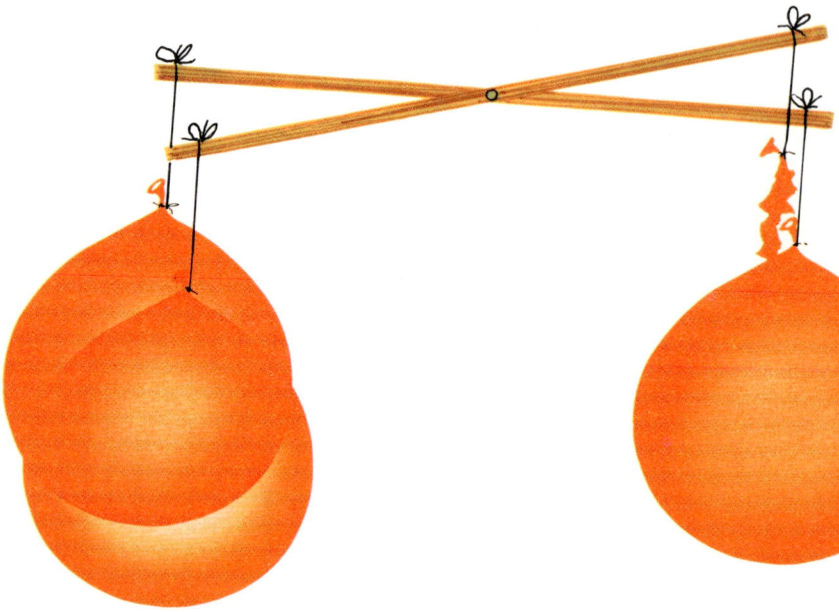

Air has Weight
Blow up two balloons and hang them at the ends of a stick that swings freely. Balance the balloons. If you then burst one of the balloons, the other will go down. The weight of the air in the full balloons pulls it down. Air has weight.

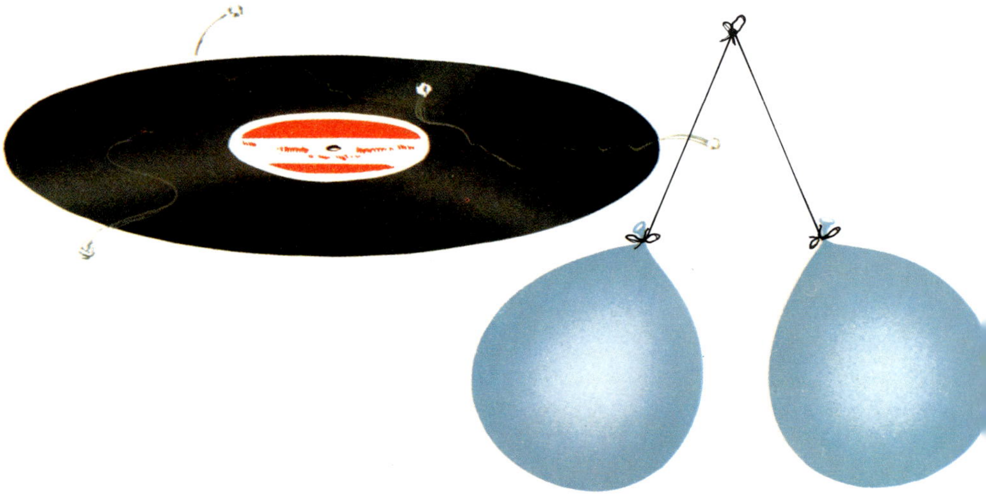

Jumping Balls
Rub an old record with a woollen cloth. Put the record on a glass, then roll up some silver paper into small balls. If you now place the balls on the record, they will jump apart. This occurs because rubbing the record charges it with electricity. And the balls become electrified too when they touch the record. As they all receive the same kind of charge from the record, they jump apart, as like charges repel one another.

The Strange Balloons
Blow up two balloons and hang them from the same point by threads of equal length. Then rub the balloons with a woollen cloth. They will then move apart from each other. For the cloth will have given them both a negative charge. And these charges repel each other.

Ringing Glasses
Take two identical wine glasses and half fill them with water. Place them close together and then rub a wet finger slowly around the rim of one of the glasses. After a while, the glass should start to emit a ringing note. For your finger will make it vibrate. And the second glass should vibrate too. If you place a piece of wire on it, you will see it vibrate. This transmission of sound energy works best if both glasses are tuned to the same note by adjusting the amount of water they contain.

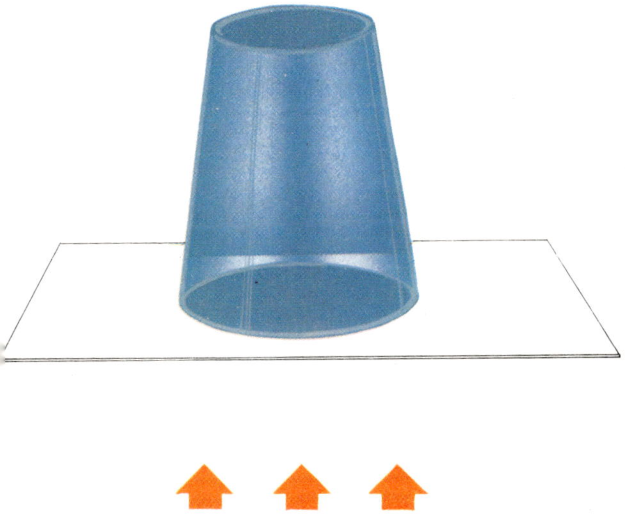

Air Presses in all Directions

Fill a glass with water and lay a piece of card on top of it. Put a hand on the card and turn the glass over. When you take your hand from the card, it stays where it is and no water comes out. This shows that the air presses up on the card with more force than the weight of the water in the glass.

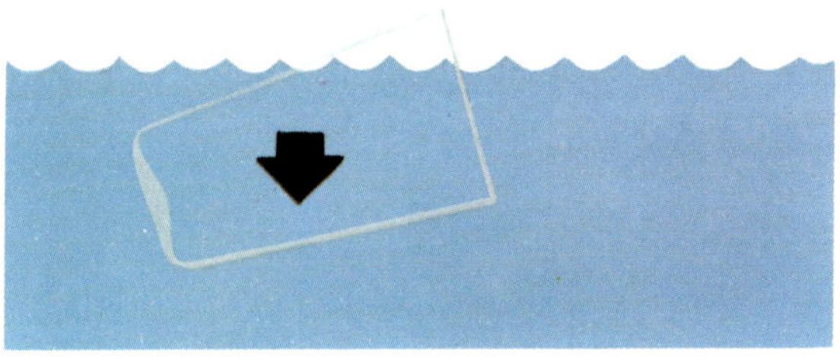

Magic Apples

Hang two apples about a centimetre apart. Blow between the apples and see what happens. They move closer together. Fast-moving air makes a lower air pressure. Blowing between the apples causes lower air pressure in the space. So the air on the other sides of the apples is able to push them together.

Powerful Air

Although we are not normally aware of it, the air exerts great pressure on the things around us. This can be demonstrated by the following simple experiment. Push a glass into a basin of water, so that the glass fills up. Then, holding the glass under the water, turn it so that its mouth points downwards. Now pull the glass almost out of the water, as shown in the lower diagram on the left. You will see that the glass stays full of water. This is because air is pressing down on the water in the basin. This downward pressure is sufficient to push the water up in the glass, as shown by the arrows.

The Magic Spiral

When air is heated, it expands. This makes it less dense, so it tends to rise. In the same way, a cork, released in water, will rise to the surface. You can demonstrate that hot air rises by making a magic spiral. Draw a spiral on stiff paper and cut it out. Then fix a needle or pin in the end of a pencil. Push the pencil into a cork, and stand it upright, with the point at the top. Now balance the spiral on the point, as shown. If you place the device on a radiator, the spiral should spin around. For the rising hot air should push on the paper strip and make it turn.

Hot Air in a Bottle

Light a small piece of paper and drop it into an empty, wide-necked bottle. As soon as the paper has finished burning, take a piece of balloon rubber and stretch it across the mouth of the bottle. Soon you will see the rubber being sucked into the bottle. This happens because, when the paper burns, it heats up the air in the bottle. The air expands on heating. Then, when the flame goes out, the air in the bottle cools once more. This makes the air contract. So the pressure inside the bottle decreases. As a result, the higher air pressure outside forces the rubber down into the bottle. For the experiment to work, the rubber must fit tightly against the mouth of the bottle. To ensure an airtight seal, it will help if you spread some petroleum jelly over the mouth of the bottle before starting.

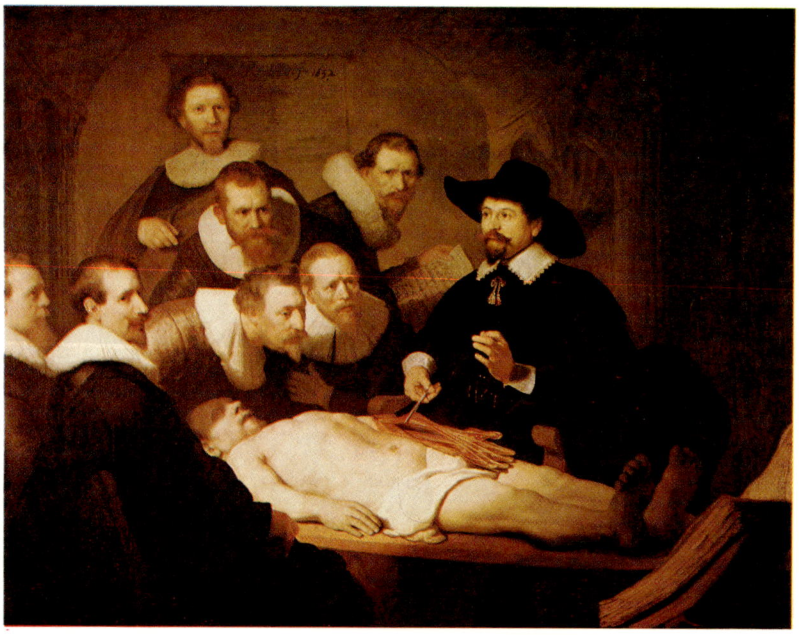

Medicine

Above: Rembrandt's painting 'The Anatomy Lesson' shows the 17th century Dutch anatomist Nicolaas Tulp.

Above: William Morton giving ether to a patient. Morton, an American dentist, began using ether as an anaesthetic in 1846.

Today, most homes have a small supply of medicines, ointments, pills and other items to deal with minor injuries and sickness. In most cases, ailments can be cured without consulting a doctor. And medical attention is usually available, where necessary. But, a few centuries ago, people were not so fortunate. Little was understood about how the body worked. And nothing was known about how disease was caused and spread. As a result, minor injury could quickly lead to serious infection. And it was often necessary to amputate a limb to prevent the infection spreading to the rest of the body. Without anaesthetics, operations were extremely painful. So the patient was usually strapped down to prevent too much movement. Not surprisingly, many patients died during the operation. Many others died as a result of infection of their new wounds. Now all this has changed. The table above shows some of the key discoveries that have revolutionized medicine during the last 400 years.

GREAT ADVANCES IN MEDICINE

Discovery	Discoverer	Date
Microscope	Zacharias Janssen	1590
Blood Circulation	William Harvey	1628
Vaccination	Edward Jenner	1796
Anaesthetic	William Morton	1846
Antiseptic surgery	Joseph Lister	1865
Germs cause disease	Louis Pasteur	1877
Psychoanalysis	Sigmund Freud	1895
X-rays	Wilhelm Roentgen	1895
Radium	Pierre and Marie Curie	1898
Penicillin	Alexander Fleming	1928

Right: Vesalius (1514-64) was the first great anatomist. He dissected human bodies and made careful drawings of what he saw.

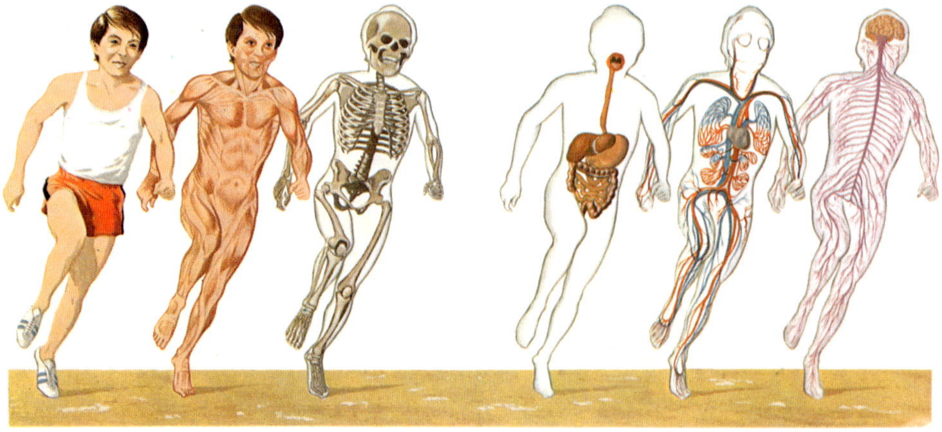

The human body has several important systems which all work together. Shown here, from left to right, are the muscles, the bones or skeleton, the digestive system, the blood system and the nervous system.

▼ With his simple microscope Leeuwenhoek was the first to see bacteria.

▼ Galileo's thermoscope (1592). It was adapted by Santorius into a thermometer in 1612.

▲ The first spectacles were held in the hand. But this 16th-century pair rests on the nose.

◀ Instead of wooden stumps and iron hooks, 16th-century surgeons designed wooden and metal artificial limbs with hinged joints.

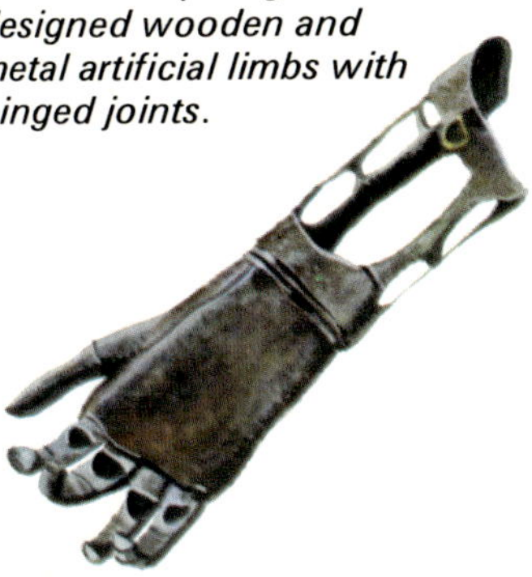

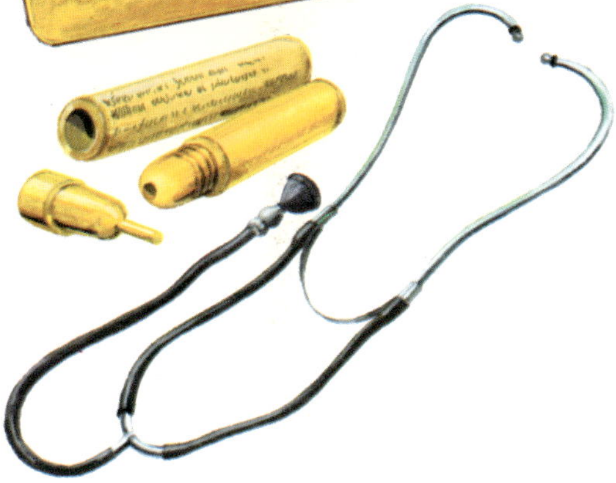

▲ Laennec's stethoscope (1816) beside one that doctors use today to listen to the heart and lungs.

MEDICAL INSTRUMENTS

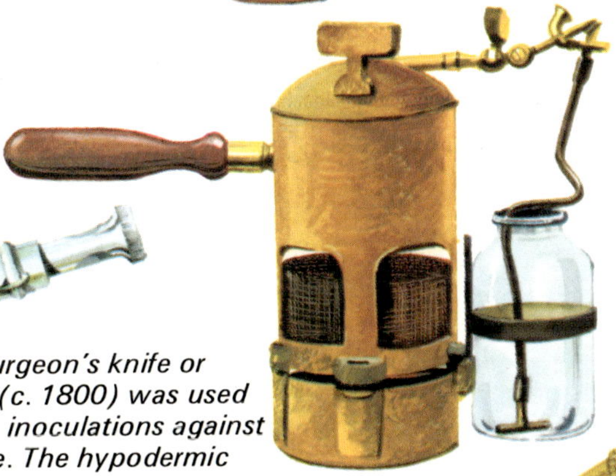

◀ Lister's carbolic spray (1875) worked by a steam kettle. Its purpose was to kill germs in the air. But better results were achieved through hygiene and sterilization.

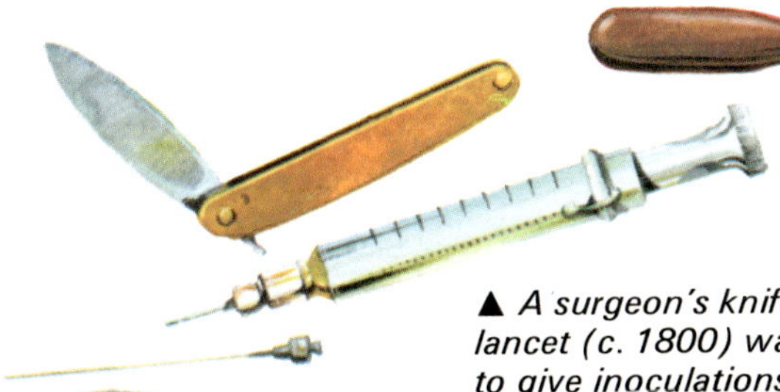

▲ A surgeon's knife or lancet (c. 1800) was used to give inoculations against disease. The hypodermic syringe, was introduced in the 1850s, to give injections.

► An inhaler which fitted over the face and a drop bottle were an anesthetist's equipment in the 1840s.

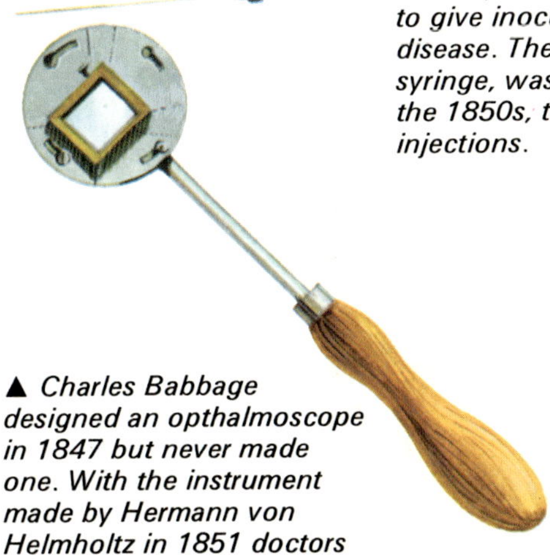

▲ Charles Babbage designed an opthalmoscope in 1847 but never made one. With the instrument made by Hermann von Helmholtz in 1851 doctors could study the human eye more closely.

► This respirator of 1876 – an ancestor of today's iron lung – was pumped by hand.

The Heart and Lungs

An adult of average size has nearly five litres of blood. The heart automatically pumps this vital liquid around the body. Many important functions are carried out by the blood. Its main purpose is to carry various substances from one part of the

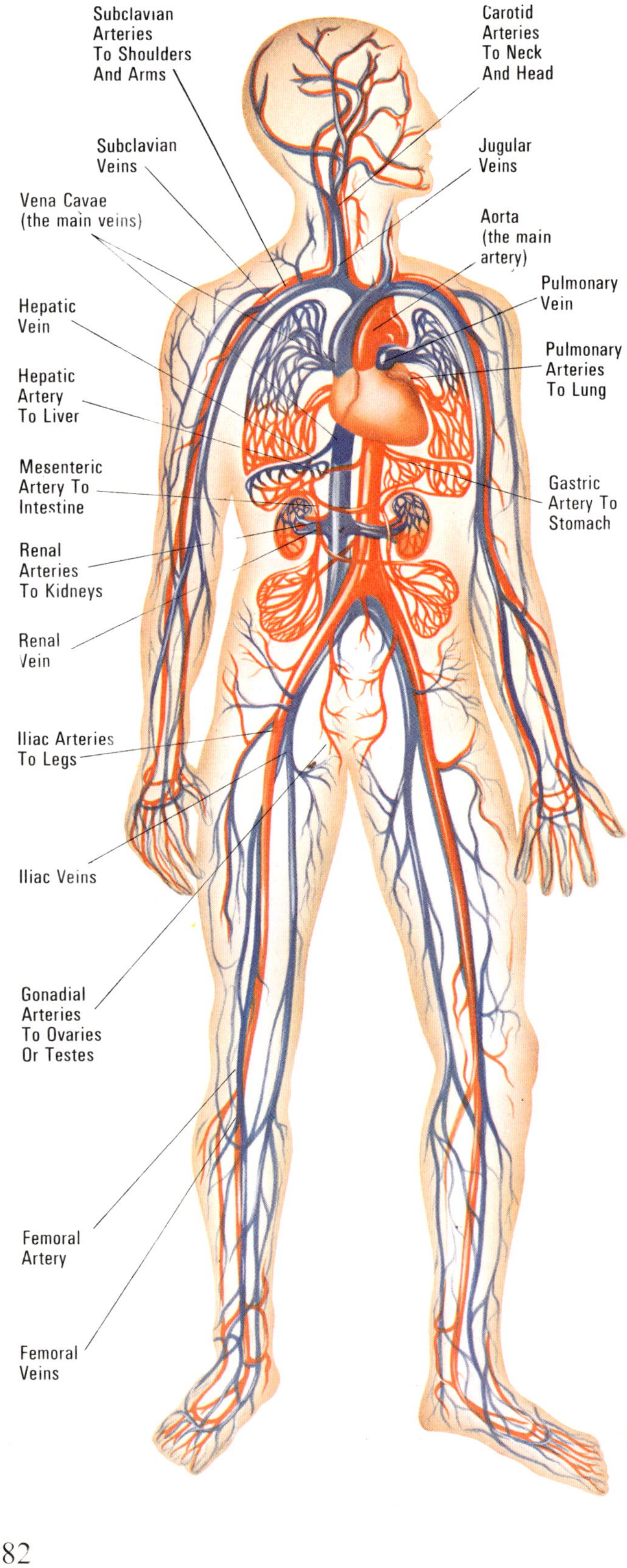

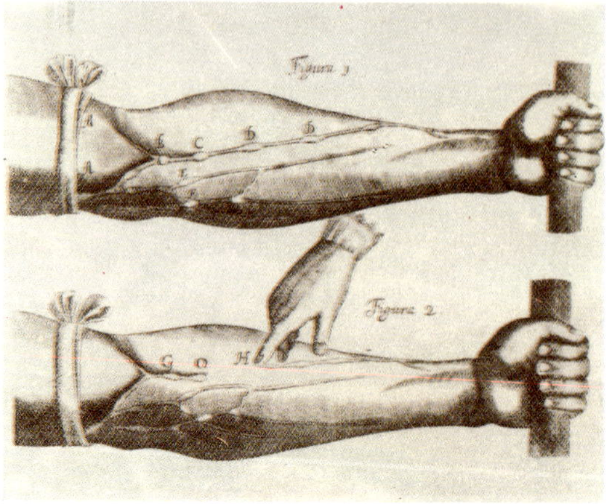

William Harvey (1578-1657) proved that blood circulates around the body. He was the first man to have the idea that the heart acted like a pump. The drawing above is from Harvey's work on the circulation of the blood, published in 1628.

The drawing on the left shows how the blood circulates round the body. The heart pumps blood out through the arteries (shown in red) to all the organs and limbs. The veins (shown in blue) carry the blood back to the heart. Tiny vessels called capillaries act as a bridge between the arteries and the veins. It is our blood that carries food and oxygen to all the cells of our body. It also collects all their waste products. An adult's body contains about 5 litres (9 pints) of blood, and it runs through more than 96,000 km (60,000 miles) of blood vessels.

Below: Many lives are saved every day by blood transfusions. Blood taken from donors is stored at a temperature of 4.5°C (40°F) and is mixed with chemicals to prevent it clotting.

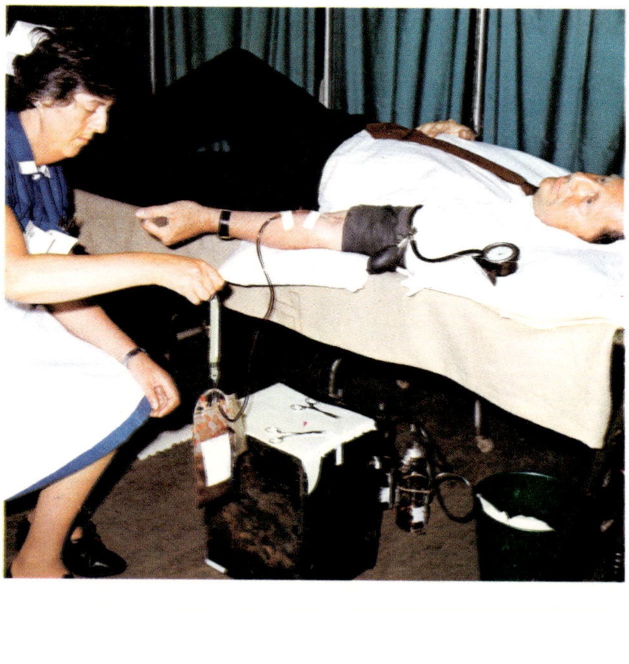

body to another. When it flows through the lungs, the blood absorbs oxygen from the air we breathe in. And, in the intestines, the blood absorbs nutrients from our food. Both oxygen and nutrients are used to nourish our bodies' cells. Waste carbon dioxide gas from the cells is absorbed by the blood and carried to the lungs. This gas is removed by the action of breathing out. When the blood cells get old they are broken down by the liver. The part of the blood that absorbs oxygen is stored for re-use and the rest is excreted. Other wastes are taken to the kidneys and passed out of the blood in the urine.

The blood also carries chemicals called hormones and enzymes around the body. Hormones help tissues, cells and organs to control various body activities, such as growth and reproduction. Enzymes are substances that control the millions of vital chemical reactions that take place in the body.

Besides carrying substances, the blood also carries heat around the body. Heat is produced internally when food substances combine with oxygen in the body cells. Most heat is produced in the liver. In addition, some heat is produced by movement of the muscles.

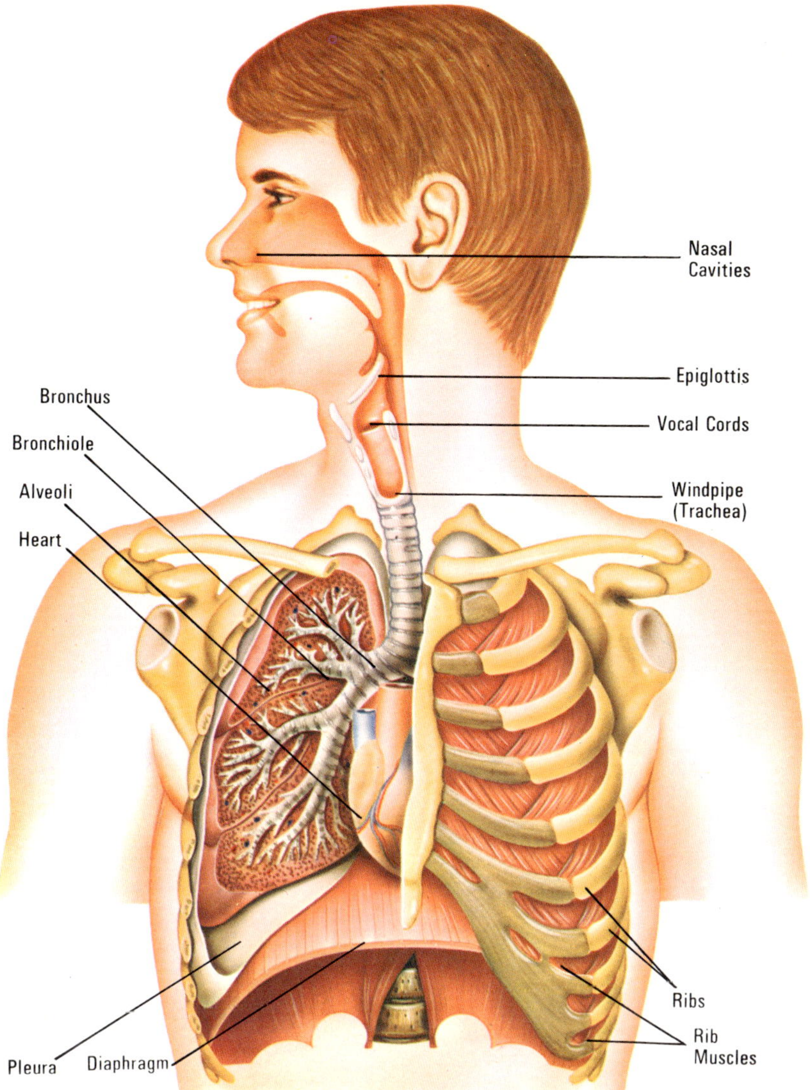

Above, right: The constant and effortless motion of our lungs draws into the body a vital supply of oxygen. The lungs are like a pair of bellows in the chest. When the diaphragm and the rib muscles contract, the space inside is enlarged and air rushes down through the nose into the lungs. When the muscles relax the lungs are squeezed and air is pushed out (below).

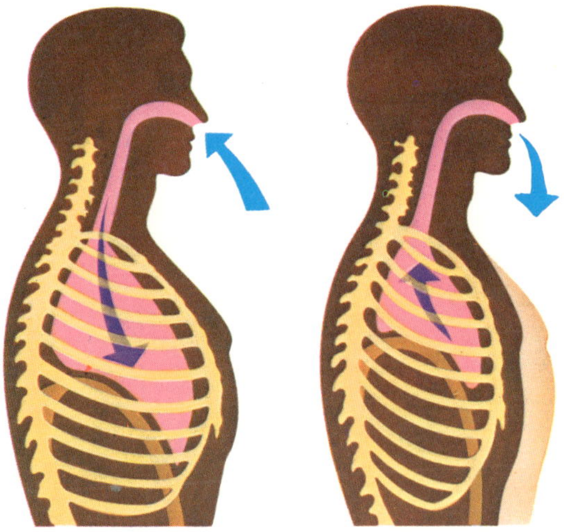

Other Functions of the Blood

Some heat may also be taken in from the Sun or some other external source. The circulation of the blood helps to keep the heat evenly distributed throughout the body. Usually, the body has more heat than it needs. So heat must be lost in order to keep the body at its normal temperature of 37°C. Most of the excess heat is lost through the skin. As the body temperature rises, more blood is passed through tiny vessels in the skin. As a result, the skin reddens, and it radiates more heat than normal. Also, increased blood supply to the sweat glands causes them to make more sweat. In evaporating from the skin, the sweat absorbs heat from the body.

Another important function of the blood is to protect the body. When the skin is wounded, blood flows out and starts to clot within a few minutes. In this way, a temporary seal is provided over the wound while the skin heals. The blood also protects us by fighting infection. For it contains white cells that can attack disease-causing organisms. Alternatively, the white cells may produce substances to counteract the poisons produced by the organisms. The blood contains five types of white cell, each providing a different form of protection.

How the Body Moves

Our skeleton serves many purposes. It provides a strong framework on which our bodies are built. It gives protection to important organs, such as the brain, heart and lungs. And it enables us to stand upright. Joints between the bones allow us to move in various ways. Movements occur when we contract muscles. These are attached to bones or other parts of our bodies. Another important function of the skeleton is the production of red blood cells. These are made in the soft marrow inside various long bones.

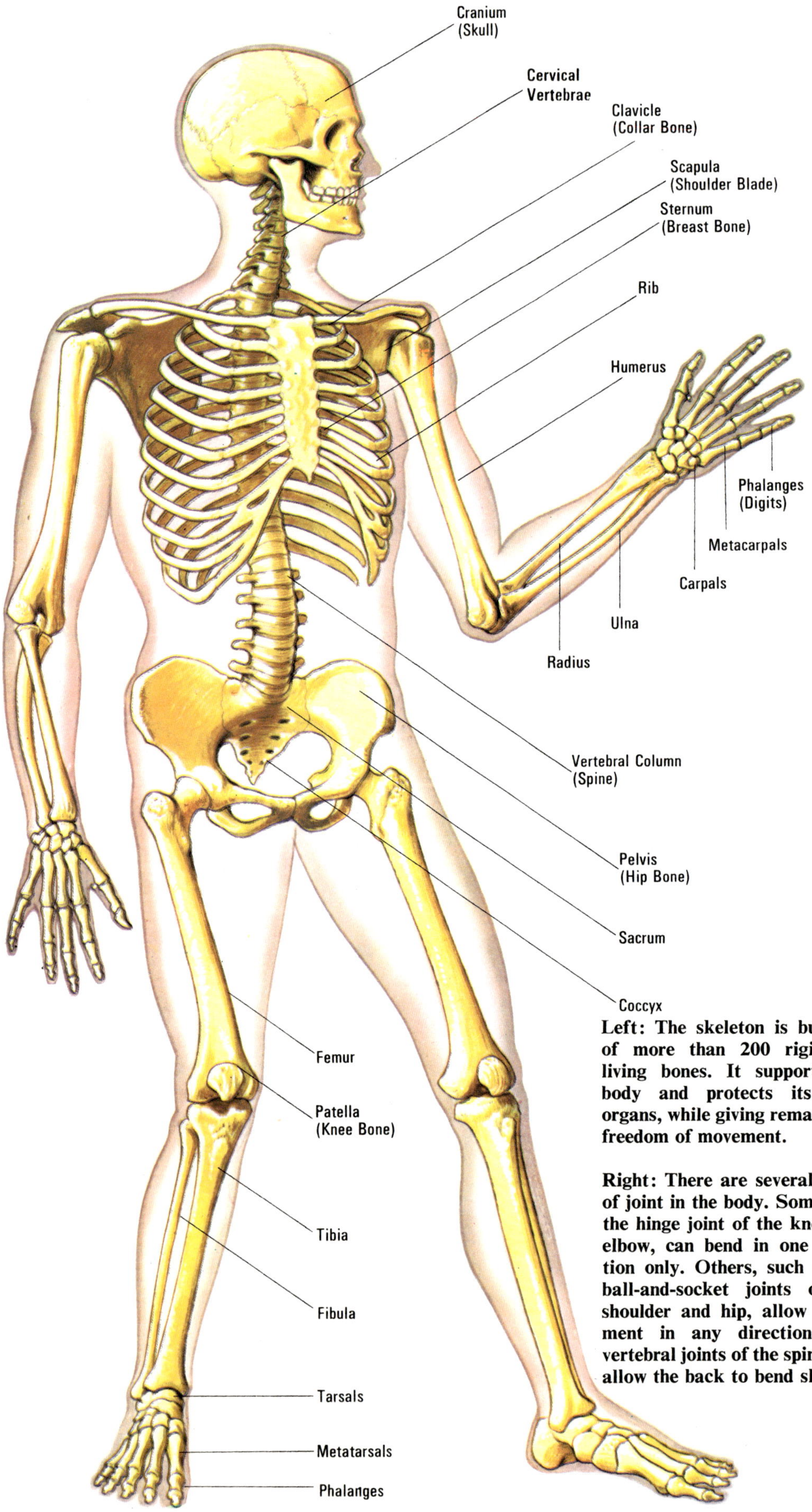

Left: The skeleton is built up of more than 200 rigid but living bones. It supports the body and protects its vital organs, while giving remarkable freedom of movement.

Right: There are several kinds of joint in the body. Some, like the hinge joint of the knee and elbow, can bend in one direction only. Others, such as the ball-and-socket joints of the shoulder and hip, allow movement in any direction. The vertebral joints of the spine only allow the back to bend slightly.

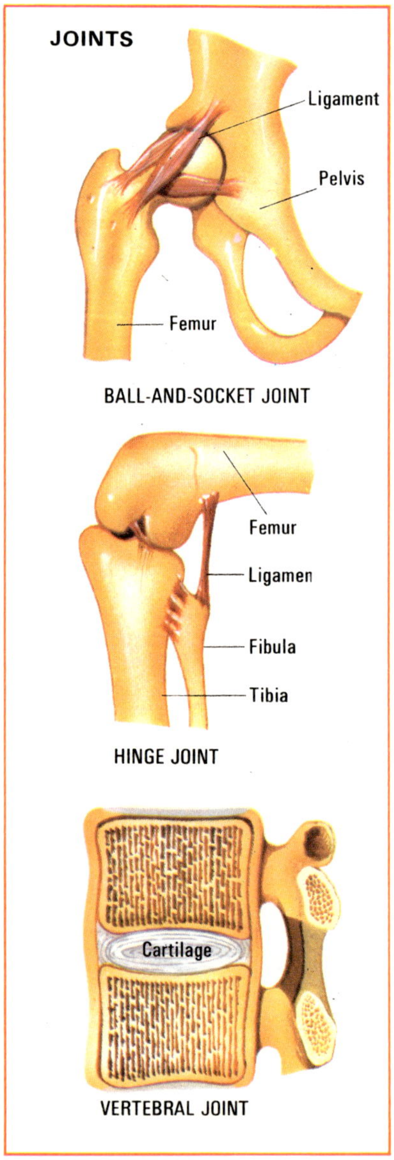

At birth, a child has over 300 bones. But many of them gradually fuse together. This reduces the number of separate bones to about 206 in the adult. Where bones fuse together, they form immovable joints. These are found, for example, in the pelvis and skull.

Four types of movable joint are found in the human skeleton. The ball-and-socket joint allows movement in many directions. Such a joint connects the leg and hip. The knee joint, which allows movement in one plane only, is a hinge type. Partial rotation of the head is allowed by a pivot joint connecting it to the spine. In the wrist and ankle, gliding joints allow bones to slide over others.

Muscles are of two main types. Involuntary muscles are normally automatically controlled by the brain with no conscious effort. Voluntary muscles are those we can easily control at will.

MUSCLE MAN

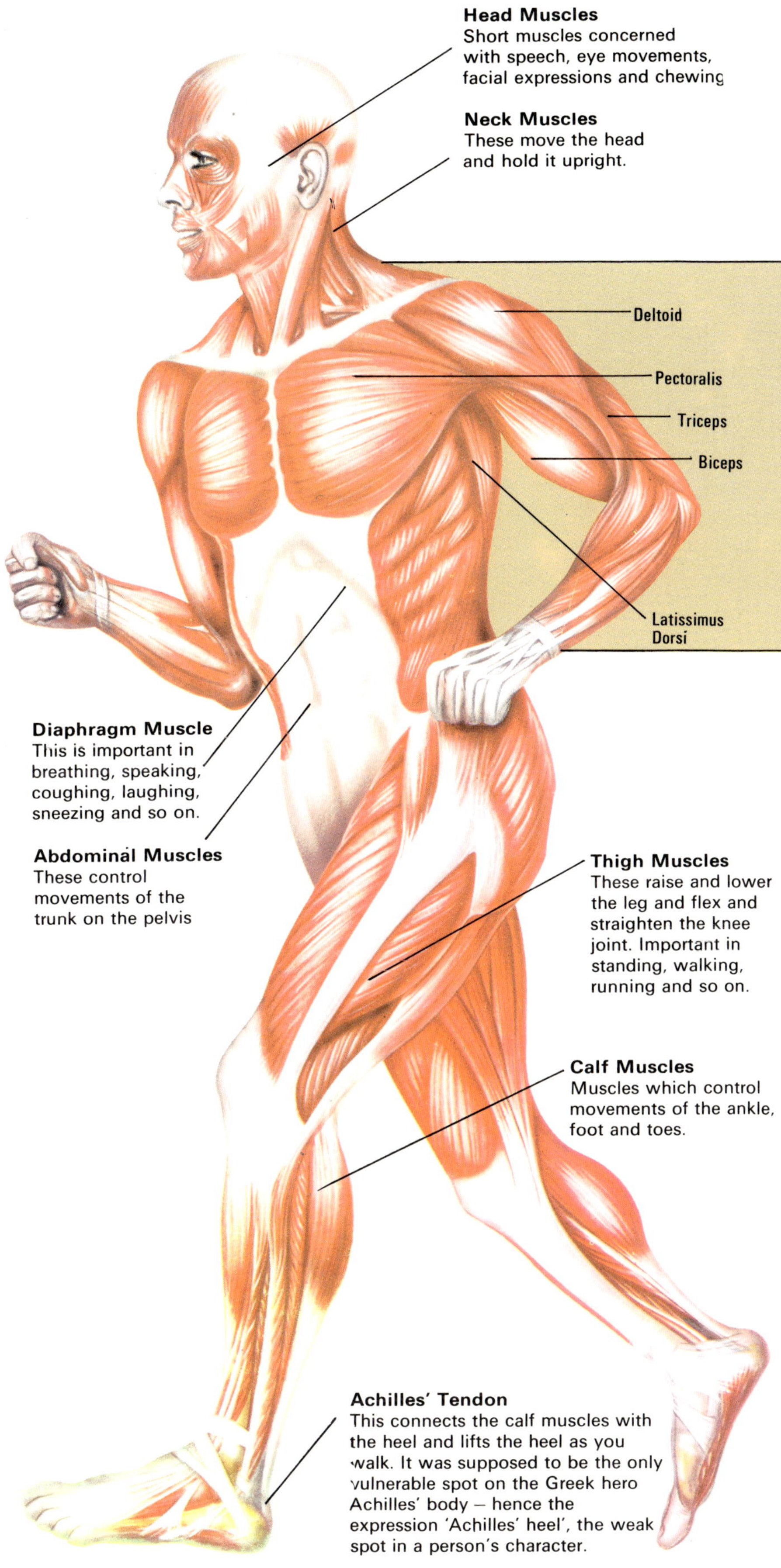

Muscles of the Arm and Shoulder

The biceps muscle flexes, or bends, the arm. The deltoid lifts the arm. The teres behind the shoulder and the latissimus dorsi pull the arm down and back. The pectoralis muscle pulls the arm forward and across the front of the body. Muscles in the forearm extend and flex the fingers, while rotator muscles enable us to rotate hand and forearm. So, to pick an object off the table: deltoid and pectoralis lift and move the arm forwards; the triceps lowers the forearm and rotator muscles turn forearm and hand; flexor muscles in the forearm bend the fingers (to grasp the object); and finally the biceps lifts the arm up.

USING YOUR MUSCLES

Clench your fist and bend your arm upwards. You can see the muscle in your upper arm swell. It does not get bigger. It only contracts or changes shape to become shorter and fatter. When you relax your arm, you can see your muscles relax too.

All muscles tire when they are used, except the heart, which goes on tirelessly.

The Nervous System

The body is active all the time, even when we are asleep. For our lungs must continue to expand and contract, so that we breathe in fresh air all the time. And our heart must keep pumping blood through our arteries and veins so that various vital processes continue. These bodily functions are controlled by the brain. When we are awake, the brain has many additional tasks to perform. Our sense organs send signals to the brain. These signals inform the brain about things we hear, see, smell, taste and touch. For example, sounds picked up by the ear are converted by our hearing mechanism into electrical signals. These stimulate the brain, so that we 'hear' the signals as sounds. If we are listening to speech, we may think about what is being said — again using the brain. Then, if we want to answer back, the brain sends signals to the throat and mouth muscles involved in speaking. Processes like this are very complicated. And yet the brain can normally carry them out quickly and reliably, while dealing with other, routine things at the same time.

The body's control system is called the nervous system. It consists of the brain, its extension, called the spinal chord, and various nerves. The nerves connect with the body's sense organs, muscles and glands. The brain and spinal chord are responsible for control, and form what is called the central nervous system. The nerves branching out from these parts make up the peripheral nervous system. They are fibres formed from two main types of cells called neurons. Sensory neurons carry signals from sense cells to the central nervous system. And motor neurons carry signals from the central nervous system to muscles or other body parts. Connector neurons in the central nervous system connect with the sensory and motor neurons.

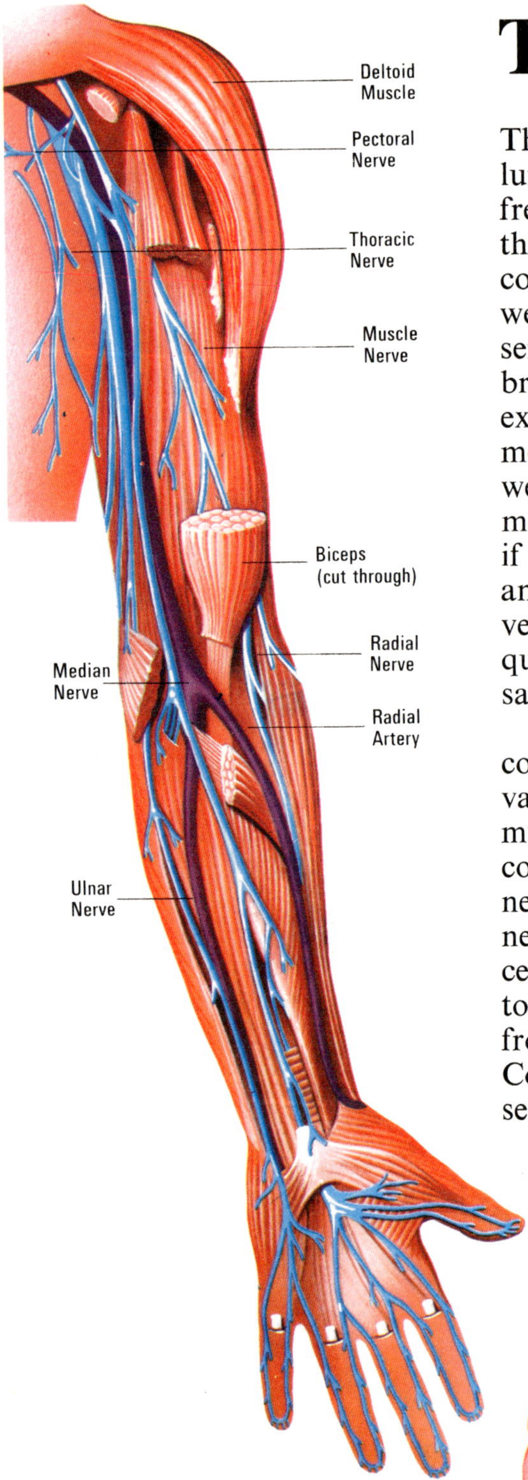

Above: The nerves in our limbs hold lots of nerve fibres, which carry electrical signals to and from the brain. Touching the skin, or changing its temperature, makes its sense cells work. They send signals along the nerves to the brain. The nerves also carry signals from the brain. These are sent to the muscles to make them move as required. Actions controlled by the brain are called voluntary movements. Involuntary movements, called reflex actions, are responses carried out automatically by the body. For example, the hand will normally move away automatically when it touches a hot object. In such cases, signals from the sensory cells travel via the spinal chord to the correct muscles. This gives the quick response necessary if injury is to be avoided. By the time the brain is aware of what has happened, we have snatched our hand away.

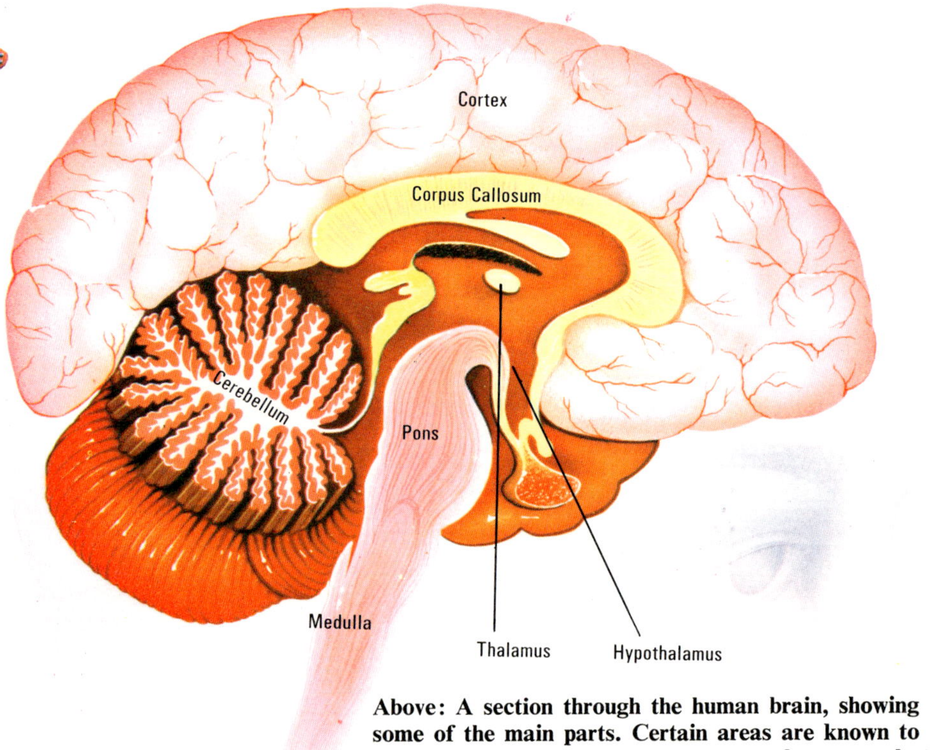

Above: A section through the human brain, showing some of the main parts. Certain areas are known to have special jobs. The cerebellum, for example, controls a person's balance and co-ordination of movements. The medulla joins the brain to the spinal cord.

Sight

Light reflected from the object passes through the cornea and lens. These bend the light rays, so that an image is formed on the retina. This sends out nerve signals that the brain interprets as a picture.

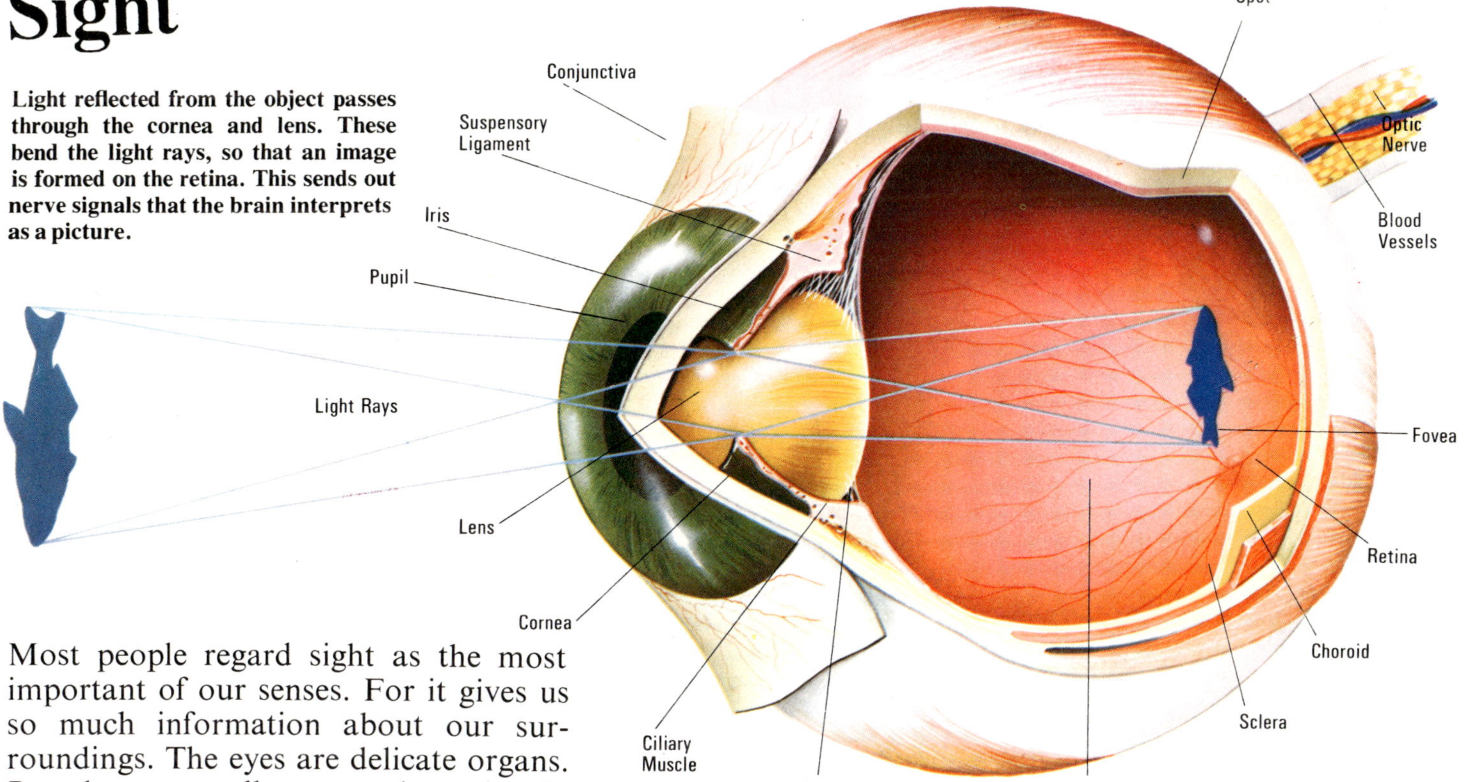

Most people regard sight as the most important of our senses. For it gives us so much information about our surroundings. The eyes are delicate organs. But they are well protected, resting in their bony sockets in the skull. At the front of each eye is the transparent cornea, through which light enters. The amount of light passing through is controlled by the iris, which has an opening called the pupil. In dim light, the pupil enlarges to let in as much light as possible. Behind the pupil is a transparent lens. The cornea and lens bend the incoming light rays so that they form an image on the retina. This is a light-sensitive layer inside the back of the eye. It contains millions of cells called rods and cones. The rods, numbering about 130 million, are extremely sensitive to light. They enable us to see in quite dim conditions. But they cannot distinguish between one colour and another. This task is performed by the cones, of which there are about seven million. As the cones are much less sensitive than the rods, we have little sensation of colour in dim lighting.

The blind spot is a small patch on the retina where there are no rods or cones. At this point is attached the optic nerve. It carries signals from the rods and cones to the brain.

The eyes form slightly different images. So the signals they send to the brain differ too. The brain uses the different signals to work out how far away from us things are.

LONG AND SHORT SIGHT

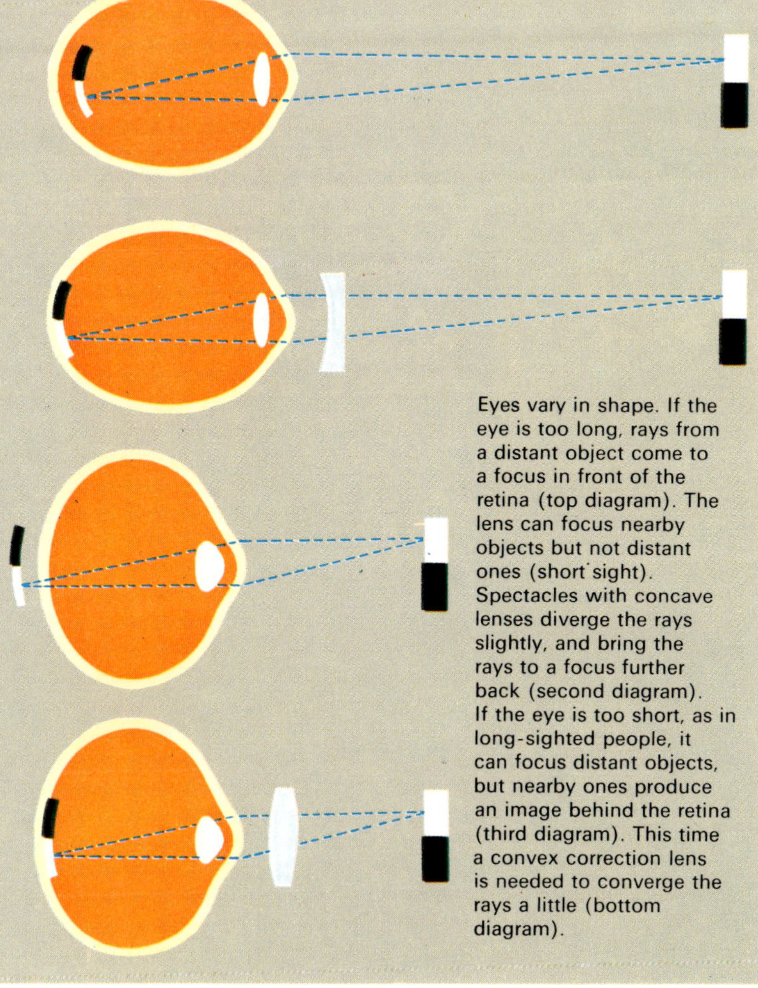

Eyes vary in shape. If the eye is too long, rays from a distant object come to a focus in front of the retina (top diagram). The lens can focus nearby objects but not distant ones (short sight). Spectacles with concave lenses diverge the rays slightly, and bring the rays to a focus further back (second diagram). If the eye is too short, as in long-sighted people, it can focus distant objects, but nearby ones produce an image behind the retina (third diagram). This time a convex correction lens is needed to converge the rays a little (bottom diagram).

Reproduction

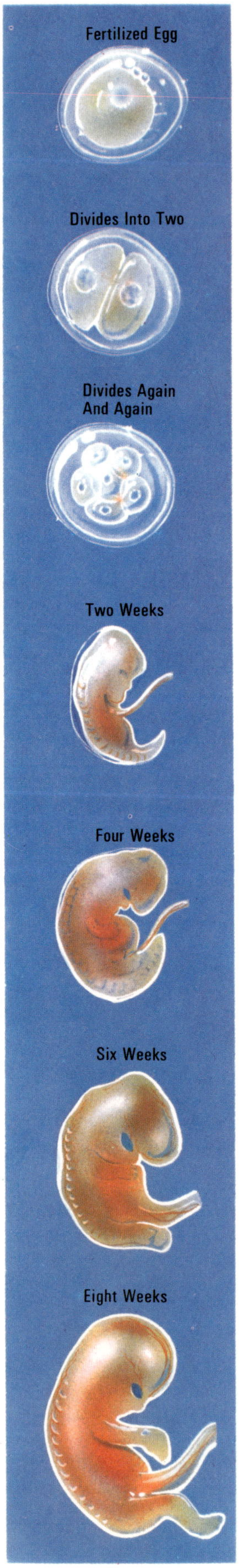

Plants and animals reproduce in various ways. Bacteria and many other single-celled creatures reproduce by splitting in half. The two parts then grow to the size of the original parent cell. This is one example of asexual reproduction. Sexual reproduction occurs in most higher plants and animals, including humans. This involves the joining of male and female gametes (sex cells) in a process called fertilization.

In humans, the male gametes are called sperms. These develop in a pair of reproductive organs called the testes. The female's two reproductive organs are called ovaries. They produce the female gametes, called ova, or eggs. Both male and female gametes are extremely small. During mating, the male's sex organ, or penis, is inserted into the female's vagina. This passage leads to the uterus, or womb. Sperms are ejected from the penis during mating and left in the female's body. They move up through the womb and may meet an egg coming down from an ovary. An egg is fertilized if a sperm manages to penetrate it.

Left: Stages in the growth of a foetus, from the first division of cells to the perfectly formed miniature human being. The drawing on the right shows the position and size of the foetus after 6½ months of pregnancy.

A fertilized egg is called a zygote. This comes down into the womb, where it starts to grow. The zygote does this by splitting in two, again and again. The number of cells thus increase rapidly, and the zygote becomes an embryo, or developing child. This becomes attached to the womb seven days after fertilization. A tube called the umbilical cord connects the embryo's abdomen with the wall of the womb. A flat, circular growth forms where the cord joins the womb. Here, the embryo's blood passes close to the mother's blood. The blood in the two systems does not mix. But oxygen and food materials necessary for the embryo's growth pass from the mother's blood into its own. Birth normally occurs after about nine months in the womb.

Above: Identical twins happen when a single fertilized egg divides into two separate embryos, each of which develops into a separate baby. The photograph on the right shows the foetus, safe in its protective sac inside the womb. It gets oxygen and food from its mother's bloodstream.

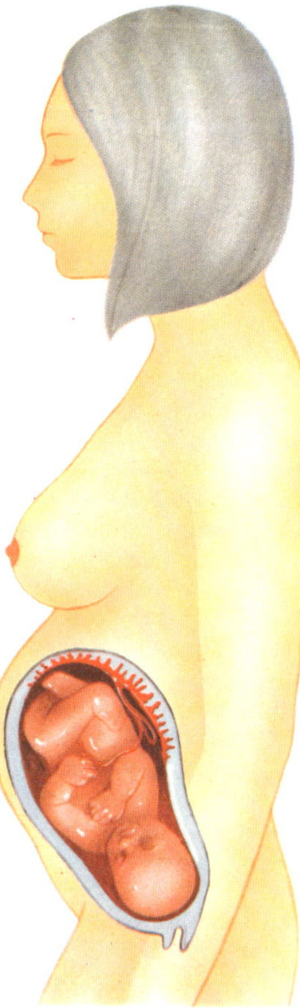

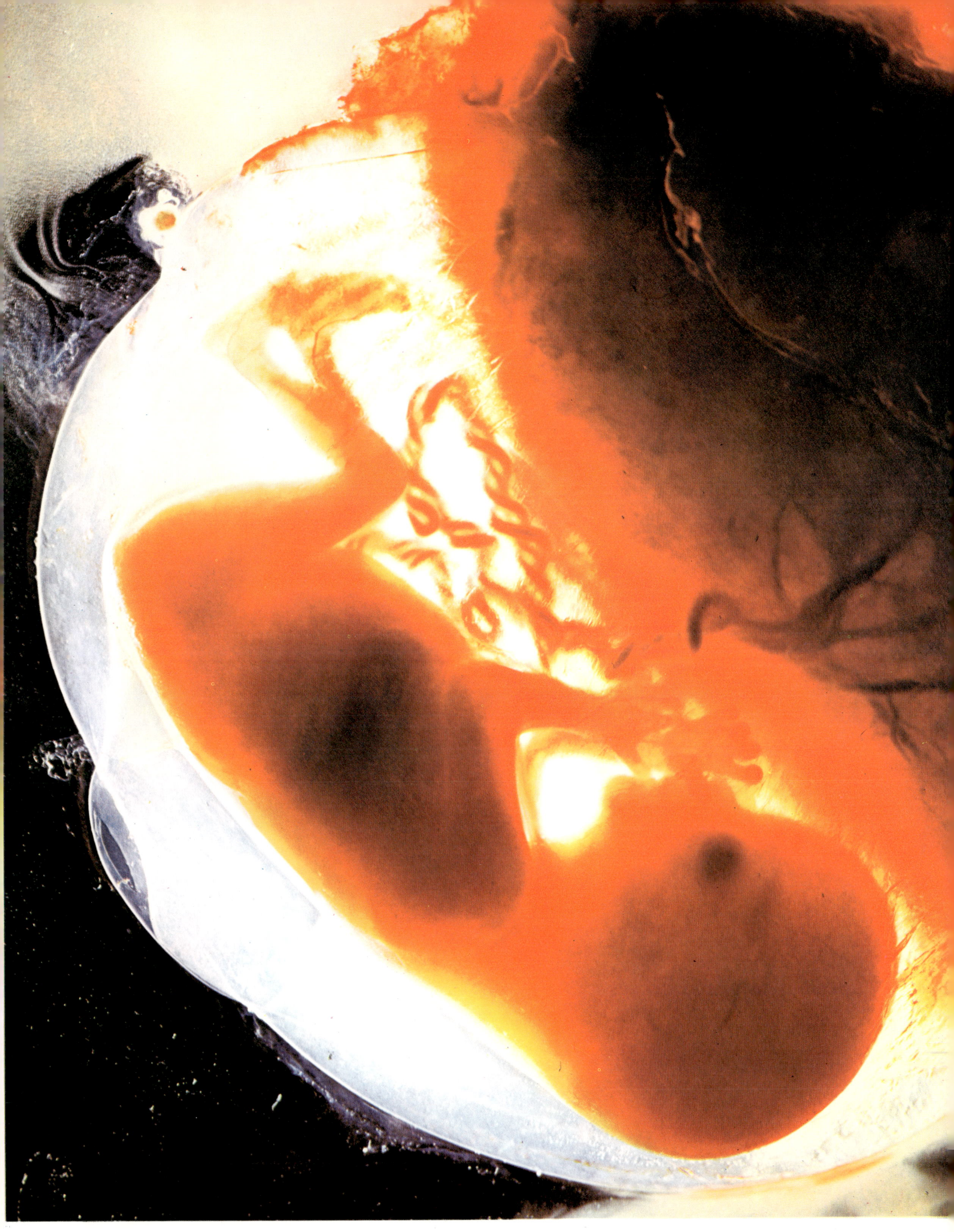

Telecommunications

Man has always needed to send messages over long distances. The most obvious way to do this was to send a runner with the information. But this was often too slow, especially for warning of an invasion or some other danger. So various signalling systems were developed.

In Africa some tribes sent messages by beating special 'talking' drums or sounding other loud instruments. Another sort of danger signal were fires or beacons lit on hill tops. The North American Indians invented a way of sending elaborate messages by means of smoke signals. They lit smokey fires on hill tops and then let the smoke out in pre-arranged ways to carry their message.

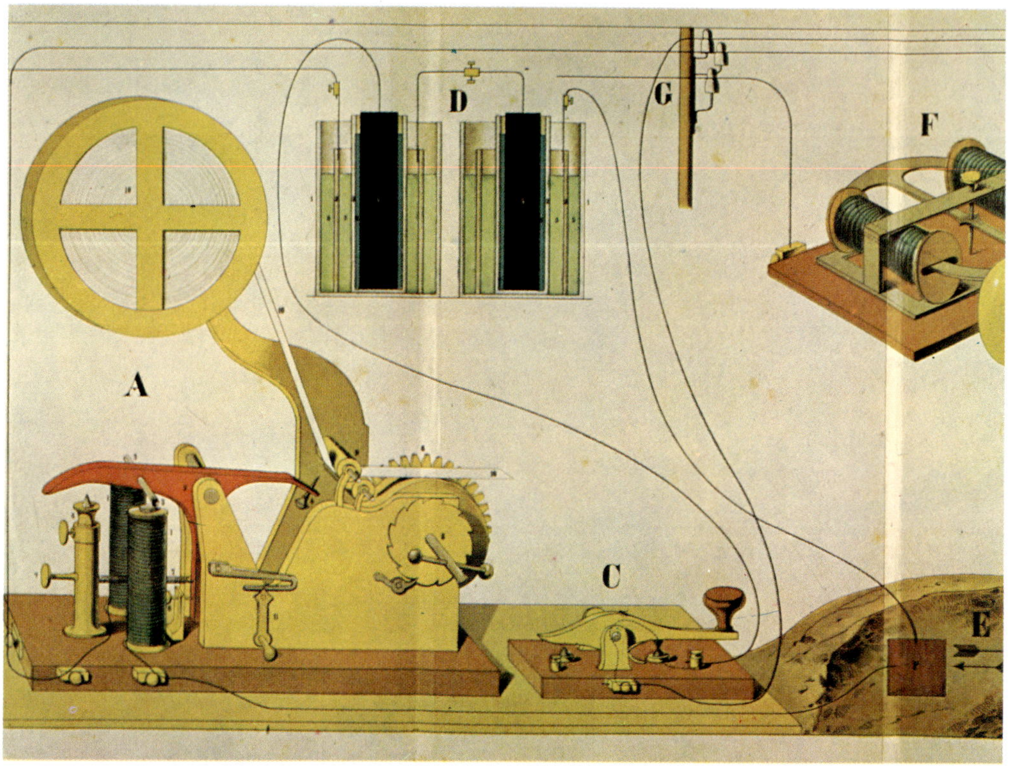

Above: A diagram showing an electric telegraph system designed by Samuel Morse in 1882. The key (C) is used to send messages in code. The recorder (A) registers incoming signals as dots and dashes on a paper tape.

Signalling Machines and Codes

From the 1600s, coded flags were hoisted to send signals between ships, and many experiments with visual signalling systems were carried out in the 1700s. A famous system was Claude Chappé's semaphore (sign-bearing) system. This was used in the 1790s, during the French Revolution.

Semaphore was used to send messages between the French army at Lille and the headquarters in Paris. The equipment had jointed arms that could be set in 192 positions to mean letters, numbers and various codes.

Signalling towers were set up at regular intervals on the route, and the messages sent from tower to tower. The system worked so well that a signal could be sent along the 240-kilometre route in two minutes. This and other semaphore systems gained popularity in the 1800s. But the electric telegraph was soon to start a great revolution in communications.

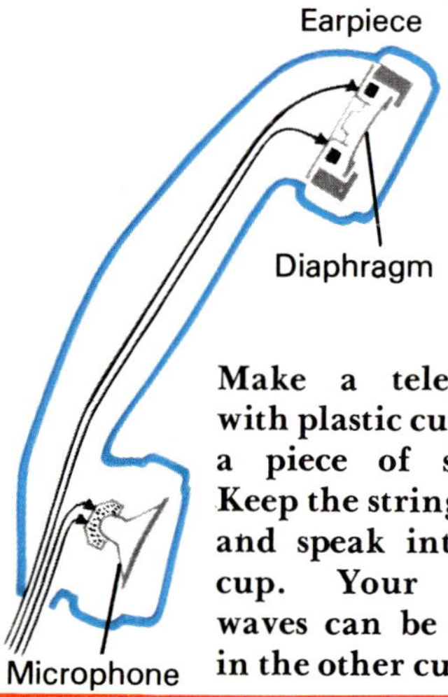

The Telephone

When you speak into a telephone your voice makes a microphone vibrate. The vibrations are turned into electrical waves that whizz down the wires to the earpiece of the person you are speaking to. There a thin *diaphragm* is made to vibrate by the electrical waves. The diaphragm vibrations are the same as those of your voice.

Make a telephone with plastic cups and a piece of string. Keep the string tight and speak into one cup. Your voice waves can be heard in the other cup.

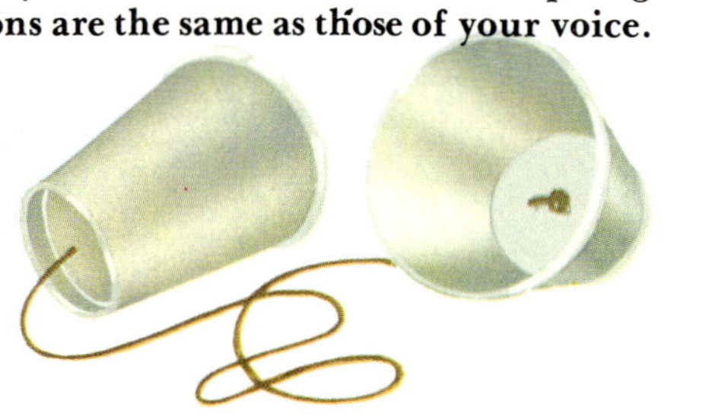

The Electric Telegraph

The first experiments in electric telegraphy took place long before Chappé invented his mechanical semaphore. In the 1700s, little was known about electricity. But sparks could be made by charging objects. When it was found that the sparks could be transmitted some distance by means of wires, it became obvious that such a system could be used for signals.

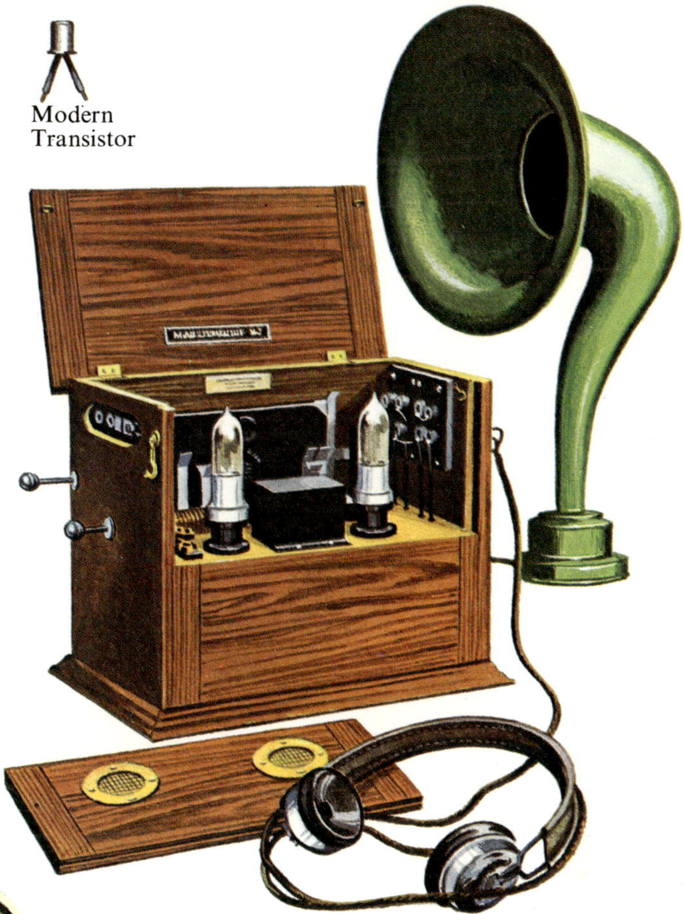

Modern Transistor

Bell's first receiver, 1875

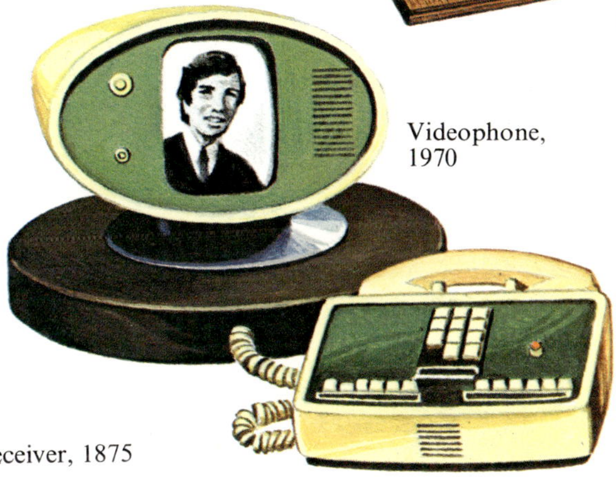

Videophone, 1970

Since Alexander Graham Bell transmitted his first telephone message in 1875, great changes have taken place in the field of telecommunications. Just four years later, London's first telephone exchange was opened. And telephone lines were gradually extended across countries throughout the world. Bell himself opened the New York-Chicago telephone line in 1892 (top left). Some callers can now see each other using the videophone (left). And the cumbersome early radio equipment (above) has been replaced by smaller, transistorized sets.

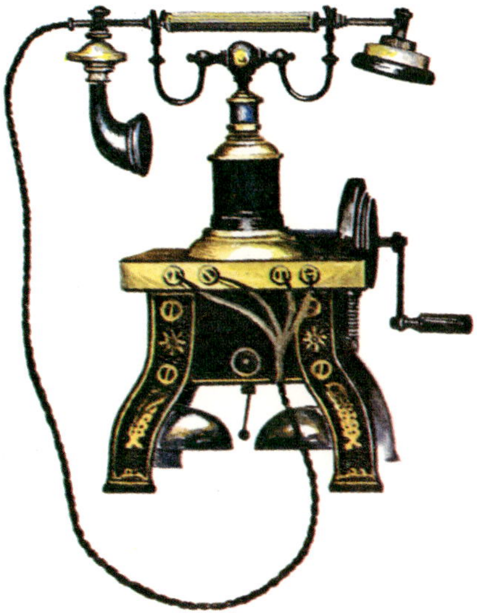

Ericsson's magneto phone, 1892

In early telegraphy the whole charge was used up to send just one pulse along the wires. It was a nuisance to have to recharge all the time. So little progress was made until the electric cell became available in the early 1800s. This gave a steady supply of electricity and could be used for a long time before it had to be replaced. In 1819, Hans Christian Oersted discovered electromagnetism. A wire carrying a current would make a compass needle deflect (swerve) and it was soon realized that these movements could be used to indicate signals. The first practical electric telegraph, invented in 1823 by the Russian Baron Schilling worked like this.

Most early electric telegraphs relied on magnetic needles being deflected to point to letters or numbers. But, in 1837, Samuel Morse demonstrated his system of sending signals by means of short and long electric pulses — dots and dashes. Morse code proved to be fast and reliable, and is still used today.

Then, in 1875, the telephone was invented by Alexander Graham Bell. At first, people regarded talking by wire as amazing. Similar reactions greeted radio communication, developed by Guglielmo Marconi around the turn of the century. But we have now become so used to technology that live television pictures bounced around the world via satellites amaze no-one.

Television and Radio

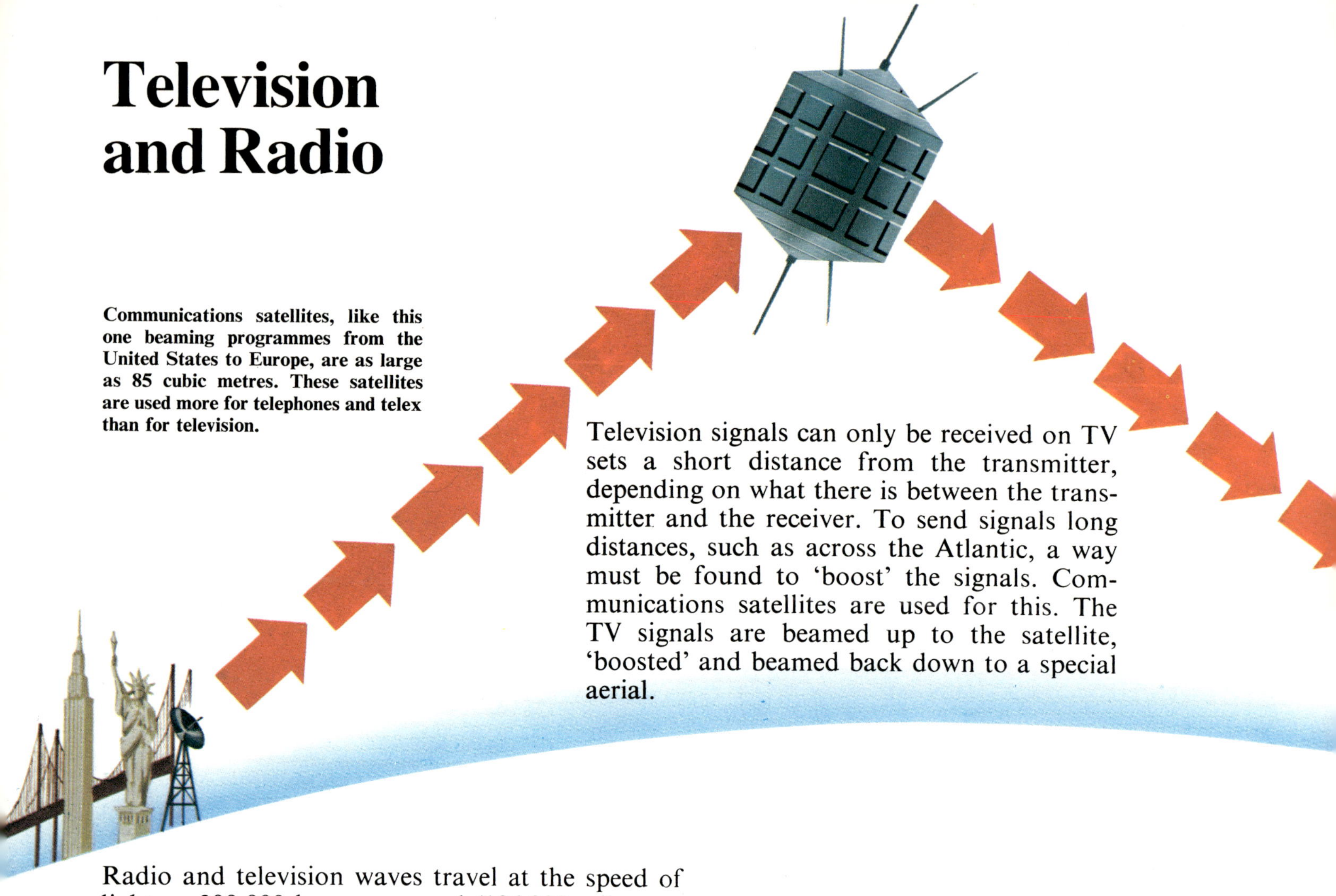

Communications satellites, like this one beaming programmes from the United States to Europe, are as large as 85 cubic metres. These satellites are used more for telephones and telex than for television.

Television signals can only be received on TV sets a short distance from the transmitter, depending on what there is between the transmitter and the receiver. To send signals long distances, such as across the Atlantic, a way must be found to 'boost' the signals. Communications satellites are used for this. The TV signals are beamed up to the satellite, 'boosted' and beamed back down to a special aerial.

Radio and television waves travel at the speed of light — 300,000 km per second (186,000 miles per second). The sound that comes from your TV set reaches you in the same way as the sound from a radio receiver. Making the colour pictures is more complicated. A special camera with three electronic tubes called image orthicons is used — one to pick up red colours, one for blue and one for green. These tubes change the light rays into electric signals. Before transmission, the colour signals are strengthened by an encoder, while an adder forms black and white signals. All these signals are sent out on a carrier wave from the transmitter. When the waves reach your TV aerial they go into your set and the set sorts out the three colours. Electron guns in your cathode ray tube shoot the three colours at the screen. The screen is coated with three kinds of dots which glow red, blue or green when they are hit by the electron beams.

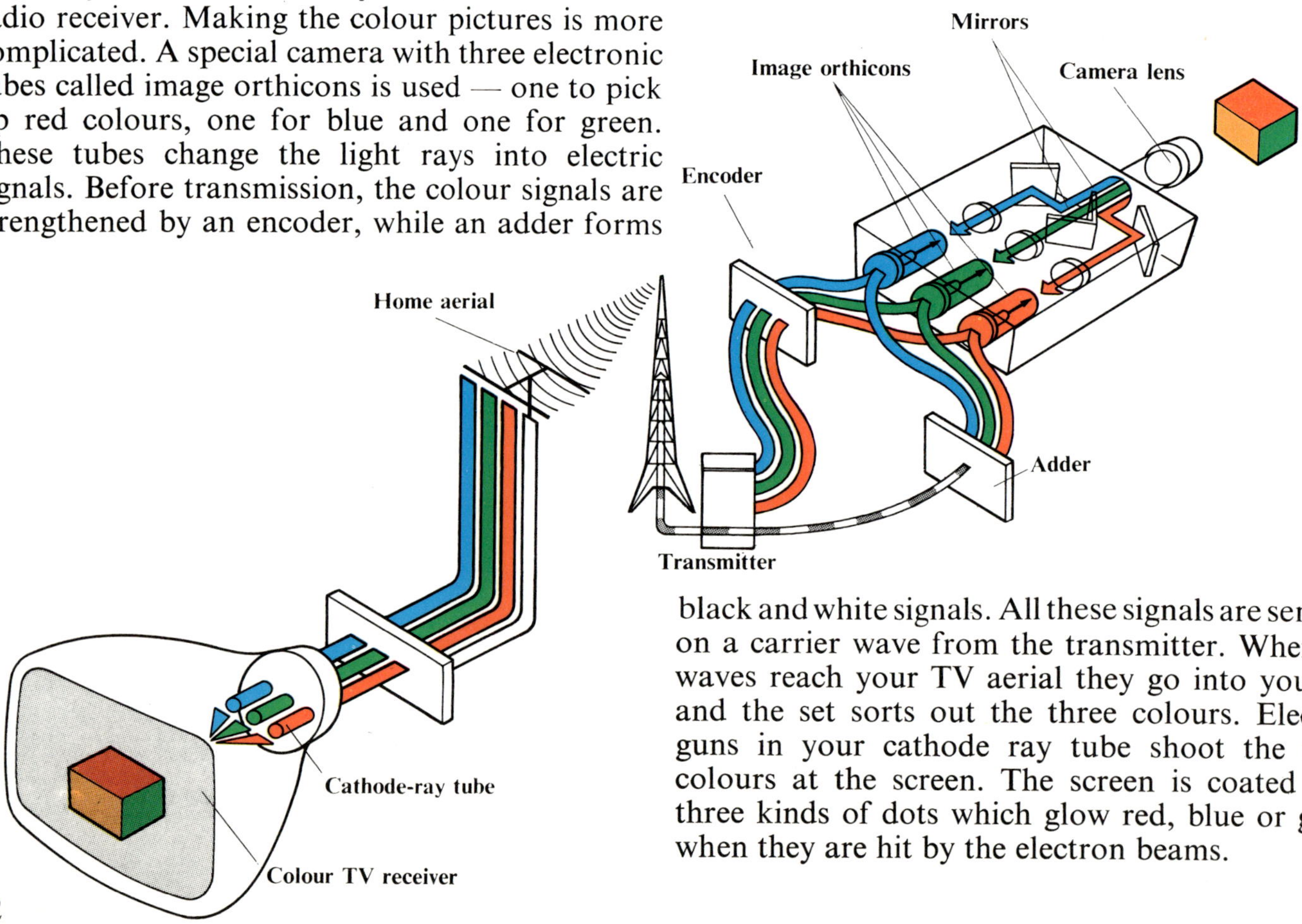

Left: The announcer speaks into the microphone. The sounds of his voice are turned into electric currents. These are broadcast by radio waves from a transmitter. Inside the radio itself the sound signals are separated from the carrier waves, and made stronger (or amplified).

How radio works. When an announcer speaks into a microphone, the sound of his voice is turned into tiny electric currents. These are made stronger by an amplifier. They are then joined up to a radio 'carrier' wave and are broadcast by the transmitter. Your radio set separates the signals made by the announcer's voice from the carrier wave. And the loud-speaker changes them back into the sound of the speaker's voice.

Radio waves have uses other than giving us TV and radio programmes. Huge radio telescopes like the ones below receive signals sent out by stars too far away to be seen by ordinary telescopes. These great movable telescopes are also used to track satellites.

Right: This radio telescope at Effelsberg, in West Germany, has a reflecting dish that is 100 metres across. Radio waves from space are collected by the giant dish, and focussed on the central receiving aerial.

Photography

Many modern cameras have complex electronic circuits for automatic exposure control and focusing. Others have numerous controls for manual adjustment. But all work in the same basic way. Light from the photographed scene forms an image on a film. The film has a light-sensitive coating called an emulsion. Exposure to light causes invisible chemical changes in the emulsion. After exposure, the film is removed from the camera and treated with chemical liquids called developer and fixer. This makes the images permanent.

Positive (reversal) film gives transparencies. These are usually mounted in frames to make slides for use in a projector.

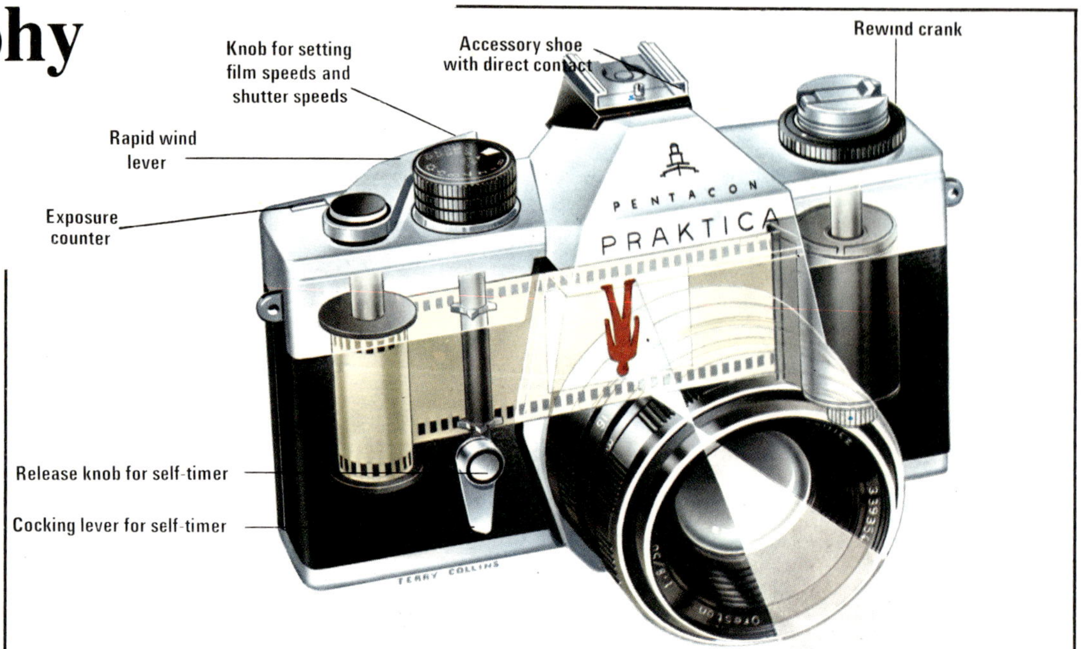

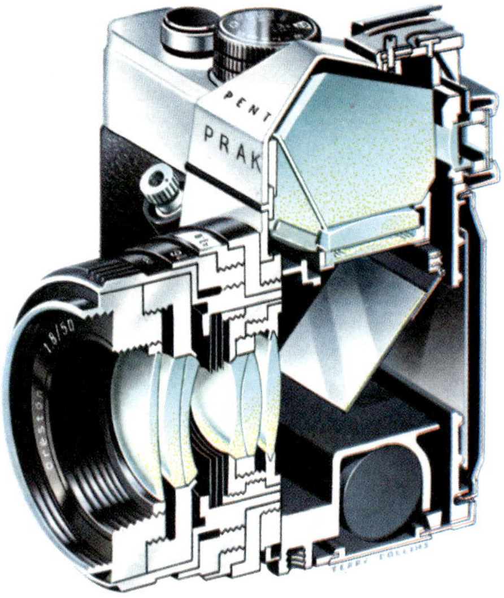

This German camera takes 35mm film. The speed of the film is set on the control on the left. It has its own built-in light meter. Not all cameras have this, and many photographers check the light of a subject with a separate battery-powered meter. Shutter speed settings vary from one second to one-thousandth of a second. The basic lens arrangement can be screwed off and replaced by special lenses such as a telescopic lens for bringing distant objects close.

Negative film gives images with the light and dark areas of the scene reversed, and, if it is a colour film, the colours are also different. The negatives are used to make prints. This is done by projecting the images onto light-sensitive paper. Developing and fixing the paper produces permanent pictures. Printing reverses the negative tones and colours, so that they are normal in the final images.

Left: Early photographers sometimes used a handcart to carry their bulky equipment. The solutions shown here were used to coat the photographic plates.

Right: Modern spectacular films often use specially designed sets and equipment costing very, very large sums of money. The realistic looking spaceship shown here was built for use in the highly successful film *Star Wars.* Many special effects for the film were created with the use of a computer.

Below: A Pathé movie camera, used in the 1920s. It was turned by hand.

Left: The Polaroid camera was invented by Edwin Land in 1947. It is used in the same way as an ordinary camera. But it uses a special film pack containing the chemicals required to develop the pictures. After a photograph is taken, the print material emerges from the camera and a picture develops automatically in seconds.

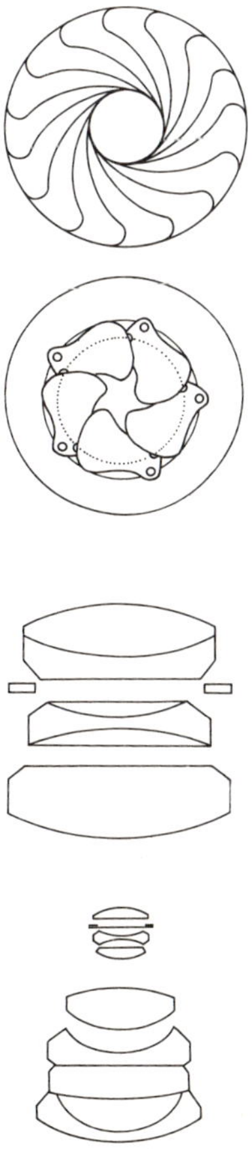

Left: A variable aperture, called an iris diaphragm (top), is used to control the amount of light passing through the camera lens. Some cameras have a shutter consisting of overlapping metal leaves (middle). These open to expose the film. A modern camera lens contains many elements (bottom).

Exposure Control

For best results, the film must receive the correct amount of light. So most cameras have controls for adjusting exposure. A device called a diaphragm provides a hole of adjustable diameter. This is used to control the amount of light passing through the camera lens, and thus controls the brightness of the image formed on the film. Another way of controlling exposure is by means of the shutter. This determines how much time the exposure needs to take.

Motion Pictures

The cine camera takes numerous photographs one after another on a long reel of film. After processing, the pictures are projected at the same high speed. They are too fast for the eye to see them separately, so there appears to be a continuous moving picture.

Above: The Lumierè brothers gave the first cinema show in Paris in 1895. Moving pictures had been demonstrated earlier. But the Lumierès were the first to project the images onto a screen.

HÆMISPHÆ
LATUM BO
ANTI
CAPRICORNVS
SAGITTARIVS
SCORPIO
AQVARIVS
Zodi
acus
Serpentarius
Anti
nous
Aquila
Circul
Equuleus
Engonasi
Æquinocti
Serpens
Delphinus
Lyra
Solstitiorum
Corona Sept.
PISCES
Cygnus
Pegasus
Draco
Bootes
Colurus
Andromeda
Cepheus
Coma
Berenices
Vrsa minor
Vrsa major
ARIES
Cetus Balena
Triangulum
Casiopea
Arcticus
Tropicus
Perseus
Auriga
TAVRUS
GEMINI
Colurus
Orion
CANCER
Apud GERARDUM VALK et PETRUM SCHENK, Amstelædami,

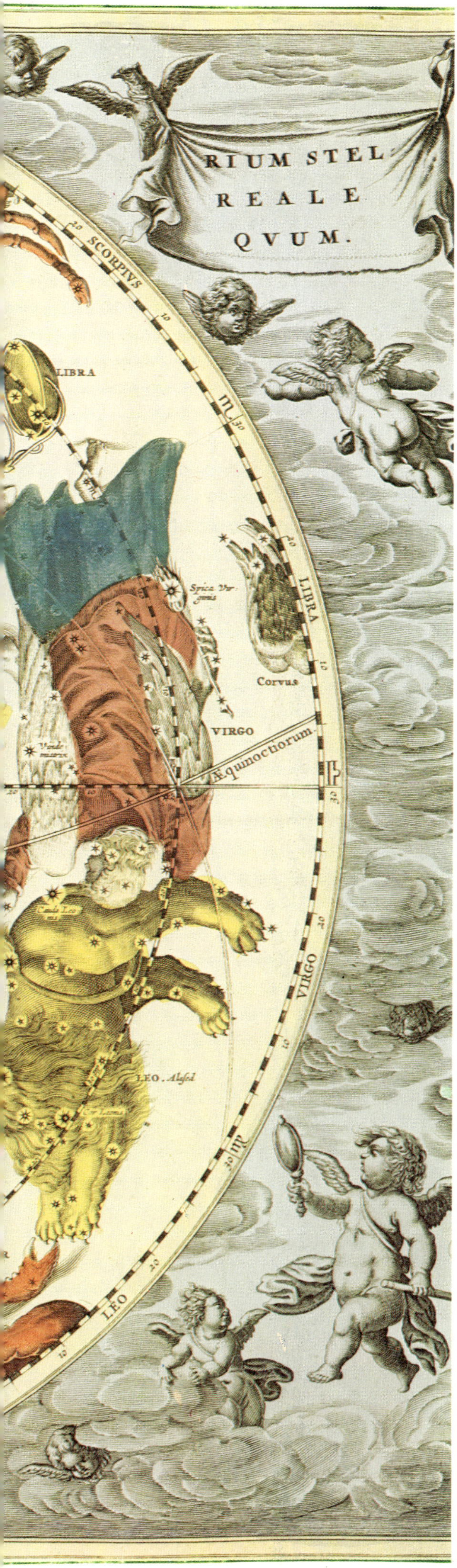

Astronomy

Movements of the Sun, Moon, stars and planets puzzled the ancient astronomers. Many of them observed and recorded these movements in a careful, scientific manner. But, throughout history, man has had a tendency to associate the unknown with religion, superstition and magic. This unfortunate habit led the astronomers to reach many incorrect conclusions about the heavenly bodies. It also often prevented new ideas from being accepted, or even suggested.

For thousands of years, the science of astronomy was hopelessly confused with astrology — the mistaken idea that events in the heavens somehow affect our lives on Earth. Astrology originated in the region called Mesopotamia, east of the Mediterranean. It was widely practised by the Chaldeans, who took control of Babylonia in the 700s BC. Various gods were thought to be associated with the stars. So there was a strong connection between astrology and religion. In the 500s BC the Persians conquered Babylonia, and the Chaldean priests fled to other lands. Soon, throughout the ancient world, they became regarded as people with special, magical powers. It seemed that, through the stars, the gods could communicate with the Chaldeans. So it was natural for people to go to the Chaldeans to seek advice on what the future might hold. Many astrologers encouraged belief in their powers of fortune telling by correctly forecasting astronomical events. From past records of hundreds of years, they could see that various events occurred at regular intervals. So they were able to predict when an eclipse of the Sun would occur, or when a particular comet would reappear in the sky. But it was the less spectacular events that proved to be of far more importance. For the regular changes seen in the heavens enabled calendars to be worked out, checked and corrected.

About every $29\frac{1}{2}$ days, the appearance of the Moon goes through a sequence of changes called phases. The dark, new Moon gradually changes to become a bright, full Moon. Then this slowly changes back to a new Moon again. The phases of the Moon provided the basis for dividing the year into months. In the Babylonian calendar, there were twelve months, alternately 29 and 30 days long. But this gave a calendar year of only 354 days. The true length of a year — the time taken for the Earth to orbit the Sun — is just over 365 days. So, with the Babylonian system, each calendar year began about eleven days too soon. Because of this error, the calendar months did not keep in step with the seasons. The Egyptian 365-day calendar proved much more satisfactory, although still about a quarter-day short. The calendar we use today is based on the Roman one worked out by Julius Caesar in 46 BC. He solved the problem of the extra quarter-day by introducing the leap year. An extra day was added to the calendar every fourth year.

Left: The stars appear to be grouped in fixed patterns called constellations. Many of them are named after animals. The painting shown here dates from the early 1700s and shows the constellations of the northern hemisphere.

In ancient times, it was assumed that the Earth lay at the centre of the universe. As the 'wandering stars' or planets moved around the sky, astronomers had to try to predict their motion on the assumption that they were moving around the Earth. The last of the great Greek astronomers, Claudius Ptolemy, who lived about AD 150, devised an elaborate system to explain the course of the planets in the sky. In this Ptolemaic system (right), each planet moves in a small circle, the centre of which moves around the Earth in a large circular orbit. Beyond this planetary system lie the fixed stars. At that time there was no understanding of the laws of the universe, and it did not matter that the system looked odd because Ptolemy was concerned only with explaining the movements of the planets, and not with understanding why they should move in this way. His attempt was so ingenious that astronomers were still using his tables over a thousand years later. The illustration (below) shows an 18th century drawing of the Ptolemaic system.

Ptolemy's Universe

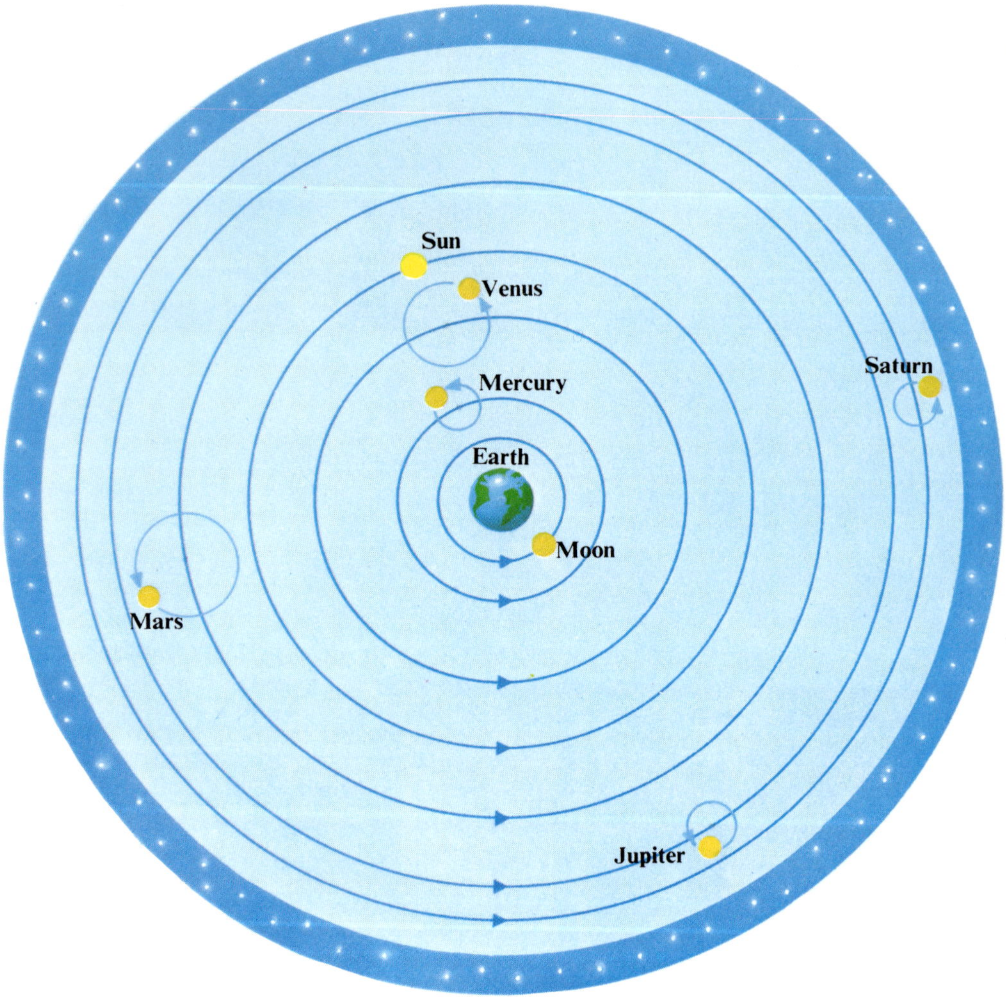

Greek Astronomy

Useful progress in astronomy came with the development of Greek philosophy. In 585 BC, Thales of Miletus achieved fame by correctly predicting an eclipse of the Sun. Thales was a great mathematician and the founder of abstract geometry. He discovered various relationships between lines and angles, and used his geometrical knowledge to work out astronomical problems. He calculated the diameter of the Sun.

Like the Egyptians, the Greeks had thought the Earth was flat. But now they began to realize that it must be curved in some way. This would account for the fact that the height of a star above the horizon varied according to the observer's position on the Earth. Around 530 BC, Pythagoras suggested that the Earth must be a sphere. This idea gradually gained supporters, including Aristotle, who lived in the 300s BC.

Evidence that the Earth really was spherical appeared during an eclipse of the Moon, when a curved shadow of the Earth could be seen moving across the Moon's surface.

Aristotle, as a philosopher, also thought that, because the Earth was so important, it would naturally be spherical, this being the most perfect shape. He was right about the shape of the Earth, but Aristotle had attached too much importance to our planet. He assumed that the Earth was at the centre of the universe, with the Sun, Moon, stars and other planets circling around it.

In the following century, Aristarchus came up with the suggestion that the Earth and other planets might, in fact, move around the Sun. But most people considered this idea to be ridiculous, and still held onto the belief that the Earth was the centre of the universe.

Right: In southern England, and in the Brittany region of France, are found groups of huge stones called megaliths. The group shown here is the megalith known as Stonehenge. It is situated on Salisbury Plain, in Wiltshire, England. Scientists think that Stonehenge was built as an astronomical observatory. It would have been used for making observations to predict eclipses of the Sun and Moon. And the movements of the heavenly bodies would have been used to work out calendars. Tests have shown that Stonehenge is at least 4,000 years old. It was built by people with an expert knowledge of geometry and measurement. For the stones were laid out with great precision.

Hipparchus, one of the greatest of all the Greek astronomers, lived in the 100s BC. One of his major achievements was the recording of more than 1000 stars. About 300 years later, Ptolemy publicized this work in his book the *Almagest* (*The Greatest*). This important record summarized the scientific knowledge of the ancient world. Although a brilliant astronomer, Ptolemy was convinced that the Earth lay at the centre of the universe. Like many other observers, he had noticed that the planets seemed to move in a strange manner. Sometimes they seemed to stop and then move backwards for a time.

Ptolemy thought that the planets, while moving in large circles around the Earth, also move in small circles. This idea was widely accepted and used by astronomers to find the positions of the planets for some 1,400 years.

Modern Astronomy

In the 1500s, a Pole called Nicolaus Copernicus wrote a book showing the planets moving around the Sun. This was a dangerous idea for it contradicted the teachings of the Church. However, the Copernican system slowly gained acceptance and formed the basis of modern astronomy.

A Sun-centred Universe

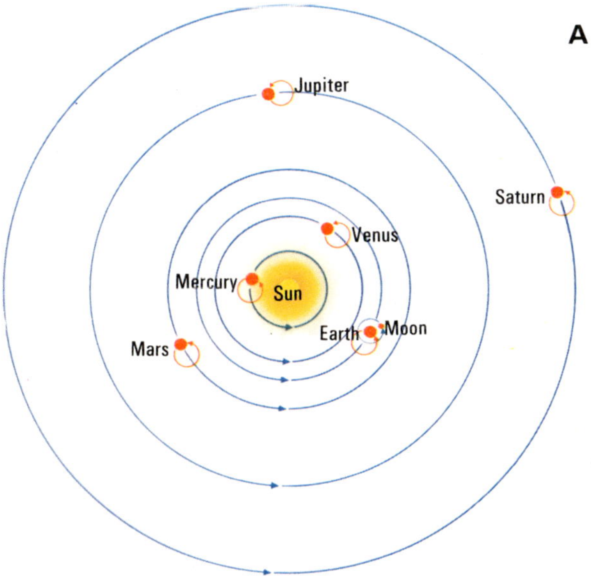

The Polish canon Nicolaus Copernicus (1473–1543) realized that the old planetary tables based on the Earth-centred universe of Ptolemy were not accurate enough. Studying the problem, he decided that the motions of the planets could be explained more precisely by supposing that they all revolve around the Sun. His book putting forward this theory was not published until his death. Since Copernicus believed, like the ancient astronomers, that the planets must move in circular orbits, his Sun-centred system still had to use the artificial epicycles of Ptolemy, and was just as complicated.

The Solar System

Right: The main features of the Solar System are the Sun and the nine planets that orbit around it. Closest to the Sun is the planet Mercury, at an average distance of 58 million kilometres. Then comes Venus (108 million km), the Earth (150 million km), Mars (228 million km), Jupiter (778 million km), Saturn (1,427 million km), Uranus (2,870 million km), Neptune (4,497 million km) and Pluto (5,900 million km).

The planets are satellites of the Sun. The closer a satellite is to the body it moves around, the shorter the time taken to complete one orbit. Because it is so close to the Sun, Mercury takes only 88 Earth days to go round it. The Earth takes just over 365 days, while Jupiter takes nearly 12 years. Distant Pluto orbits the Sun only once in 248 years.

The ancient astronomers had no telescopes So, to them, the planets appeared as tiny specks of light, just like the stars. But they behaved in a quite different way. They seemed to move in relation to the fixed patterns formed by the stars. The term 'planet' comes from the Greek word meaning 'wanderer'.

We now know that the Sun is at the centre of the planetary family we call the Solar System. Besides the nine major planets, many other bodies orbit around the Sun. These include thousands of asteroids — minor planets mainly between the orbits of Mars and Jupiter. Comets also orbit the Sun, but travel along extremely irregular paths. The majority of comets spend most of the time millions of millions of kilometres beyond the outermost planets. However, from time to time, a comet becomes visible as it passes close to the Sun. Then it disappears back into the depths of outer space.

Other members of the Solar System include the moons that orbit some of the planets. There are many man-made satellites too. Around the Earth we have put into orbit satellites which relay information to us.

Gravity holds the Solar System together. The Sun's gravitational pull keeps the planets and other bodies in orbit around it, and the gravitational pull of the planets prevents their moons and satellites from drifting away. Gravity also causes the planets to disturb one another's orbits. Such disturbances are called perturbations. Unexpected perturbations in the orbit of Uranus eventually led to the discovery of its neighbour Neptune. John Couch Adams and Urbain Le Verrier worked independently to calculate the position of the planet causing Uranus to move as it did. Their results agreed and, in September 1846, observers in Berlin found that Neptune was in its expected place.

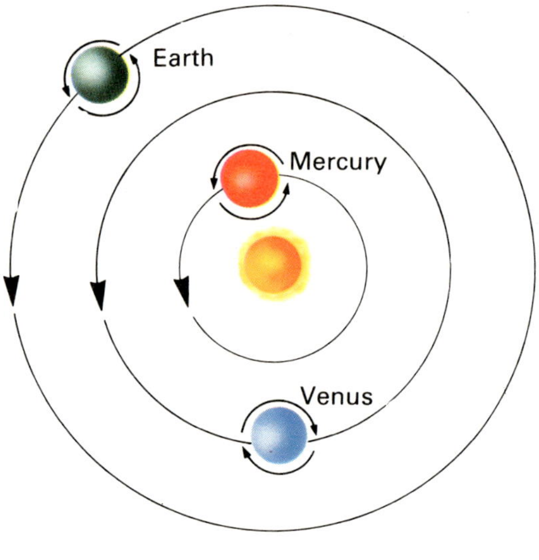

Far right and right: The nine major planets are shown drawn to about the same scale so that their sizes can be compared. The planets are shown in order of their average distances from the Sun. They can be identified by the numbers on the small diagram. Planet 1 is Mercury, with a diameter of 4,800 kilometres. Next comes Venus (2), diameter 12,104 km; the Earth (3), 12,756 km; Mars (4), 6,787 km; Jupiter (5), 142,200 km; Saturn (6) 119,300 km; Uranus (7), 47,000 km; Neptune (8), 48,000 km; and Pluto (9), about 6,000 km.

Left: As viewed from the Pole Star, the planets appear to move in an anti-clockwise direction around the Sun. They also spin on their axes. Most of them spin in an anti-clockwise direction. But Venus turns the other way.

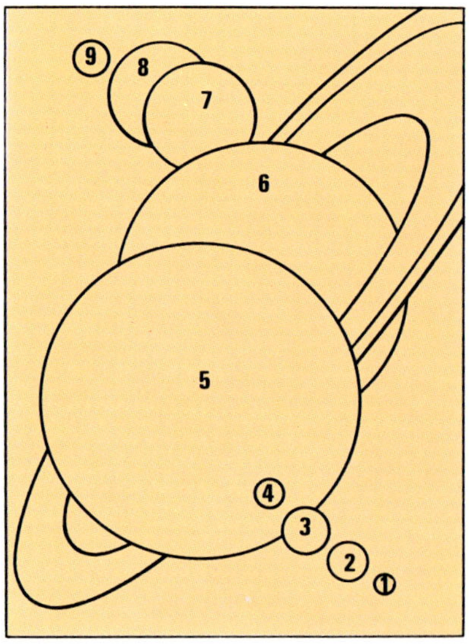

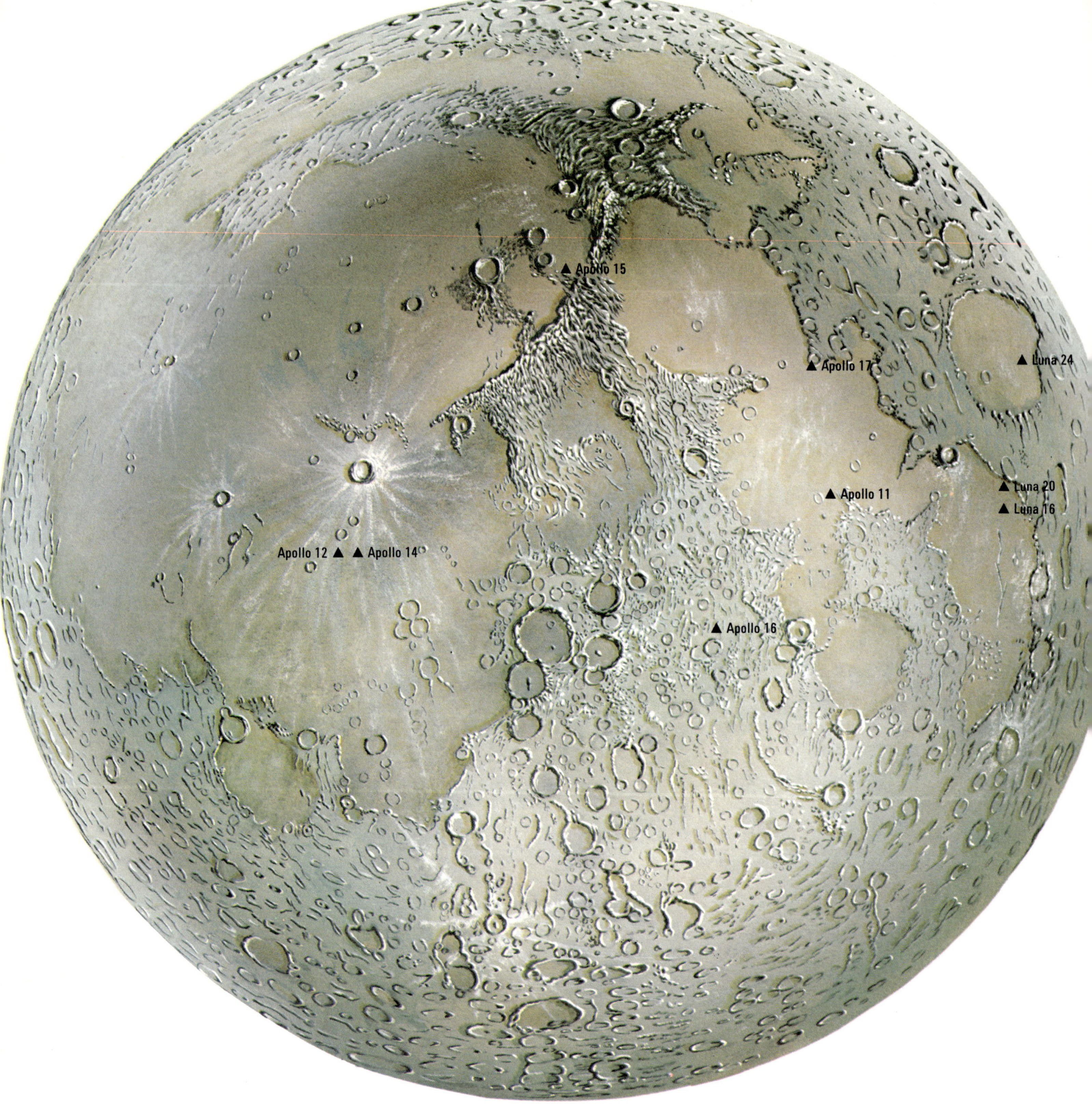

The above map shows the full Moon as it appears from the Earth when viewed through a telescope. The same side of the Moon always faces the Earth. This is because the time taken for the Moon to spin once on its axis is exactly equal to the time it takes to orbit the Earth. If you walk around a person, and turn so that you face them all the time, you will be moving in the same way as the Moon. The first maps of the Moon were produced in the early 1600s, when the Italian Galileo, introduced the telscope to astronomy. Over the years, telescope power and design were improved. And so astronomers were able to see more and more detail in the lunar surface. The Moon has mountains and valleys. And it also has some large, flat areas, once thought to be seas. But, in other ways, the Moon looks quite different from the Earth. Scientists developed many theories about the Moon, how it was formed and how its surface features were produced. But only in recent years did it become possible to test these theories. Space probes and manned missions have revealed much about the Moon. American Apollo and Russian Luna landing sites are indicated on the map. Just how small the Moon is can be seen by comparing it with Australia (right).

Above: A close view of Copernicus, one of the thousands of craters marking the surface of the Moon. This photograph was taken by the American Orbiter 2 spacecraft in 1966. The horizontal lines show where separate pictures have been joined together to make up this composite view. Copernicus measures about 90 kilometres across. In the centre of the crater is a group of mountains. They rise about one kilometre above the floor of the crater. Between August 1966 and August 1967, five Orbiter spacecraft were sent to the Moon. All of them went into orbit and transmitted pictures of the lunar surface back to Earth. The photographs enabled scientists to build up the first detailed Moon map.

The Moon

Detailed study of the Moon began in the early 1600s. In October 1608, a Dutch spectacle-maker called Hans Lippershey demonstrated his invention — the telescope. News of this remarkable instrument spread to Italy, and came to the attention of a professor of mathematics called Galileo Galilei. He had a keen interest in astronomy and realized how useful the telescope would be in his studies. So he built a telescope for himself, and turned it first towards the Moon. This observation, in 1609, marked the beginning of telescopic astronomy. Soon, Galileo was able to draw a map of the Moon, showing its mountain ranges, valleys, plains and craters. But there was still much to learn about the surface of the Moon.

Galileo's map could only show one side of the Moon. For it is this same side which always faces the Earth. This is because the Moon spins on its axis while it is moving around the Earth. Both rotations take exactly the same length of time — just over 27.3 days. So what the far side of the Moon looked like was a complete mystery, although there was no reason to think that it would be much different from the side which faced the Earth.

Over the years, improvements in telescope design enabled astronomers to observe the lunar surface in greater detail. Accurate calculations were made of its size and mass. Some astronomers had thought that the dark, flat areas were seas. But it became clear that they were plains, as Galileo had suspected. However, these regions had been named as seas on Moon maps, and we still use the same names today.

Below: Apollo astronauts brought back nearly half a tonne of Moon rock to the Earth. Scientists in many countries have had samples to study. Geologists have estimated the age of this sample at 4,600 million years. This means that it was formed very early in the Moon's history. The youngest rock found on the Moon was formed about 3,000 million years ago. Since then, little change has taken place on the Moon.

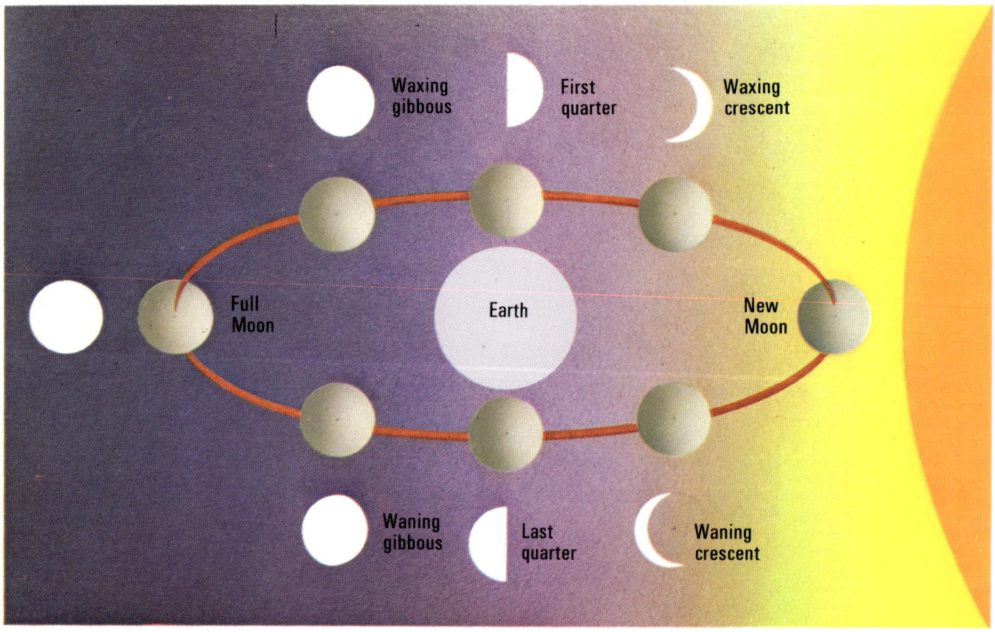

Left: In this diagram, the Moon moves in an anti-clockwise direction around the Earth. At new Moon, the side of the Moon facing the Earth is in darkness. Then, as the Moon moves around the Earth, a slim crescent is seen. This gradually increases, or waxes, through the first quarter and gibbous phases. Eventually, at full Moon, the side facing us is totally illuminated by the Sun. Then the bright area seen from the Earth decreases, or wanes. It passes through the gibbous and last quarter phases to become a slim crescent and, finally, a new Moon again. The diagram, which is not drawn to scale, shows how the Moon appears at each stage in its journey around the Earth. As the Earth is orbiting the Sun, this 29½ day cycle of phases is slightly longer than the time taken for the Moon to orbit the Earth.

In 1959, the Moon's greatest mystery was revealed when a Russian space probe called Lunik 3 photographed the side hidden from the Earth. The pictures sent back to Earth by satellite astonished astronomers. For the far side of the Moon was quite different from the side facing us. Almost the entire surface was mountainous, covered with craters and with no large 'seas' at all. No explanation has yet been found for this marked difference. But other space probes and manned missions have given us a wealth of information about the Moon.

Facts about the Moon

Equatorial diameter	3,476 kilometres
Volume	1/49 Earth's volume
Mean density	3.34 (water = 1)
Mass	1/81 Earth's mass
Gravity	1/6 Earth's gravity
Perigee	356,400 kilometres
Apogee	406,700 kilometres
Mean distance from the Earth	384,400 kilometres
Spins on axis in	27.3 days
Orbits Earth in (sidereal month)	27.3 days
Completes phases in (synodic month)	29.5 days
Escape velocity	2.4 kilometres/second

The Lunar Surface

We cannot be sure how the Moon formed. But it probably condensed from a cloud of hot matter soon after the Earth formed, over 4000 million years ago. Scientists think that the two bodies were formed separately because their surface rocks contain different amounts of various elements. This makes it unlikely that, as was once thought, the Moon was formed by material breaking away from the Earth. As the Moon cooled down, a solid shell of rock hardened on its surface. Huge rocks from space were attracted by the Moon's gravity. These crashed onto the lunar surface, blasting out enormous craters. The shocks threw up vast amounts of material which grew into rugged mountain ranges. Sometimes, molten lava oozed through the surface rock layer and hardened to form the dark, flat 'seas'.

The Moon is much smaller than the Earth, so its gravitational pull is comparatively weak and unable to hold an atmosphere around it. On Earth, the atmosphere acts as a kind of 'blanket', keeping in heat and preventing great variation in the surface temperature. But the Moon, with no such protection, has a night-time temperature of around −150°C. After the long night — equal to nearly two weeks on Earth — the temperature climbs steadily to reach 100°C at mid-day. The Moon's surface has changed little in some 3,000 million years. With no water or atmosphere, it has not been subjected to the powerful weathering that has gradually changed the face of the Earth.

Left: During a total eclipse of the Sun, the Moon passes directly between the Sun and the Earth. Although the Moon is much smaller than the Sun, it is much closer to us. By chance, this makes the Moon appear almost exactly the same size as the Sun, when viewed from the Earth. So, during an eclipse, the Moon can completely cover the Sun, but only for a few minutes. The maximum duration of a total eclipse is $7\frac{1}{2}$ minutes. As the distance from the Moon to the Earth varies slightly, the Moon's apparent size varies too. When the Moon is at its farthest distance from the Earth, it cannot completely cover the Sun's disc. So, when it passes directly in front of the Sun, a bright, narrow ring is seen around its edge. This is known as an annular eclipse.

Below: The diagram shows how eclipses of the Sun and Moon occur. Both types of eclipse are determined by the position of the Moon. A solar eclipse occurs when the Moon passes directly in front of the Sun. And a lunar eclipse occurs when the Moon moves into the shadow of the Earth.

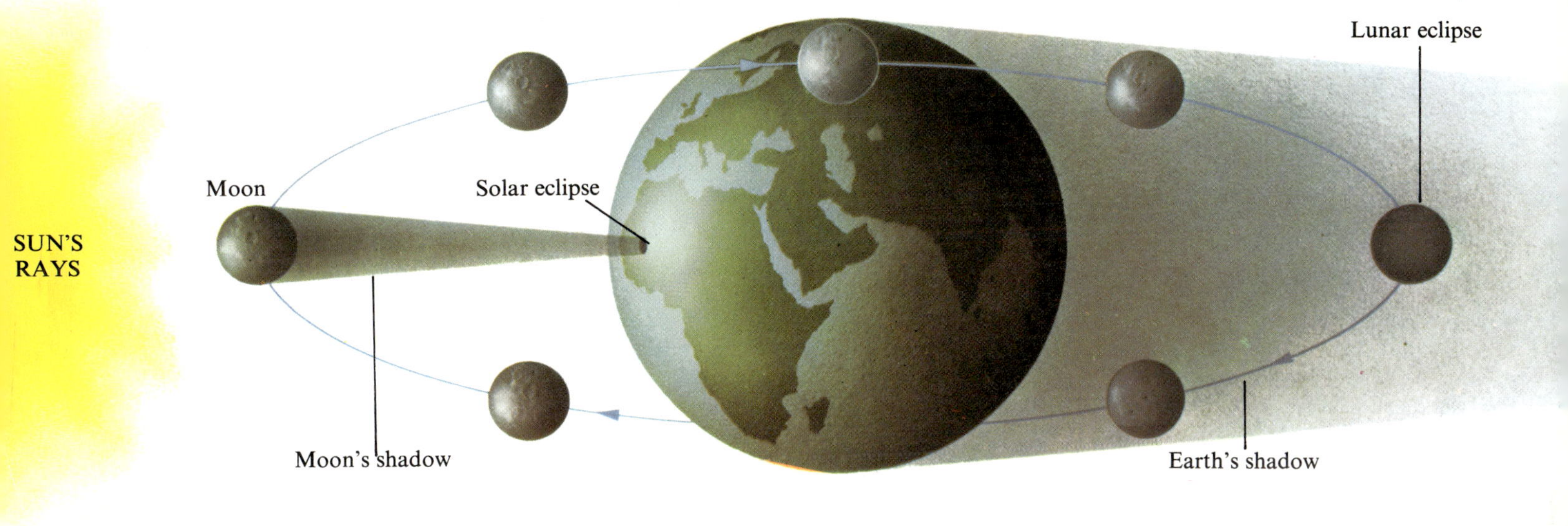

Left: A view of the far side of the Moon, taken from an orbiting spacecraft. The large crater measures about 80 kilometres across. Like many large craters, it contains a group of mountains.

Right: A photograph of the Moon, taken during a lunar eclipse. At the stage shown here, the Moon is just starting to emerge from the shadow of the Earth. The part of the Moon still shaded by the Earth is not absolutely dark. This is because some light from the Sun passes around the Earth and is refracted, or bent inwards by the Earth's atmosphere. This light falls on the Moon, lightening the shadow and giving it the dull copper colour shown here. Even when the Moon is totally eclipsed, it is usually visible as a dim, brownish disc.

The Sun

The Sun consists mainly of hydrogen, yet it is over 300,000 times as heavy as the Earth. It is also by far the largest body in the Solar System, with a volume well over one million times that of the Earth. Because the Sun is so massive, it has an extremely strong gravitational pull, with enormous pressure at its centre. When the Sun was formed, about 4600 million years ago, this internal pressure caused so much heat that the hydrogen started to undergo a nuclear reaction. This caused hydrogen to be changed into helium, and a great deal of energy was given out as heat, light and other radiation. The vast mass had become a star. Since the Sun started to shine, about 600 million tonnes of hydrogen have been used up each second. There is still enough hydrogen left for the Sun to shine for a further 5000 million years.

The surface temperature of the Sun is about 6000°C — high enough to melt all known materials. But this is cool when compared with the temperature at its centre — an incredible 15,000,000°C. Although the Sun is the brightest body we can see in the sky, if compared with many other stars it is relatively small and dim. In fact, astronomers know it as the type of star they call a yellow dwarf. Some of the largest stars — the supergiants — are so enormous that more than 25 thousand million bodies the size of the Sun could fit into the space they occupy. The reason why the Sun appears to be so big and bright is that it is so much closer to us than any other star. It is about 150 million kilometres from the Earth — less than one-quarter-millionth of the distance to the next nearest star, Proxima Centauri.

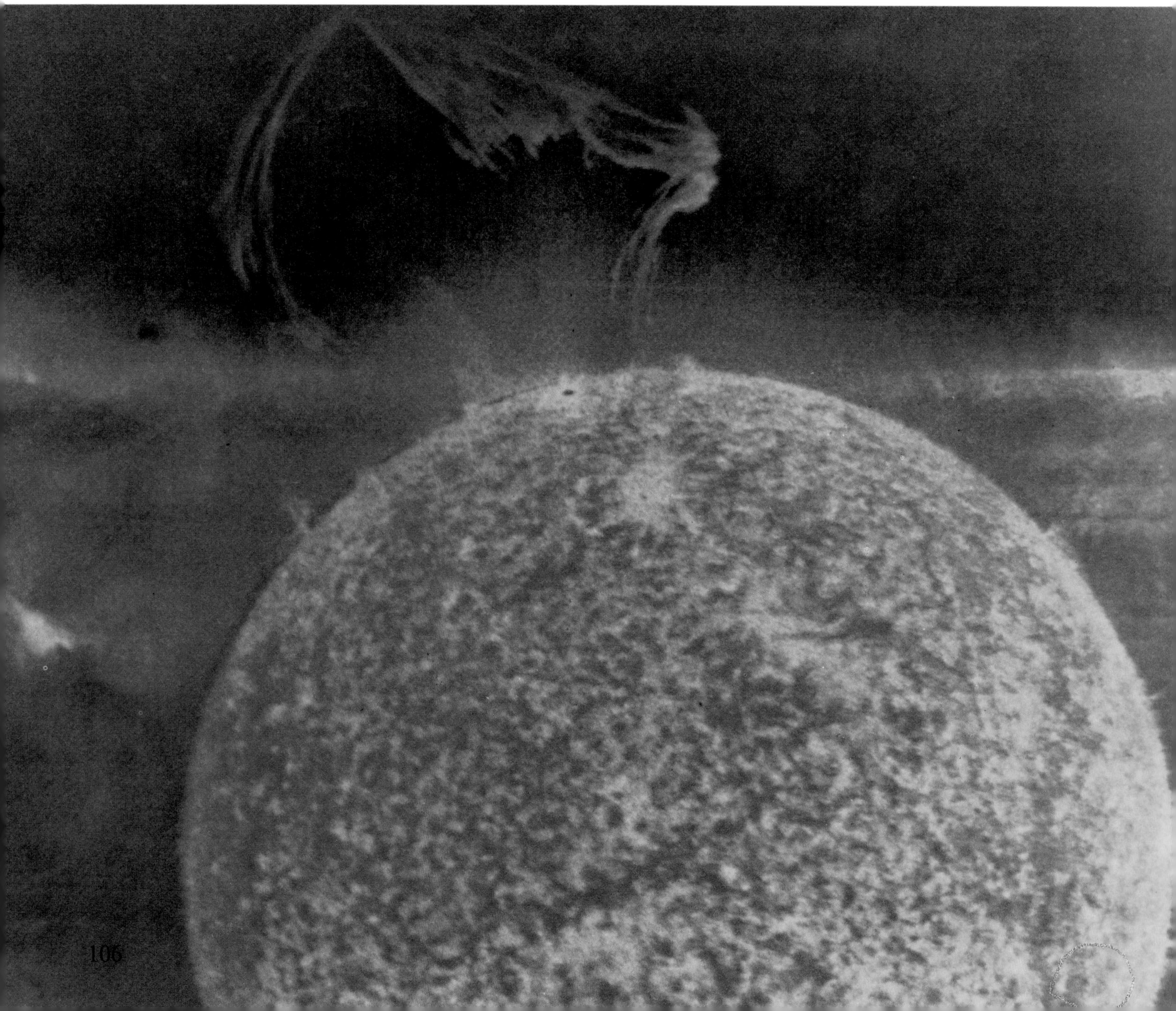

Earth

Left: A giant trail of glowing gases, called a prominence, bursts from the surface of the Sun.

Below: An eclipse of the Sun occurs when the Moon's shadow falls on the Earth. In a total eclipse, the whole of the Sun is hidden from some observers. People in surrounding areas see a partial eclipse. When the Moon does not pass directly between the Sun and Earth, only a partial eclipse may be seen.

Above: The dark patches are sunspots. They are not really dark, but appear so compared with the surrounding surface, which is about 2,000°C hotter. The appearance of sunspots, solar flares and prominences varies over an 11-year period called the solar cycle. Maximum activity occurred in 1969, so 1980 and 1991 are expected to be active years too. When great eruptions called flares occur, the powerful radiation emitted interferes with radio signals.

The Solar Surface

The Sun's bright surface is called the photosphere. From time to time, patches called sunspots appear on it. These can be observed by using a telescope to project an image of the Sun onto a piece of white card. The telescope should be mounted on a tripod so that a steady image is obtained. Never look directly through a telescope at the Sun. The powerful rays can quickly damage the eyes. Dark filters for viewing the Sun can be bought, but some of these are unsafe. However, with a projected image, there is no danger.

Sunspots appear darker than the surrounding photosphere. This is because their temperature is about 2,000°C lower. The cooling is caused by magnetic disturbances in the Sun's swirling surface gases. Large sunspots may last for several months, although the smallest can disappear after just a few hours. When sunspots occur, other disturbances are often seen too. Brilliant eruptions, called flares, may take place. These normally disappear within an hour. Sometimes, trails of glowing hydrogen hundreds of thousands of kilometres long are thrown up from the surface. These streamers, called prominences, may last for weeks.

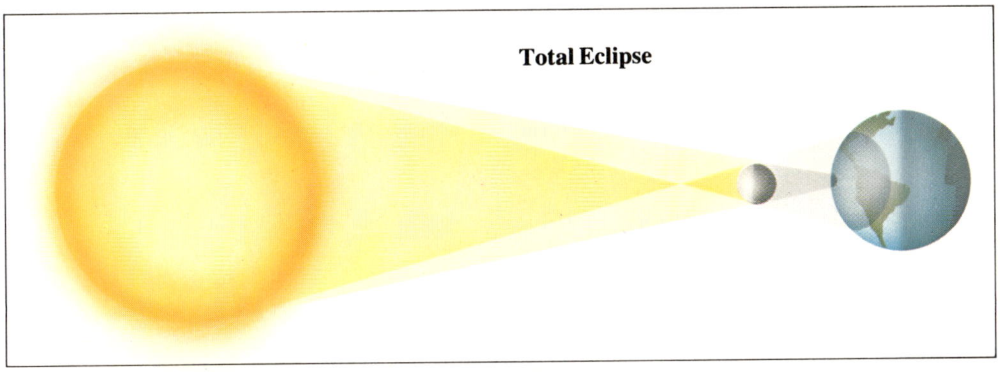

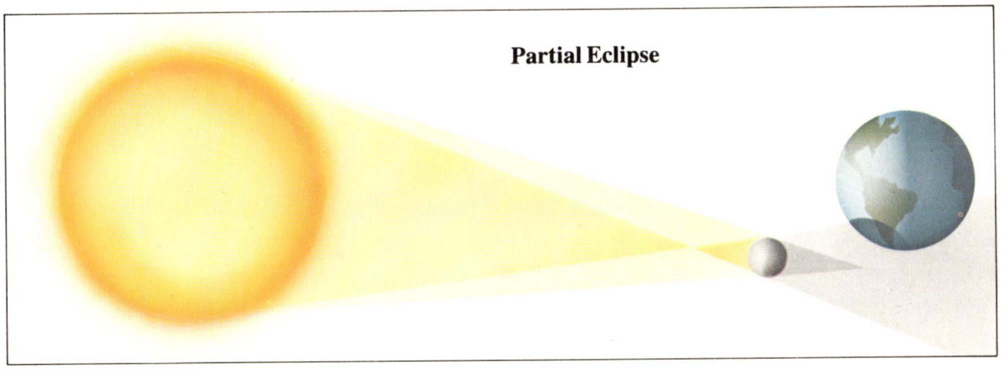

Mercury: The Inner Planet

Mercury, the planet closest to the Sun, is also the smallest. In diameter, it measures 4880 kilometres — only 40 per cent larger than the Moon. Like the Moon, Mercury shows changes in its appearance, as it moves in its orbit. This is because it is an inferior planet — that is, one whose orbit lies inside that of the Earth. When Mercury is on the far side of the Sun, the planet appears to an observer on Earth as a complete disc. But, as it approaches the Earth, less and less of it is lit by the sun and it eventually appears as a narrow crescent.

Mercury is like the Moon in other ways too. Its surface is covered with craters — the result of bombardment by meteorites soon after it was formed. There are also some plains on one side. These were formed by larva coming up from the interior and hardening on the surface.

Because Mercury has no atmosphere or surface water, it is a lifeless, virtually unchanging world. The lack of an atmosphere also means that, like the Moon, it experiences extremes of temperature. During the night, Mercury's surface temperature drops to a bitter 170°C below zero. But its closeness to the Sun causes the daytime temperature to go up to about 350°C, which is higher than the melting point of lead!

Mercury spins quite slowly on its axis, one rotation taking 59 Earth-days. But its year — the time it takes to go around the Sun — is only 88 Earth-days long. Such a short year is to be expected for a planet that is, on average, only 58 million kilometres from the Sun. If Mercury did not orbit so quickly, it would not develop sufficient centrifugal (outward) force to balance the Sun's strong gravitational pull.

Above: The planet Mercury, compared in size with the Earth. Mercury is the smallest of the planets. Its diameter is little more than one-third that of the Earth.

Right: In this picture of Mercury, a section has been cut away to show the planet's inside. The core probably contains a lot of iron, as Mercury is known to have a high density.

Left: An artist's impression of a Mercurian landscape. The planet has a greater temperature variation than any other planet. As Mercury is the closest planet to the Sun, its daytime temperature rises to around 350°C. But there is no atmosphere to help retain heat. So the night-time temperature drops to about —170°C. These great temperature changes have caused giant cracks to open up over the surface of the planet. As on the Moon, the lack of an atmosphere makes the sky appear black.

Below: The surface of Mercury, as photographed by the Mariner 10 space probe. The craters were formed long ago by meteorites.

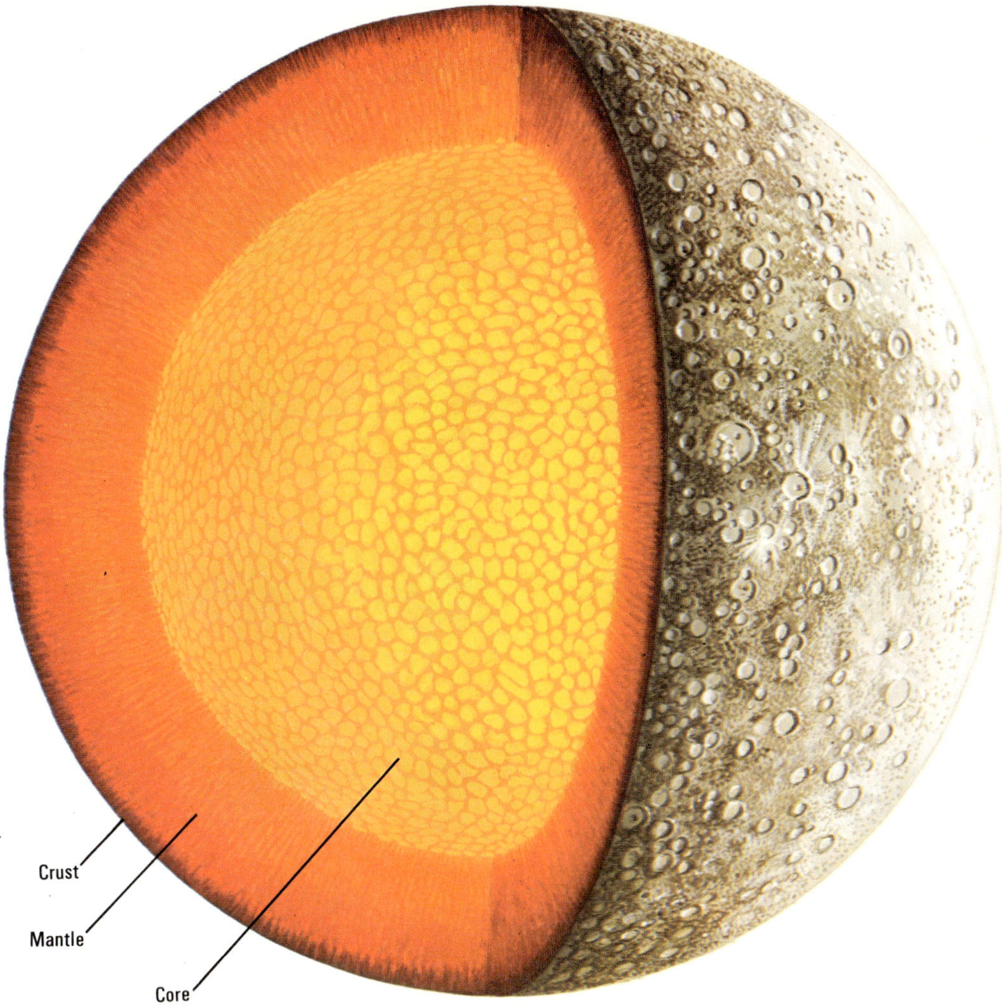

Above: The flight-path of Mariner 10, which was the first spacecraft to use the gravity of one planet, Venus, to reach another, Mercury. It produced the first close-up pictures of Mercury in March 1974.

Venus: The Cloudy Planet

Below: An instrument capsule, released from a Russian space probe, descends through the Venusian atmosphere on a parachute.

Venus is often visible to the naked eye, appearing like an extremely brilliant star. Being so bright, it can be seen as the Sun starts to set. It also remains visible for some time after the Sun has started to rise again. For this reason, Venus is sometimes called the Evening Star or the Morning Star. However, it is really a planet, and is seen by the light it reflects. (Stars give out their own light.) Venus has a covering of dense, white clouds. These reflect light well and account for the planet's brilliance.

Venus lies between the orbits of Mercury and the Earth, at an average distance of 108 million kilometres from the Sun. Venus alters in appearance, like Mercury, as it is also an inferior planet. With a diameter of just over 12,000 kilometres, Venus is almost the same size as the Earth. Its gravitational pull is strong enough to hold an atmosphere around it. The Venusian atmosphere is quite different from that around the Earth, and is made up mainly of carbon dioxide. Although Mercury is closer to the Sun, Venus has a higher temperature. This is because its atmosphere holds heat. In the daytime, its temperature reaches about 480°C. Photographs taken by Russian space probes show that the planet has a rocky surface that may have undergone much erosion. Venus orbits the Sun once every 225 days, and takes 243 days to spin on its axis.

Venus is only slightly smaller than the Earth (above), and its internal structure is probably similar. Apart from the surface conditions, the main difference is its lack of a strong magnetic field and radiation belts.

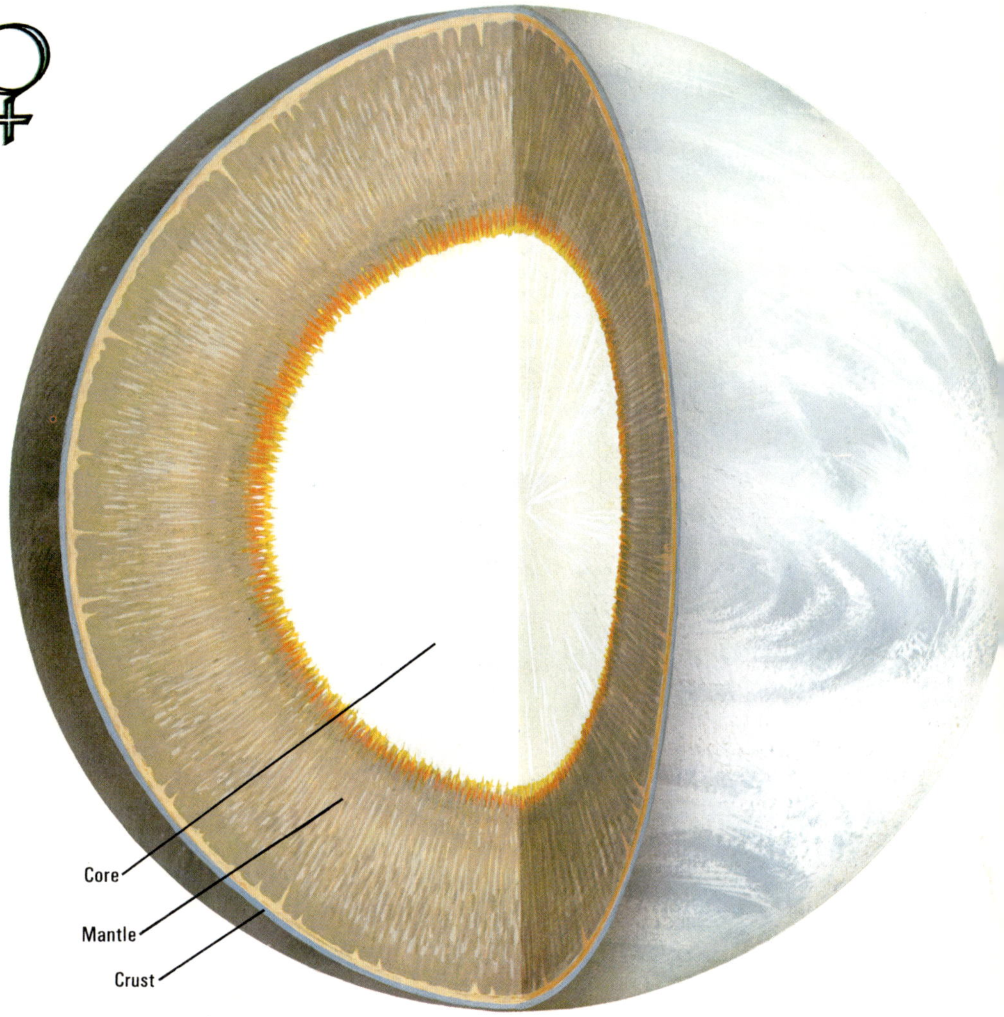

VENUS FACTS

Diameter: 12,104 kilometres
Orbital period: 225 days
Rotation period: 243 days
Length of day: 2760 days
Average distance from Sun:
108·2 million kilometres
Surface temperature: 480°C
Main atmospheric content: Carbon dioxide
Moons: None

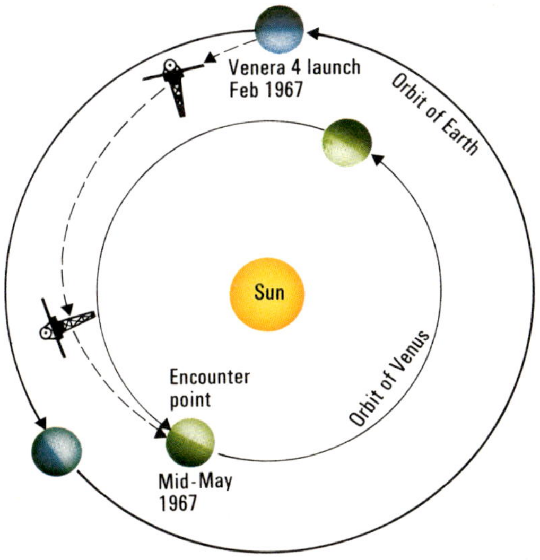

PROBES TO VENUS

Right: Venera 4, the Russian space probe, which sent back signals from 30 kilometres above the surface of Venus in 1967.

Until the Space Age, Venus was a mystery planet. We knew nothing about its appearance, for it has a dense, cloudy atmosphere that completely hides its surface. So, when it became possible to send space probes to other planets, Venus was an obvious target. So far, Venus has been visited by 15 spacecraft. But some of the early missions failed, or were only partly successful. For the probes were unable to withstand the turbulent atmosphere and very high temperatures. In 1962, 1967 and 1974, American probes flew close to Venus and sent back pictures to Earth. Meanwhile, the Russians concentrated on soft-landing instruments on the Venusian surface. Their probe Venera 4, managed to send signals until only about 30 kilometres above the surface. Venera 7 transmitted from the surface in 1970.

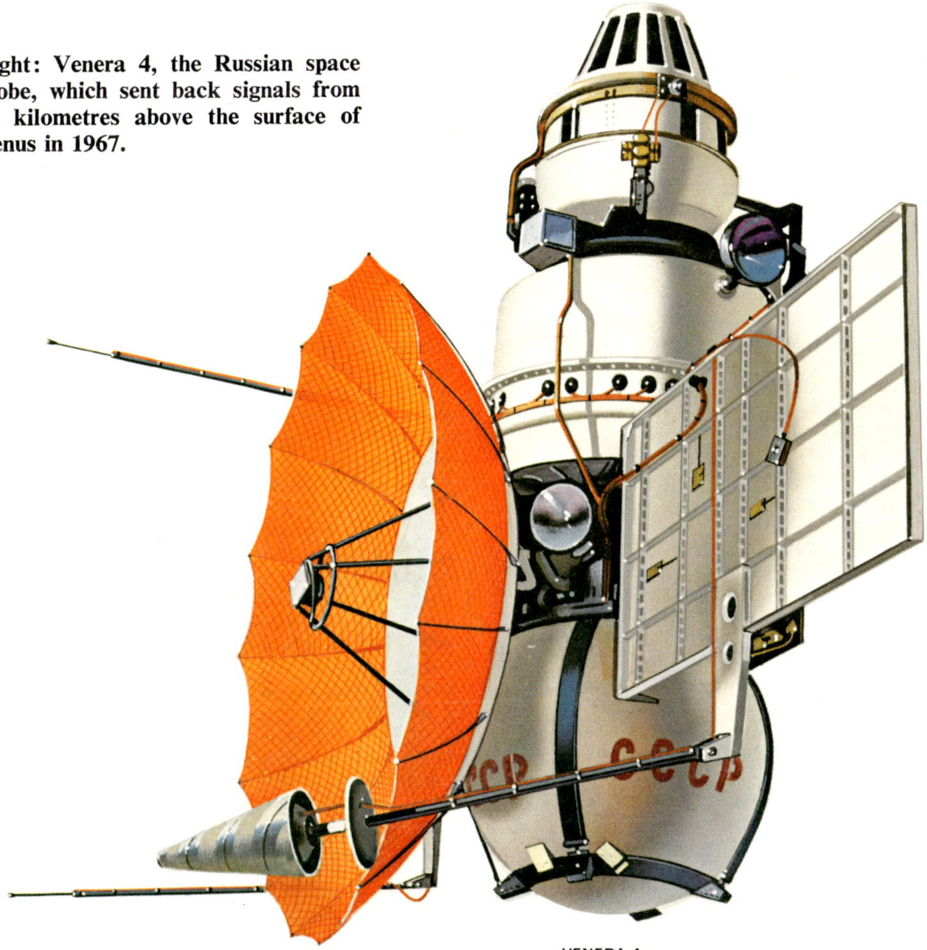

VENERA 4

Mars: The Red Planet

If life exists on any other planet in the Solar System, that planet is Mars. Since the telescope was invented, astronomers have noticed some similarities between Mars and the Earth, and have imagined many others. Like our planet, Mars has brilliant white caps at its poles. Most of the surface is light reddish-brown, with some large, darker patches. Early observers thought that the lighter areas were huge deserts, and straight lines running through them were imagined to be irrigation canals. The darker regions seemed to be seas or lakes.

This last idea was rejected when astronomers realized there was little water vapour in the Martian atmosphere. Also, the dark patches kept changing in size and shape in a way that indicated they were not areas of water. The changes were observed to be seasonal, for the areas increased in spring and shrank in winter.

The seasonal changes on Mars gave rise to the idea that it had some form of vegetation, tending to grow in spring and die away in winter.

Originally, it had been assumed that, as on Earth, the white polar caps consisted of frozen water. But the discovery that the Martian atmosphere contained a large proportion of carbon dioxide seemed to disprove this theory. Instead, astronomers assumed that the polar regions must be covered with frozen carbon dioxide — otherwise known as dry ice.

Astronomers have discovered much more about Mars by observations and measurements made from the Earth. We know that the diameter of Mars is 6,787 kilometres — just over one half the diameter of the Earth. Mars takes about 24½ days to spin on its axis. It orbits the Sun in 687 days at an average distance of 228 million kilometres.

Above: Mars, one of our neighbouring planets, has a volume less than one-sixth that of the Earth. Because Mars is quite close to us, and has a clear atmosphere, its surface markings can be seen from the Earth. The white region at the top of the picture is one of the polar caps. It consists of a thin layer of frozen carbon dioxide. The area of the polar caps varies according to the season.

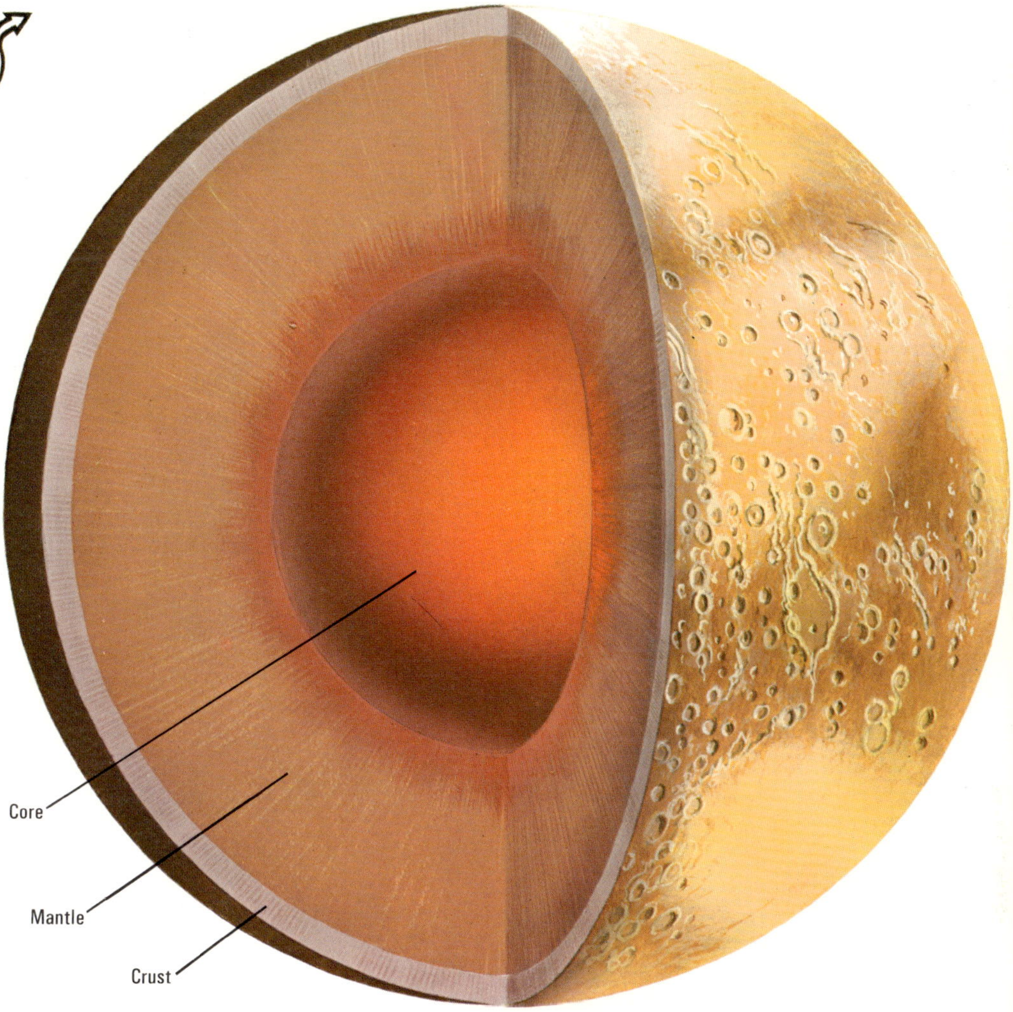

Right: A cut-away view of Mars, showing the relative sizes of core, mantle and crust. The core is thought to contain a lot of iron.

Left: The American space probe Viking 1 took this photograph of a Martian landscape in July 1976. The rocks measure up to about one metre across. The dusty soil is rust coloured as it has a high proportion of iron oxide. Winds have formed dunes from the dust in some regions. And windborn dust gives the Martian sky a permanent pinkish tinge. Viking 2 landed on Mars in August 1976. One of the main objectives of the Viking probes was to search for signs of life. The two craft took soil samples and carried out various tests. But no real evidence of life was found.

The orbits of most planets are almost circular, but Mars has an oval orbit. Because its distance from the Sun varies a lot there are great temperature differences — the main cause of the seasons on Mars. Winter occurs at the same time in both hemispheres when the planet is farthest from the Sun. Both polar caps grow larger, the southern cap sometimes reaching half-way to the Martian equator. But it may disappear completely in summer, when the warmer weather makes the caps retreat.

Mars has two tiny moons — Phobos and Deimos. In 1971 America's Mariner 9 space probe zoomed towards them to investigate.

Mariner 9 orbited Mars sending back pictures of the surface to scientists on Earth. Two American Viking space probes landed on Mars in 1976, and they obtained much more information on the planet. It was already known that the 'canals' must be mountain ridges, or some other natural feature, and scientists were sure that the dark patches were not vegetation. But the big question remained — did life exist on Mars? Tests carried out on the Martian soil failed to confirm the presence of organic (living) matter. But the existence of life on Mars has not yet been proved impossible. So the mystery of the red planet still remains hidden.

Probes to Mars

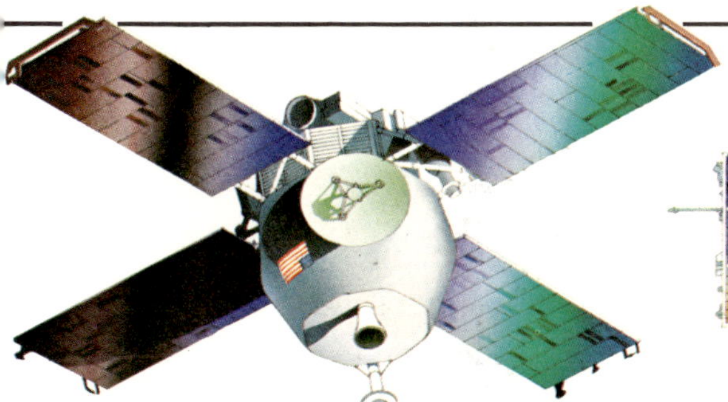

Mariner 9 went into orbit around Mars in November 1971, and sent back the first photographs to give a really good idea of the surface.

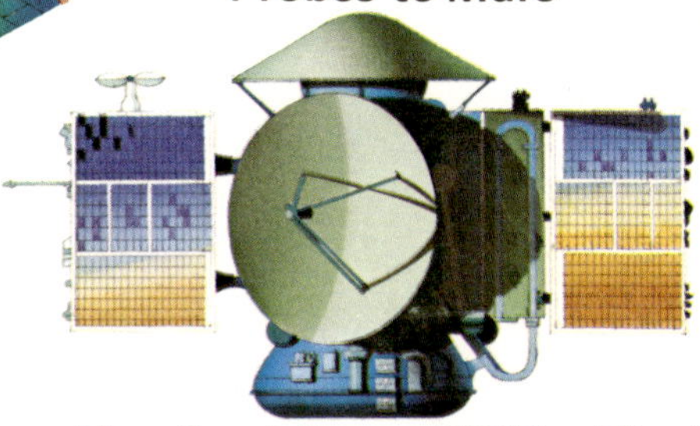

Mars 2 and 3 were USSR orbiter/lander spacecraft. Only Mars 3 landed safely, but ceased working after two minutes on the surface.

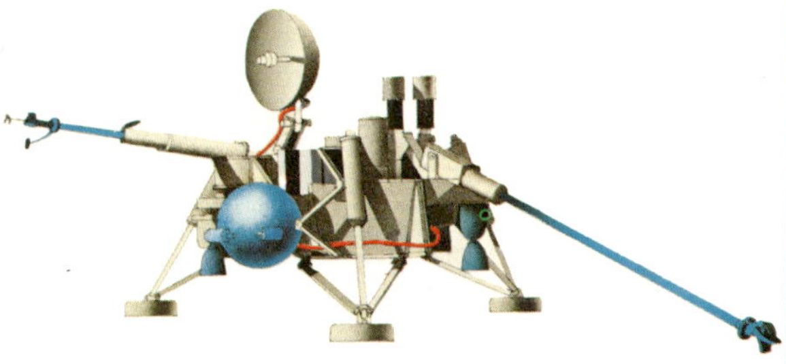

Two Viking landers reached the surface in July and September 1976. They took photographs and sampled the surface conditions, while their parent orbiters took detailed photographs.

Jupiter

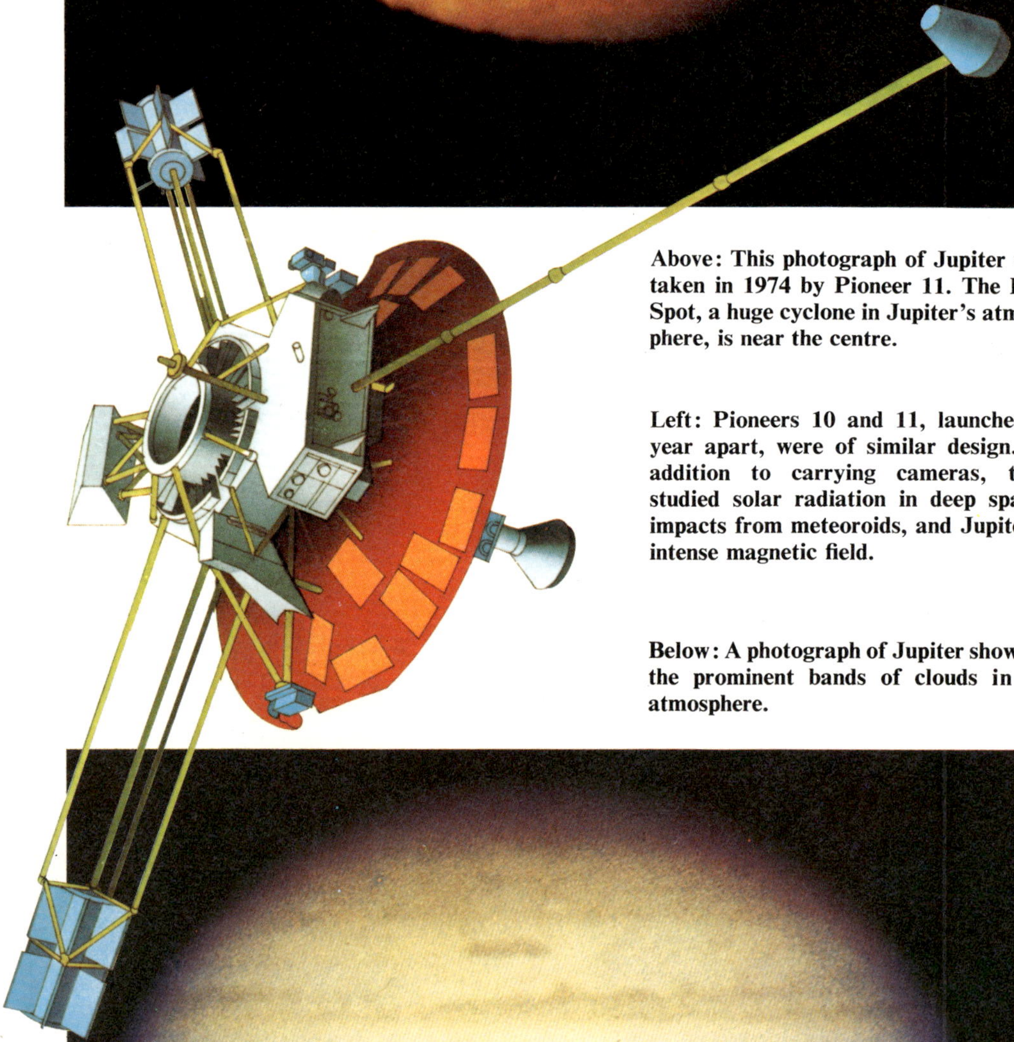

Above: This photograph of Jupiter was taken in 1974 by Pioneer 11. The Red Spot, a huge cyclone in Jupiter's atmosphere, is near the centre.

Left: Pioneers 10 and 11, launched a year apart, were of similar design. In addition to carrying cameras, they studied solar radiation in deep space, impacts from meteoroids, and Jupiter's intense magnetic field.

Below: A photograph of Jupiter showing the prominent bands of clouds in its atmosphere.

With a diameter of 142,800 kilometres, Jupiter is the largest planet in the Solar System. Its mass is more than twice that of all the other planets together. Astronomers believe that this giant planet has a relatively small rocky core of iron silicate. Around this is a vast ocean of liquid hydrogen that makes up most of the planet. Above the liquid is Jupiter's atmosphere. The lower part is made up of cloud layers, containing crystals of various hydrogen compounds, including water (ice) and ammonia. The top of the ammonia cloud layer is thought of as the surface of the planet, although there is an upper atmosphere of hot gases.

Jupiter orbits the Sun at an average distance of 778 million kilometres. This is over eleven times the distance between Earth and the Sun. As Jupiter is so far from the Sun, its surface is extremely cold—around −150°C. Yet it is warmer than might be expected. In fact, measurements show that Jupiter radiates more heat than it receives from the Sun. This is because the enormous pressure at its centre is causing the core to collapse. Tremendous heat generated by this keeps the core much hotter than the Sun's surface. The extreme pressure also prevents the core from turning into gas. Jupiter's great red spot is a gigantic storm which has lasted for centuries far above the clouds.

♃

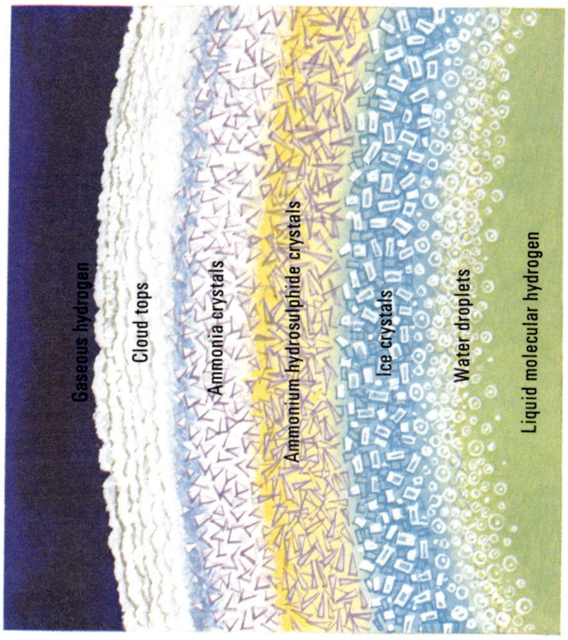

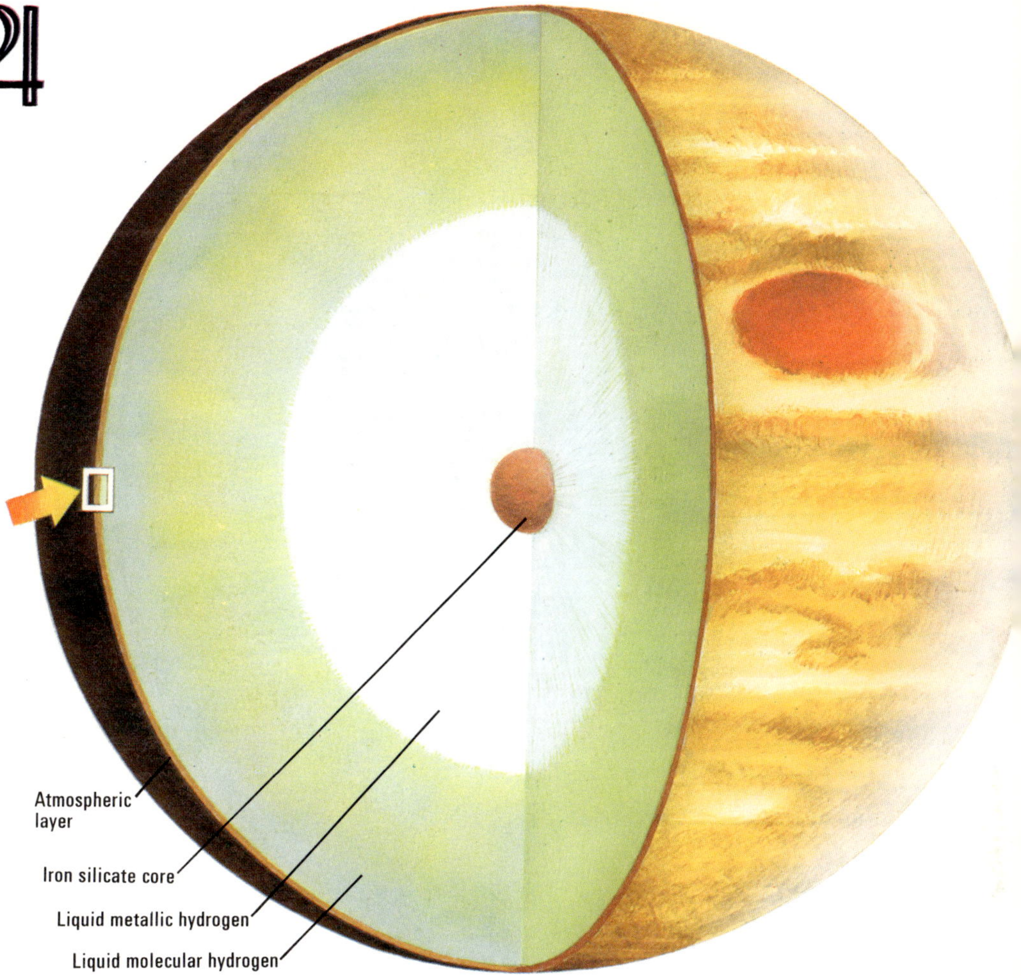

THE MOONS OF JUPITER

The 13 moons, or satellites, of Jupiter are listed below. The Roman numerals show the order in which the satellites were discovered. The four largest satellites—Ganymede, Callisto, Io and Europa were discovered in 1610 by Galileo. Lena was discovered as recently as 1974. And space probes may well reveal the presence of other, smaller satellites in the future. Amalthea, the innermost satellite, takes only half a day to orbit the giant planet. But Sinope, the outer satellite, takes over two years to complete one orbit.

Jupiter's moons from inner orbits to outer orbits.

V	Amalthea
I	Io
II	Europa
III	Ganymede
IV	Callisto
VI	Himalia
VII	Alara
X	Lysithea
XII	Ananke
XIII	Lena
XI	Carme
VIII	Pasiphae
IX	Sinope

Top left: Just how gigantic Jupiter is can be seen from this illustration, which compares it with the Earth. Although Jupiter consists almost entirely of the light element hydrogen, it is still, by far, the most massive of all the planets. Most of the hydrogen is in liquid form. But various hydrogen compounds, in solid, liquid and gas form, are present in the planet's atmosphere.

Above and above left: Jupiter has a relatively small core of iron silicate surrounded by liquid hydrogen. Details of the planet's atmosphere are shown on the left. The outer cloud layer is regarded as the planet's surface.

Below: Jupiter and its family of satellites. Details of the satellites are given in the information box (left).

Inside Saturn (above) and a comparison with the Earth (below).

Opposite page: A view of the planet Saturn from Titan, its largest moon. Titan has an atmosphere which makes the sky appear blue.

Below: Because Saturn's rings are tilted, their appearance changes as the planet moves in its orbit.

Saturn

In many ways, Saturn resembles Jupiter. With a diameter of 120,200 kilometres, Saturn is a giant planet almost as large as Jupiter. It consists mainly of hydrogen, with a relatively small core of rocky material. On the surface are cloud belts like those on Jupiter. But Saturn is a much cooler planet, with less activity in its atmosphere. The most outstanding feature of Saturn is the beautiful ring system around it. The rings extend more than 76,000 kilometres above the planet's surface. They consist of countless chunks of rock or ice, but are only a few kilometres thick, so cannot be seen from the Earth when they are edge-on to us. Saturn has ten satellites. The largest is Titan, with a diameter of nearly 6000 kilo metres.

The Outer Planets

The outer worlds of the solar system are too far away to be examined in detail. Uranus and Neptune, though smaller, appear to be built on the same pattern as Jupiter and Saturn, with thick hydrogen atmospheres and no true 'surface' at all. Faint markings have been detected on their tiny discs. Pluto is hardly larger than a star-like point, but astronomers believe it may have a frosty coating of methane, probably overlying a rocky surface like that of Mercury or Mars.

Uranus was discovered in 1781, after having been mistaken several times for a faint star. This cold giant is unique in the way it spins. The axes of the other planets are more or less 'upright', but Uranus lies over on its side. During the long time it takes to orbit the Sun (equivalent to 84 Earth years), first one pole and then the other points almost directly at the Sun. This means that a large part of each hemisphere has continual night for about 40 years, followed by a day of equal length.

The outstanding discovery in nearly two centuries of observation was made on 10 March 1977. Uranus passed in front of a faint star, and observers were surprised to see the star dim down and brighten again several times both before and after the planet itself blocked out the star. Sensitive scientific instruments showed that five narrow, faint rings, about 10 kilometres wide and some 20,000 kilometres above the planet's surface, must have caused the effect. Much dimmer

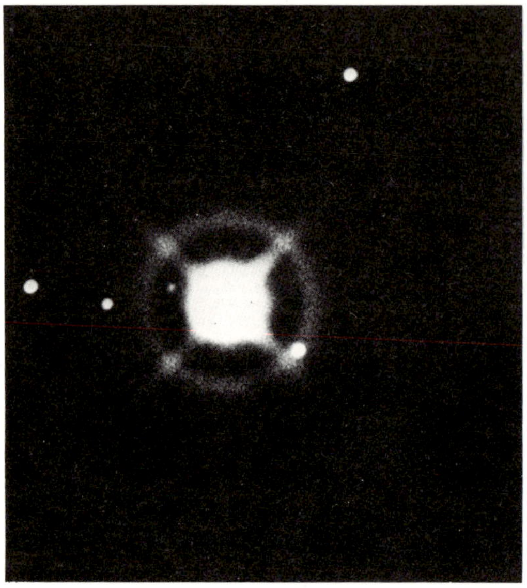

Above: Uranus and its five satellites. None of them exceeds 1000 km (620 mi) in diameter.

Below: The two satellites of Neptune are indicated by arrows. The image of Neptune, like that of Uranus, is enlarged and winged because of light scattered in the telescope. It should appear as a tiny spot.

Below: Pluto was discovered in 1930 by comparing these two photographs, taken three days apart. Every star in the view is in the same place, except for one spot: the moving planet.

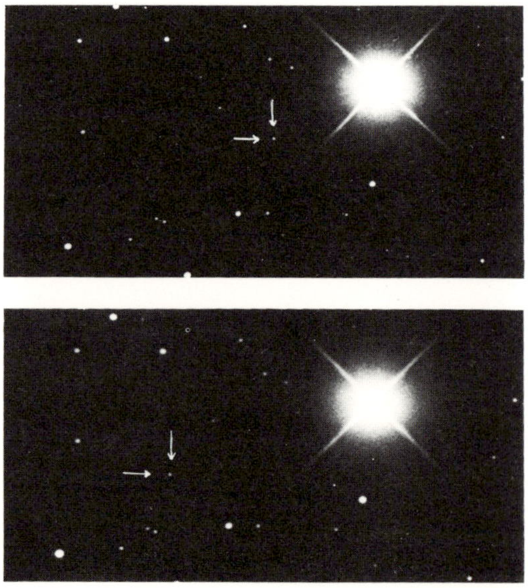

The orbits of the three outer planets. The orbit of Pluto is so eccentric that between the years 1969 and 2009 its distance from the Sun is less than that of Neptune. However the plane of Pluto's orbit is tilted to that of Neptune, like two hoops loosely interlinked, and the planets never come very near one another. (Not to scale.)

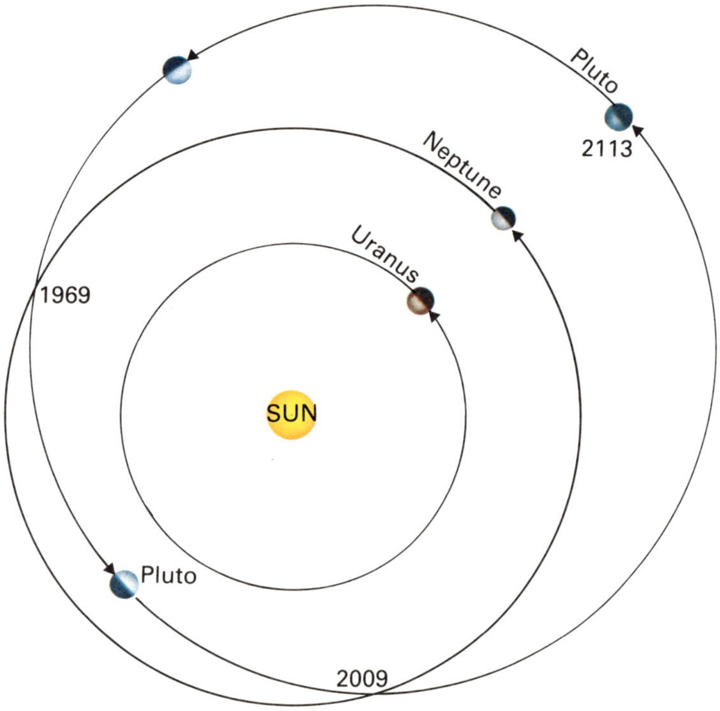

than Saturn's rings, there seems little hope of observing them directly from the Earth's surface through a telescope.

Whether Neptune, too, has rings, remains to be seen. Astronomers hope that the 2.4-metre Space Telescope, due to be launched in 1983, will be able to photograph faint details of this kind.

The Unseen Planet

When Neptune was found, in 1846, it was after a search for a new outer planet whose gravitational pull was affecting the orbit of Uranus. With Neptune's discovery, the wandering of Uranus seemed to have been cleared up. But further slight errors in the positions of both Uranus and Neptune made astronomers believe there must be an even more remote planet. Several searches were made, and Pluto was finally discovered in 1930. But the new planet came as something of a surprise. Astronomers had calculated that it would be much larger than the Earth; in fact it turned out to be slightly smaller than Mars, with a diameter of about 6,000 kilometres.

In 1969 Pluto came closer than Neptune to the Sun, and it will not become the outermost planet again for another 40 years. After that it will swing away to its most distant position — 50 times the distance of the Earth from the Sun — in the year 2113. Pluto is such a strange planet that some scientists believe it may be an escaped moon of Neptune.

Some astronomers have predicted the existence of another planet, far beyond Pluto, which is affecting the orbits of some comets. But even if a tenth planet does exist it will be so faint that it is unlikely ever to be seen through a telescope.

Uranus is about four times the diameter of the Earth, and is probably made up of liquid hydrogen surrounding a rock and ice core, which is about the same size as the Earth.

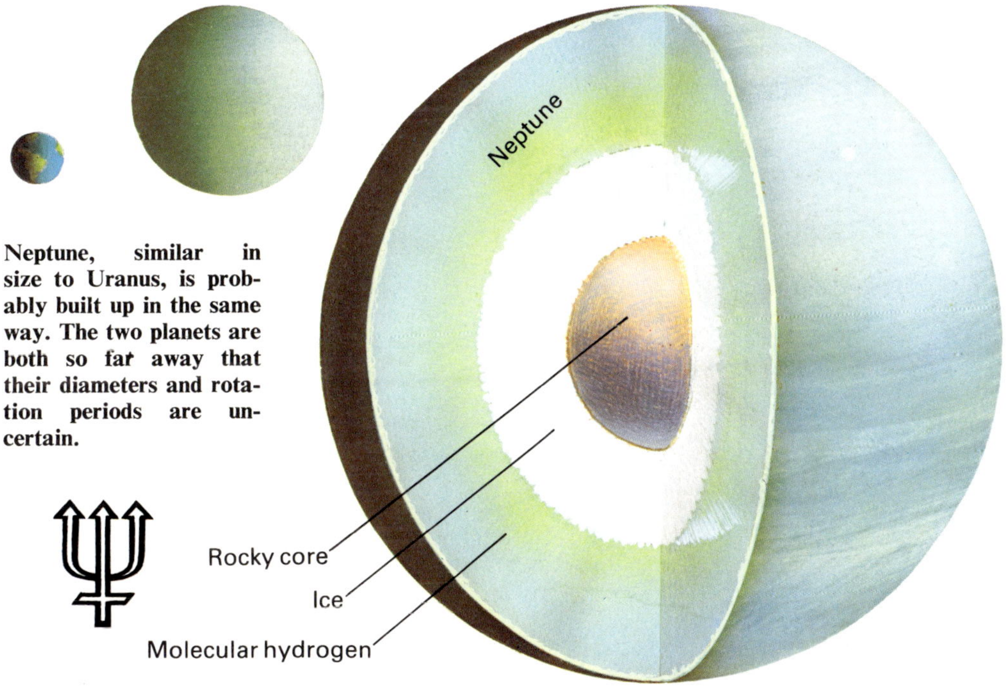

Neptune, similar in size to Uranus, is probably built up in the same way. The two planets are both so far away that their diameters and rotation periods are uncertain.

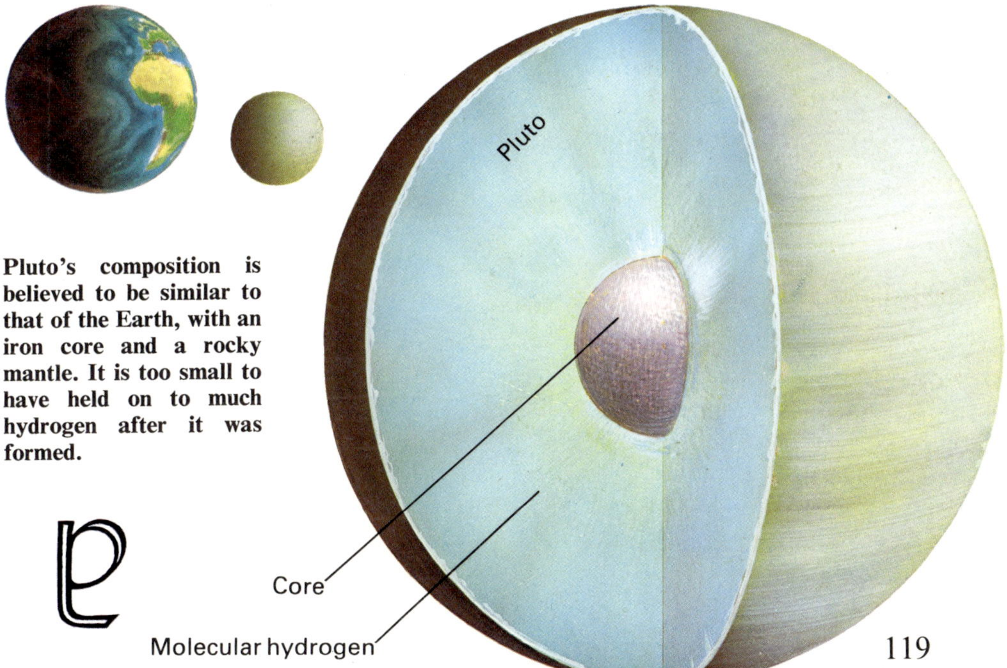

Pluto's composition is believed to be similar to that of the Earth, with an iron core and a rocky mantle. It is too small to have held on to much hydrogen after it was formed.

Rocks in Space

The total number of planets in the Solar System is unknown. Besides the nine major planets, there are numerous minor planets called asteroids. Few are more than 150 kilometres across, and some are less than one kilometre. Most of the asteroids are found in a broad band between the orbits of Mars and Jupiter. But some move in long, narrow orbits that cross the paths of other planets. Icarus, for example, sometimes crosses the orbits of the inner planets and passes close to the Sun. Hidalgo, on the other hand, travels out almost as far as Saturn. The total number of asteroids has been estimated at between 40,000 and 100,000.

Above: The asteroids are quite small bodies. Here, some of the largest asteroids are compared in size with the Moon.

Below: The appearance of Halley's comet in 1066, recorded on the Bayeux tapestry.

THE LARGEST ASTEROIDS

	(km)	Distance from Sun (million km)	Length of year
Ceres	1003	414	4·6 years
Pallas	608	414	4·6 years
Vesta	538	353	3·6 years
Hygeia	450	471	5·6 years
Euphrosyne	370	473	5·6 years

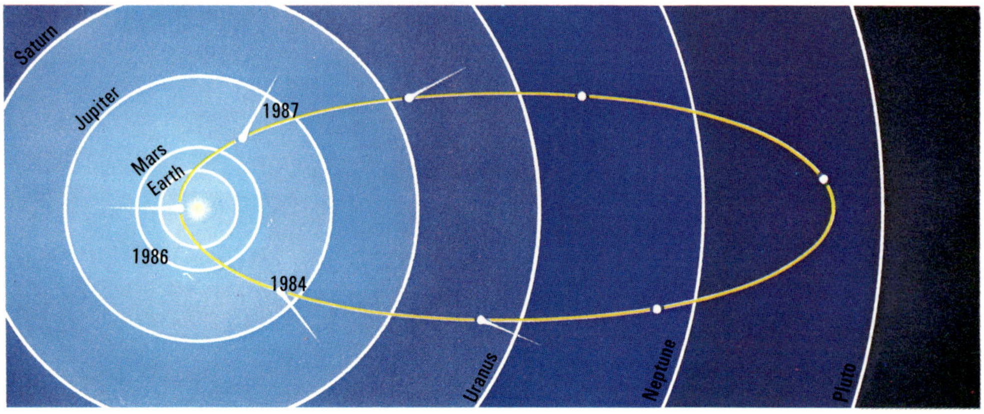

Above left: Comet Humason was the fifth comet discovered in 1961. It will not be seen again until about 4860.

Left: The orbit of Halley's comet. It will be visible to the naked eye when it passes close to the Sun in 1986.

Above right: Particles called meteoroids orbit the Sun. Meteor showers are seen when the Earth passes through their path.

Right: The largest known meteorite crater on Earth is the Barringer, or Coon Butte crater in Arizona. It is 1.3 km across.

Above: Comet West, photographed in March 1976, from the Kitt Peak National Observatory, near Tucson, Arizona.

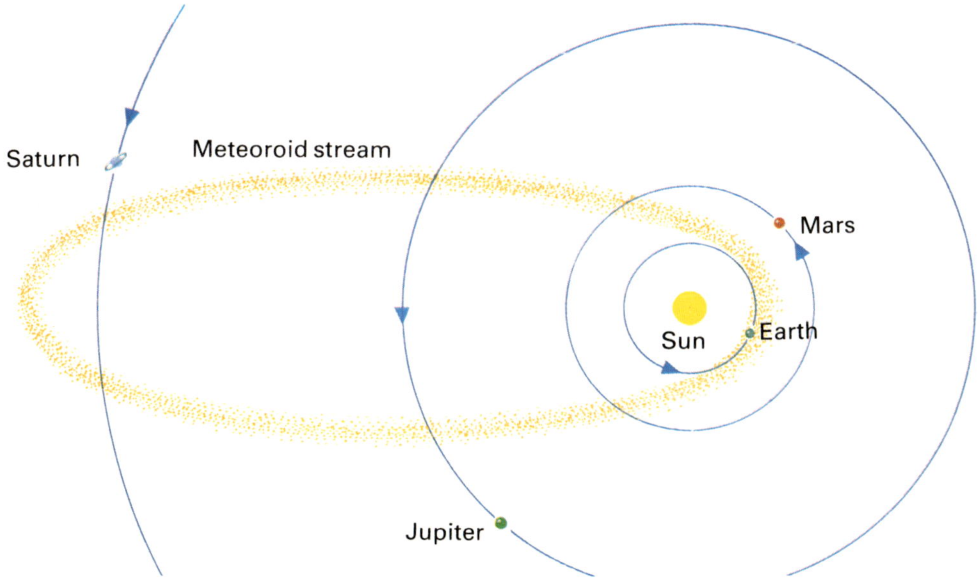

Comets and Meteoroids

Comets are often described as 'dirty snowballs'. They consist of a ball of dust, rock, ice and frozen gases only about ten kilometres across. Most comets are usually a long way from the Sun. But their unusual orbits regularly take them close to it. Then radiation makes some of the frozen gases evaporate and glow. These gases form the comet's bright tail, which may extend more than 100 million kilometres from the head of the comet.

Dust and rock that break away from comets are called meteoroids. These continually enter our atmosphere, where friction makes them glow white hot. The resulting streaks in the night sky are called meteors, or shooting stars. Meteoroids that hit the ground are called meteorites.

Telescopes

Left: An astronomer is dwarfed by the 508 centimetre Hale reflecting telescope at Mount Palomar Observatory, near Pasadena in California.

Below: A replica of the reflecting telescope invented by Isaac Newton. By using a curved mirror instead of an objective lens, he overcame the defect called chromatic aberration (colour distortion).

Below: The 100 centimetre refracting telescope at Yerkes Observatory, near Chicago.

Until the 1600s, astronomers were concerned mainly with the positions and movements of the Sun, Moon, stars and planets. But then the invention of the telescope opened up many new possibilities. For the first time, astronomers could observe the Sun and Moon in detail. They could look for the moons of other planets. They could also investigate thousands of stars that they had not been able to see with the naked eye.

The first telescope was made in 1608 by a Dutch spectacle-maker called Hans Lippershey. The Dutchman had no interest in astronomy, but news of his invention reached the Italian scientist Galileo Galilei, who decided to make an instrument for himself. Galileo finished his telescope in 1609 and, immediately, began to make important discoveries in astronomy. He saw that the Moon has mountains, craters and flat areas, and drew a map of the lunar surface. The following year, Galileo discovered four of Jupiter's moons. He also saw that the planet Venus, like our Moon, undergoes phases. Galileo realized that the particular changes in appearance that he observed could be explained only if the Sun was at the centre of our planetary system, as Copernicus had suggested.

By modern standards, Galileo's telescope was a poor instrument. Yet he discovered so much. Today, astronomers can delve deep into the universe with optical telescopes of incredible power. Radio telescopes help them to learn about the stars by studying the radio signals they give out.

OBSERVING THE SUN

It is easy to study the Sun, even with a simple telescope. To do this, the telescope is mounted on a stand and pointed, through closed curtains, out of an open window. When the instrument is correctly positioned, an image of the Sun will be projected onto a white screen placed behind the eyepiece. You will then be able to study the nature of sunspots. This is the only safe way of observing the Sun. Never look directly at it through the telescope. Many dark filters supplied for this purpose do not give enough protection.

MAKE A TELESCOPE

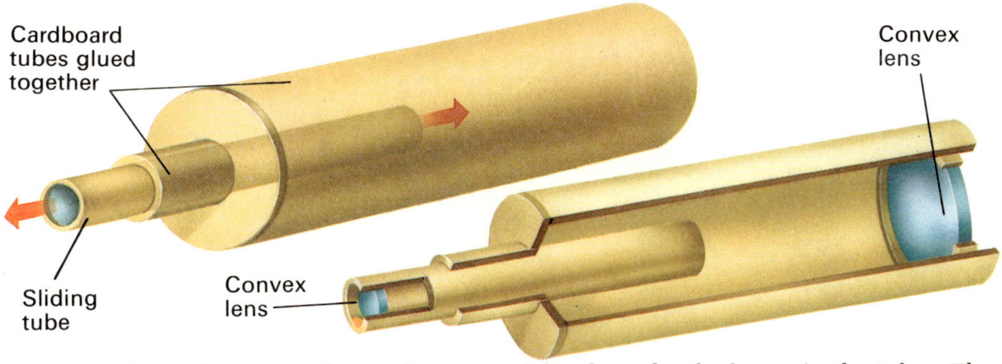

You can make a refracting, or lens, telescope quite simply. You will need two cheap magnifying glasses or old spectacle lenses, which are convex (fatter in the middle), and two sturdy cardboard tubes. Fit the lenses into the tubes as shown in the picture and arrange for the eyepiece tube to move in and out so that you can focus properly. You will have to experiment to find the right places for the lenses in the tubes. The image you see with the telescope will be upside-down, but this does not matter for astronomical work.

Another kind of telescope is the reflector, which uses a curved mirror to gather light rays. This is the kind most astronomers use; they give a better optical image and can also be made much larger.

Only the upper part of the Kitt Peak solar telescope pokes up above the ground. The rest is buried in the cool earth. This is important because small temperature changes would upset the delicate measurements. The telescope uses three mirrors (below). The upper mirror is driven by a motor to follow the Sun. The Sun's light is reflected on to the concave mirror deep below the surface, then on to a third mirror which directs it on to a table in the observation room.

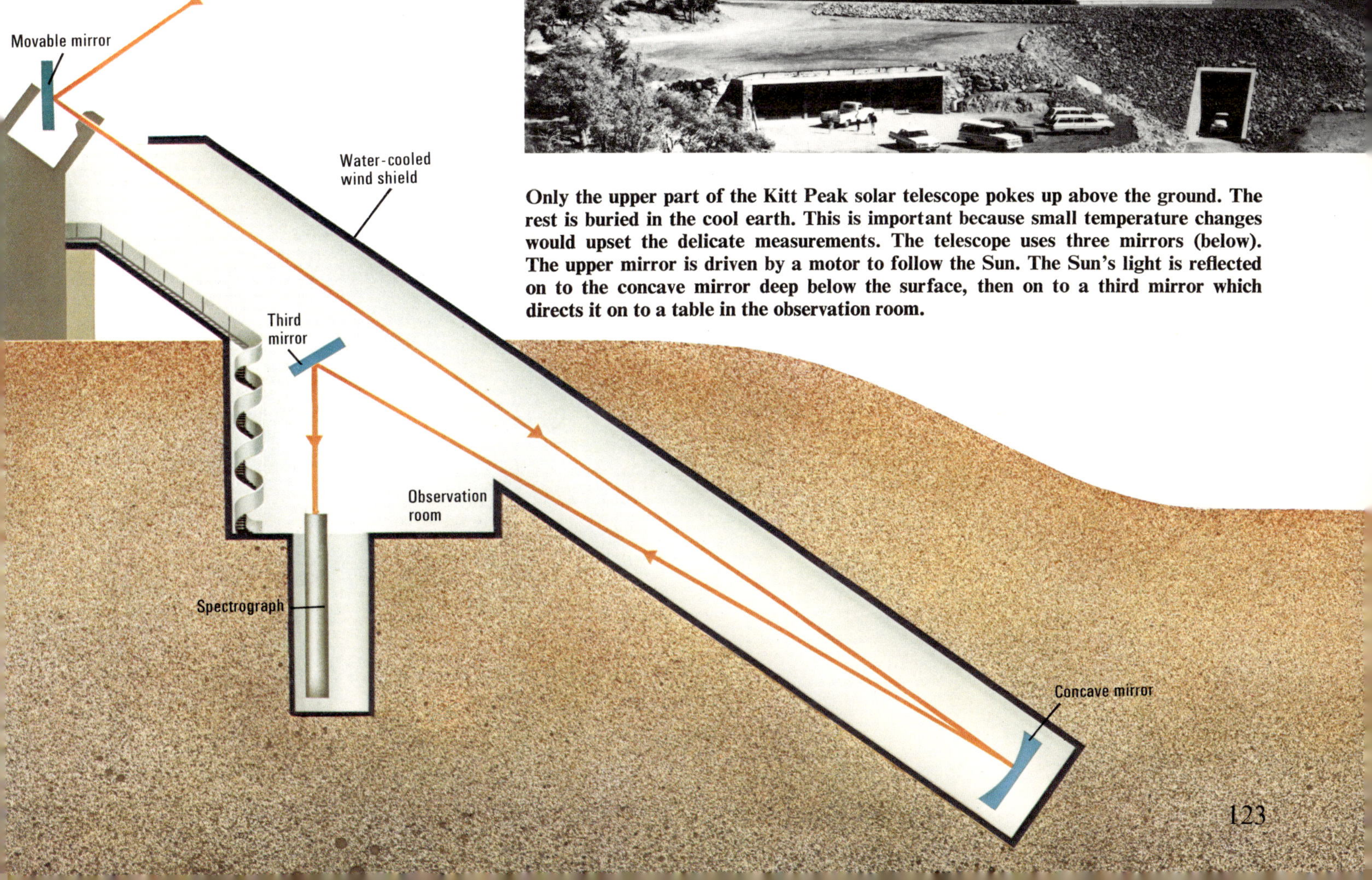

Stars and Galaxies

Most scientists think that the universe was created in one enormous explosion that happened between 12 and 25 thousand million years ago. This is called the big-bang theory. In the explosion, vast amounts of material were scattered in space. Gradually, this material formed the star systems, or galaxies. We know that the universe contains at least 1,000 million galaxies. A typical galaxy is our own — the Milky Way. It contains about 100,000 million stars, which are arranged in a flat, double-spiral formation. The distance across the spiral is about one million million million kilometres, or 100,000 light-years. (One light-year is the distance that light travels in one year and is equal to nearly ten million million kilometres.)

Although extremely large compared with the Earth, the Sun is actually one of the smaller stars in our Galaxy. It is called a dwarf star. The largest stars are the supergiants, which are up to 3,000 times bigger than the Sun. As we can see, the Sun is a single star. But only about 30 per cent of the specks of light we think of as stars are, in fact, single bodies. Nearly half of them are *binaries* — pairs of stars orbiting around each other. The rest are *multiple* systems which contain three or more stars.

When we speak about stars we think of them as parts of groups called constellations. But these are not true groups. The stars in a constellation appear to us to be in the same part of the sky, but they may be far apart from each other and from the Earth.

Above: Two views of our galaxy, which is called the Milky Way. It consists of some 100,000 million stars arranged in a vast spiral. The position of the Sun and Solar System is shown by the arrows. As the top illustration shows, the stars are concentrated in one plane, like a plate. As a result, a faint, whitish band can be seen across the night sky. This is why the galaxy is called the Milky Way.

Right: The Andromeda galaxy is the closest spiral star system to our Milky Way. Both are members of the Local Group, a cluster of over 20 galaxies. This is quite a small cluster. Some clusters contain thousands of galaxies.

Below: Our Sun appears extremely large and bright. But this is because it is much closer to us than are the other stars. In fact, the Sun is of moderate size, having a diameter of nearly 1,400,000 kilometres. It is a type of star known as a yellow dwarf. Compared with the Sun, some stars are tiny, while others are enormous. Syrius B, one of the white dwarfs, is only 39,000 kilometres across. But the giant star Capella has a diameter more than 10 times that of the Sun. And the largest supergiants are around 3,000 times greater than the Sun in diameter.

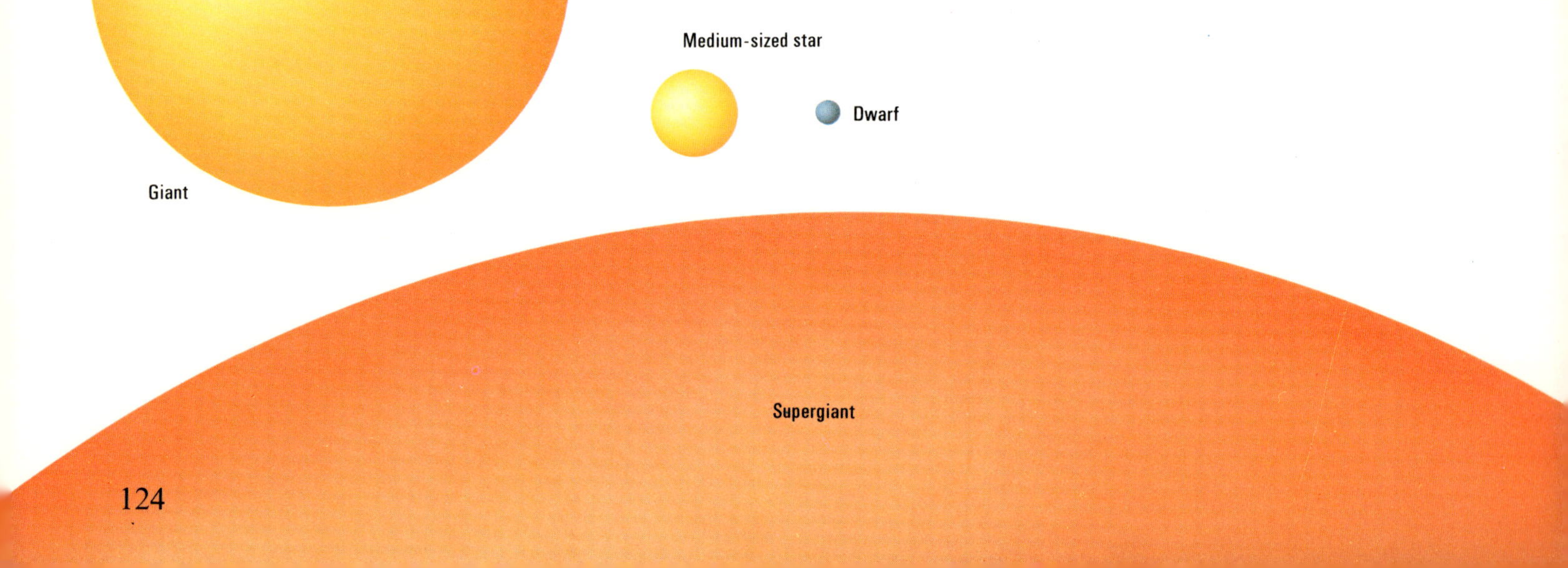

Journey into Space

Right: **Astronaut Edwin Aldrin followed Neil Armstrong onto the lunar surface in July 1969.**

Below and right: Putting a spacecraft into orbit by means of a multistage rocket, such as the Saturn V. For a spacecraft to enter orbit, it must reach a very high speed. This cannot be attained using one rocket. The multistage rocket is able to reach the required speed as it reduces its weight by dumping used rocket stages.

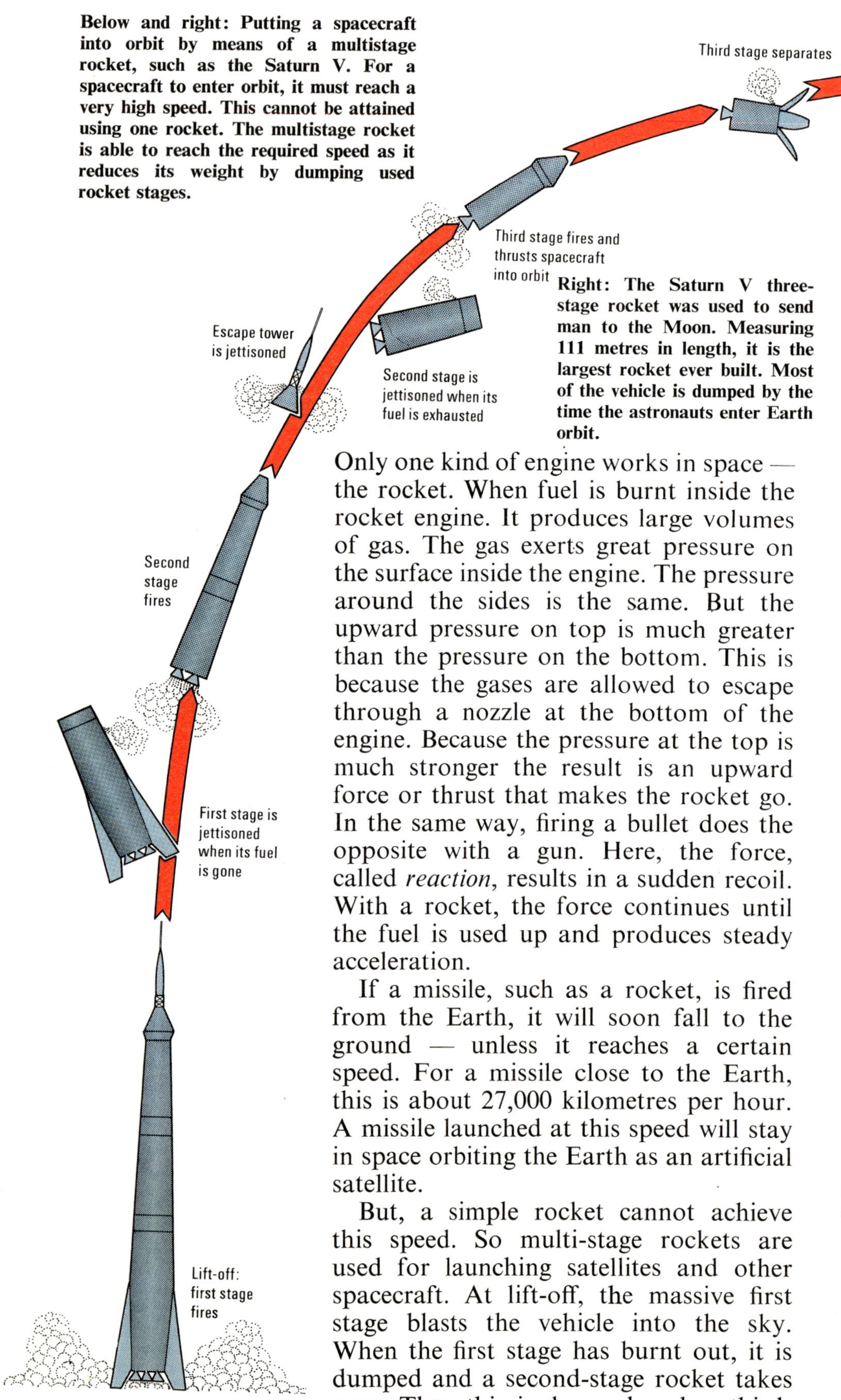

Right: The Saturn V three-stage rocket was used to send man to the Moon. Measuring 111 metres in length, it is the largest rocket ever built. Most of the vehicle is dumped by the time the astronauts enter Earth orbit.

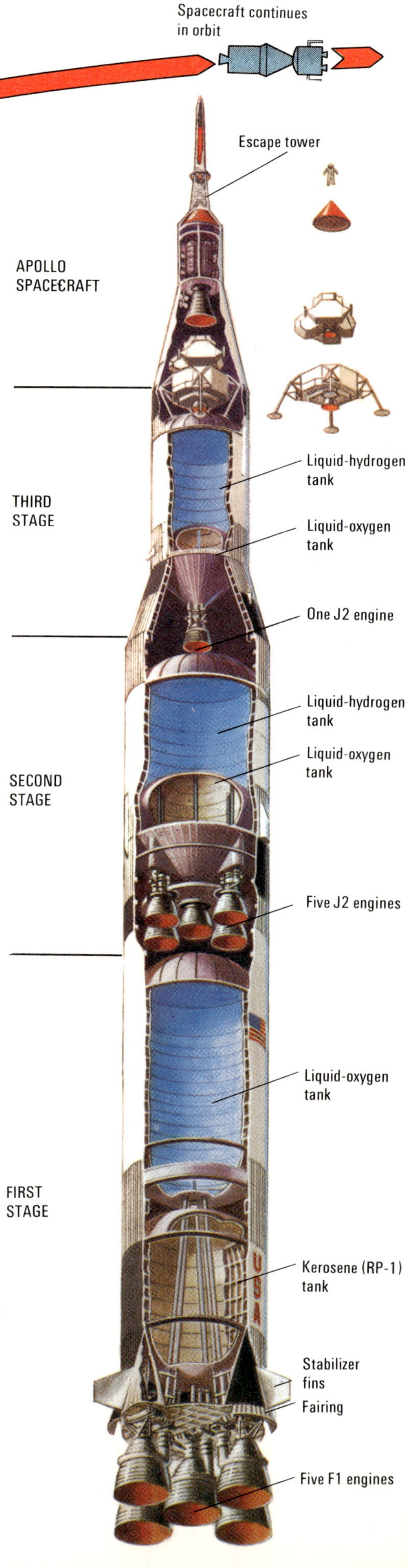

Only one kind of engine works in space — the rocket. When fuel is burnt inside the rocket engine. It produces large volumes of gas. The gas exerts great pressure on the surface inside the engine. The pressure around the sides is the same. But the upward pressure on top is much greater than the pressure on the bottom. This is because the gases are allowed to escape through a nozzle at the bottom of the engine. Because the pressure at the top is much stronger the result is an upward force or thrust that makes the rocket go. In the same way, firing a bullet does the opposite with a gun. Here, the force, called *reaction*, results in a sudden recoil. With a rocket, the force continues until the fuel is used up and produces steady acceleration.

If a missile, such as a rocket, is fired from the Earth, it will soon fall to the ground — unless it reaches a certain speed. For a missile close to the Earth, this is about 27,000 kilometres per hour. A missile launched at this speed will stay in space orbiting the Earth as an artificial satellite.

But, a simple rocket cannot achieve this speed. So multi-stage rockets are used for launching satellites and other spacecraft. At lift-off, the massive first stage blasts the vehicle into the sky. When the first stage has burnt out, it is dumped and a second-stage rocket takes over. Then this is dumped and, a third-stage rocket provides the final burst of acceleration.

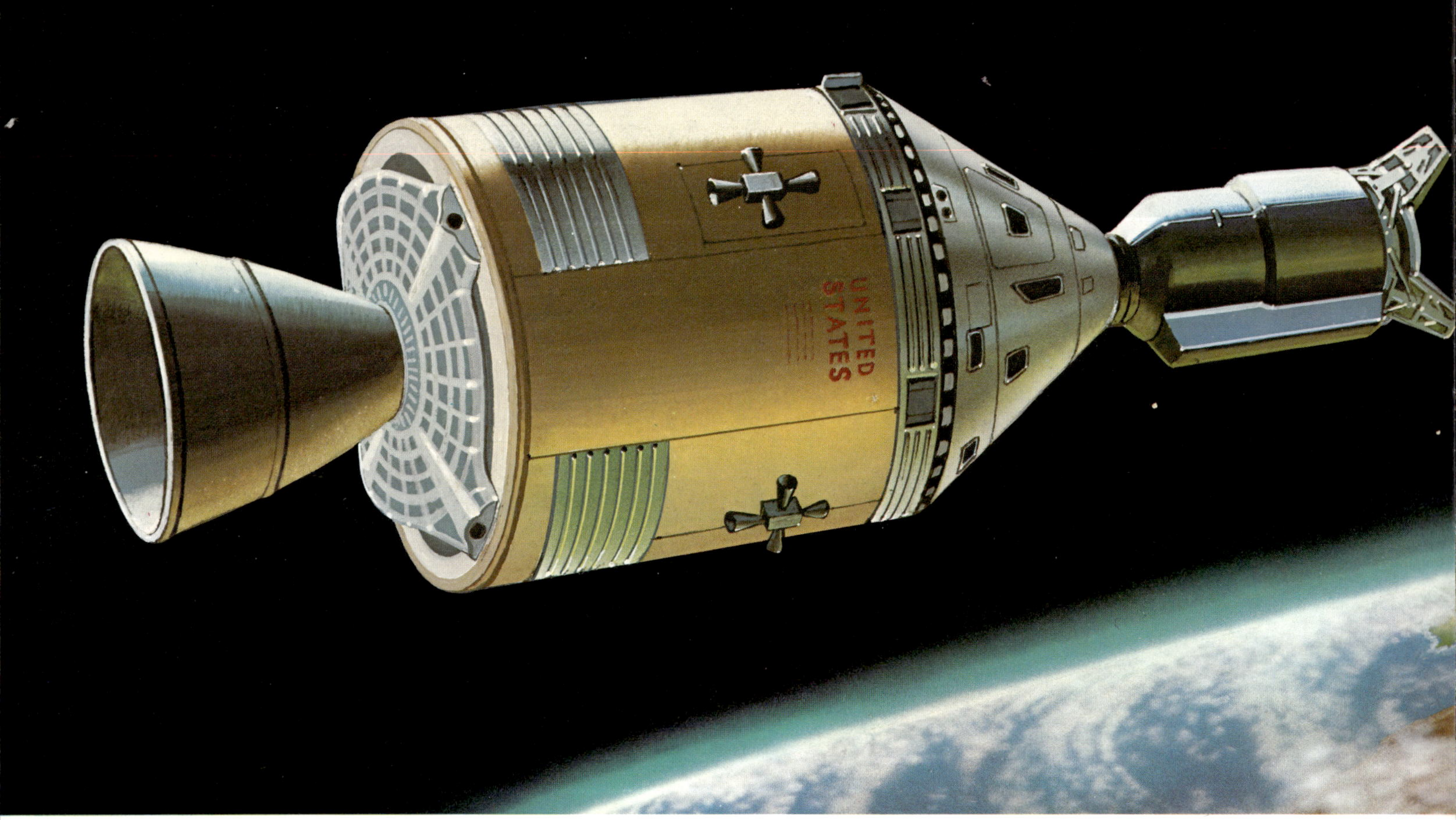

Exploring Space

October 1957 is generally regarded as the beginning of the Space Age. For that was when the Russians amazed the world with the launch of Sputnik 1 — the first artificial satellite. This tiny aluminium sphere, less than 60 centimetres across, carried a few scientific instruments and sent back information to the Earth. Although a simple device by modern standards, Sputnik 1 was the start of a great 'space race' between Russia and the United States. Advances in space technology were rapid. In November 1957, a Russian dog called Laika became the first satellite passenger. Then, in the following January, the Americans launched their first satellite, Explorer 1. After developing safe techniques for getting satellites back to Earth it became possible to send man into space.

In 1961, the Russian Yuri Gagarin became the first man to orbit the Earth. The following year, John Glenn became the first American in orbit. Then the Americans planned a space programme with the aim of landing man on the Moon. Success came in July 1969, when Neil Armstrong set foot on the lunar surface with the words: 'That's one small step for a man, one giant leap for mankind.'

While the Americans were busy with their Moon programme, the Russians concentrated on developing unmanned space probes. After 1969, the Americans did the same. For the conditions on most planets would make a manned mission dangerous, if not impossible. The cost of sending people so far would be enormous.

Of particular interest were the two American Viking probes, which soft-landed on Mars in 1976. The Viking craft carried out soil tests to see if any primitive form of life existed on the planet. But the tests did not give a clear result. One of the most rewarding probes has been the American Pioneer 11 spacecraft. Launched in April 1973, it reached Jupiter in December 1974. It then went on to provide the first close-up pictures of Saturn in September 1979. Current interest is focussed on the American Voyager spacecraft due to reach Uranus in 1986 and Neptune in 1989.

Left: The first joint American-Soviet space experiment took place in July 1975. Here, the American Apollo and Russian Soyez spacecraft are shown slowly approaching each other. Seconds later, the two craft were firmly locked together as they orbited some 225 kilometres above the Earth. A special docking module was used to link the two spacecraft. The American astronauts and Russian cosmonauts passed through the docking module in order to visit each others' spacecraft. The experience gained during this experiment may prove useful if ever a space rescue mission becomes necessary in the future.

Below left: The American Skylab space laboratory was launched in 1974. The three-man crew reached Skylab by means of an Apollo spacecraft (shown attached on the left). Three crews took turns to man the laboratory. Skylab burnt up on re-entering the atmosphere in 1979.

Below: A photograph of a Viking lander, as it would have appeared on the surface of Mars. Two such probes touched down on the red planet in July and August, 1976. They photographed the Martian surface, made various scientific measurements and searched for signs of life in the soil.

Bottom left: Many spacecraft are used to study the Earth. This Nimbus satellite records world weather conditions and transmits details back to Earth.

The Space Shuttle

Spacecraft have to reach very high speeds in order to get into orbit or to escape completely from the Earth's gravitational pull. The required speed cannot be achieved using a single-stage rocket. So, a multi-stage rocket is used. The first stage provides lift-off and initial acceleration. Subsequent stages accelerate the spacecraft further. With ordinary rockets, the cost is enormous. For powerful, high-precision rocket motors are extremely expensive items. Yet they are dumped once their fuel has run out. Only the relatively small spacecraft, mounted on the tip of the giant launch vehicle, completes the mission. The American space shuttle is a means of launching spacecraft at relatively low cost.

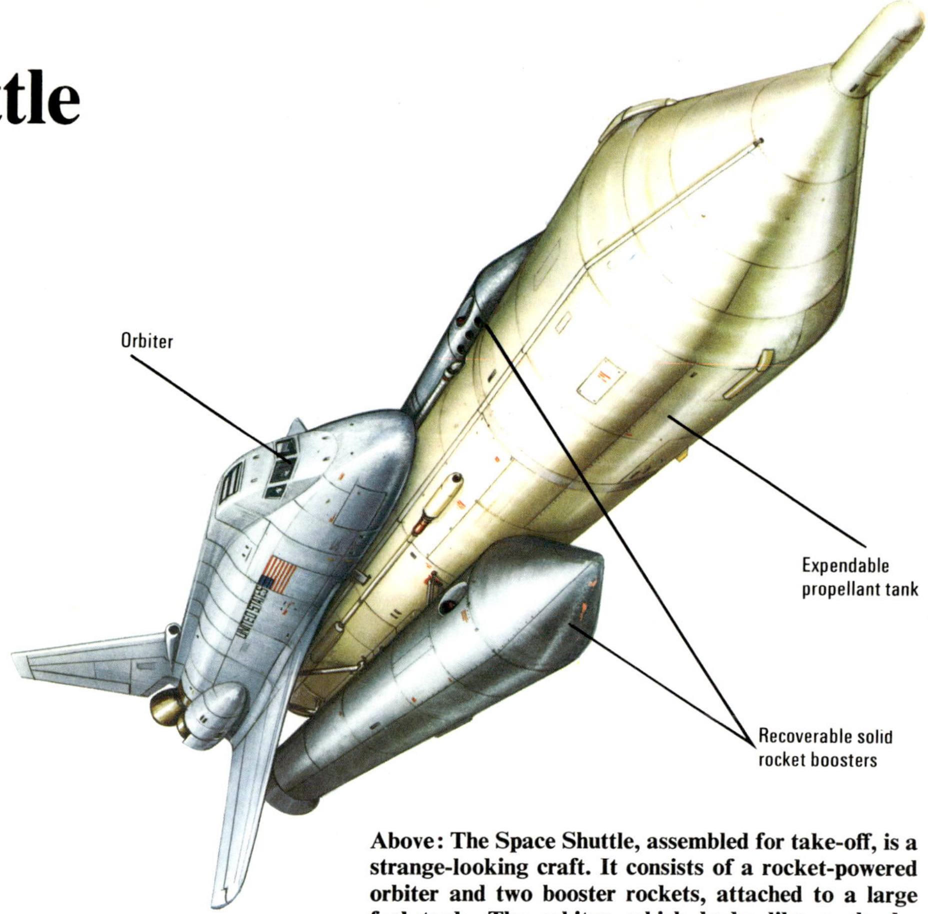

Above: The Space Shuttle, assembled for take-off, is a strange-looking craft. It consists of a rocket-powered orbiter and two booster rockets, attached to a large fuel tank. The orbiter, which looks like a chunky aircraft, will be used to take satellites, people and equipment into orbit around the Earth.

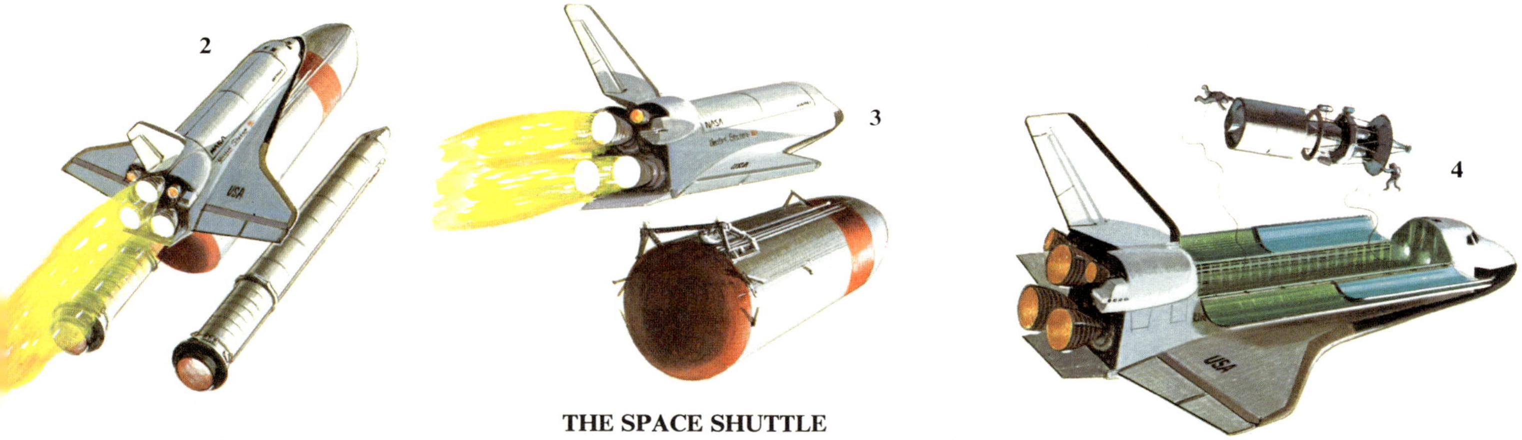

THE SPACE SHUTTLE

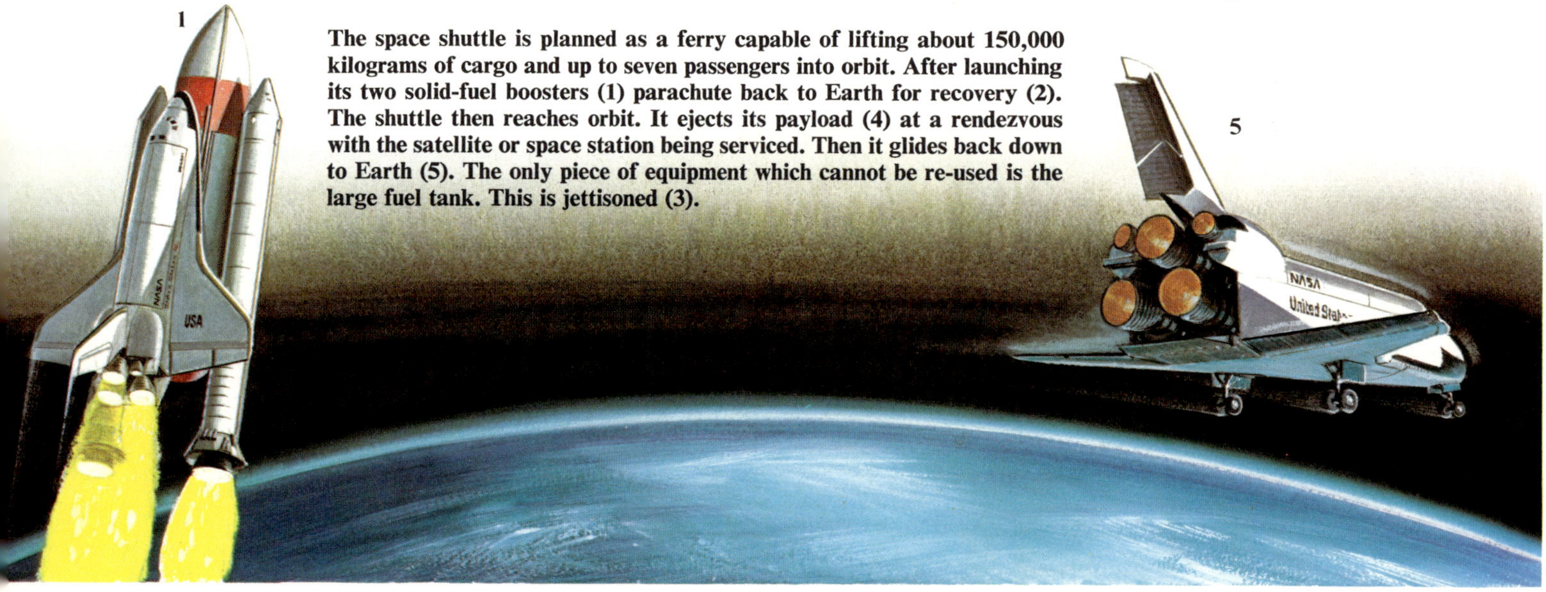

The space shuttle is planned as a ferry capable of lifting about 150,000 kilograms of cargo and up to seven passengers into orbit. After launching its two solid-fuel boosters (1) parachute back to Earth for recovery (2). The shuttle then reaches orbit. It ejects its payload (4) at a rendezvous with the satellite or space station being serviced. Then it glides back down to Earth (5). The only piece of equipment which cannot be re-used is the large fuel tank. This is jettisoned (3).

The complete shuttle looks rather strange. It consists of a rocket-powered aircraft fixed to the side of a huge fuel tank. Also attached to the tank are two booster rockets. The space shuttle is, in effect, a multi-stage rocket. But the most expensive parts return safely to Earth, and can be used over and over again. Only the fuel tank — the cheapest part of the shuttle — is dumped.

The aircraft-like part of the shuttle is called the orbiter. It has three powerful rocket engines that use liquid hydrogen and liquid oxygen, stored in the 47-metre-long fuel tank. The booster rockets, which are a little longer than the orbiter, contain solid fuel.

To get lift-off the main rockets on the orbiter, and the two booster rockets are fired. At a height of about 45 kilometres above the Earth, the boosters' solid fuel supply runs out. Then, the empty rockets are separated from the shuttle and parachuted into the sea.

Above: Having entered orbit around the Earth, the orbiter of the Space Shuttle ejects a satellite from its equipment bay. The orbiter then returns to Earth.

Below: The Shuttle orbiter will be used to carry a space telescope into orbit sometime in the 1980s.

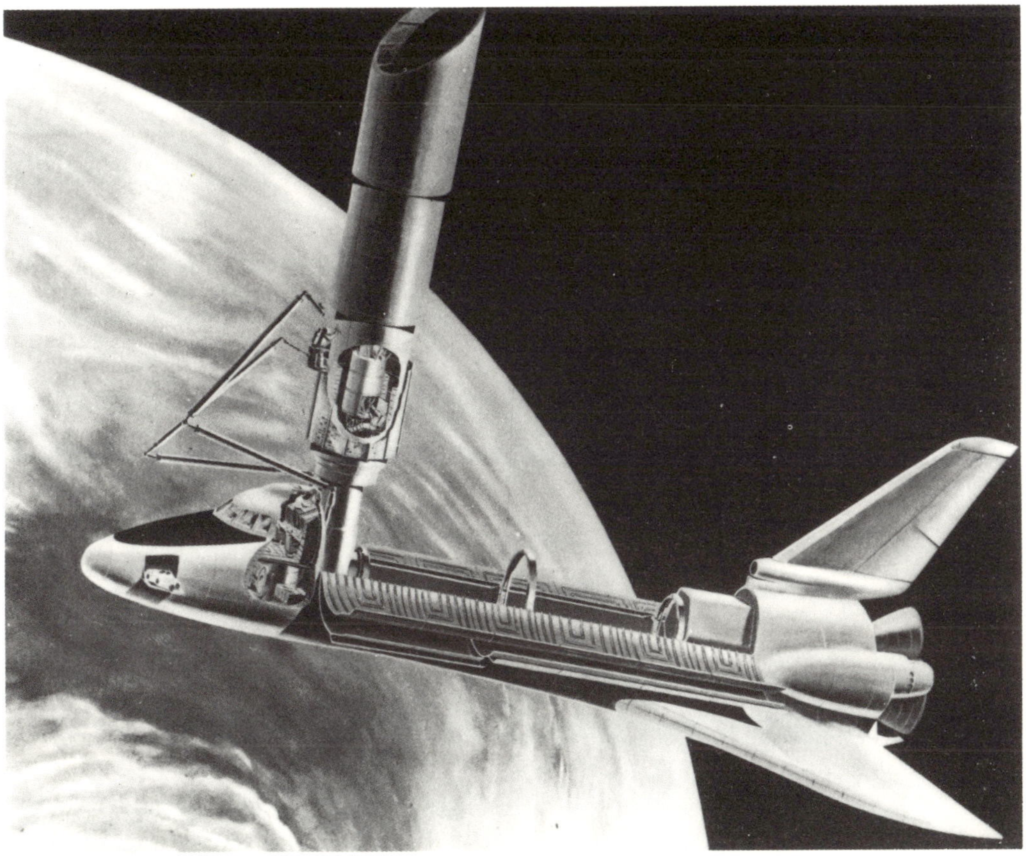

A recovery vessel picks up the boosters, which are later serviced before re-use. After dropping the empty boosters, the orbiter continues its ascent, powered by its own main rockets. When the liquid fuel supply runs out, the fuel tank is separated and falls into the sea. By this time, the orbiter has enough speed for its orbit, 1,000 kilometres above the ground.

Most of the orbiter's body consists of a huge cargo hold for loads weighing up to 150 tonnes. The cargo may consist of ordinary satellites, a space laboratory, or materials for building a giant space station. After ejecting its load, the orbiter drops into the atmosphere and glides to the ground. Besides cargo, the orbiter can also ferry up to seven passengers between the ground and an orbiting spacecraft.

Our Future in Space

Above: An artist's impression of a future base on the Moon. The lunar rocks contain useful minerals which, as the supplies on the Earth are used up, may become worth exploiting. The spacecraft would take the raw material up to a space station in Earth orbit for processing.

Below: If a moon base or space colony is established, it will have to be served by vehicles bringing in supplies. Such a ship, like the one shown here, would act as a ferry to bring people and cargo from Earth-orbit out to the moon base or colony. The ship would be powered by solar energy.

There are many reasons why man will one day set up colonies on the Moon, and on suitable planets and in space. As the Earth's own mineral supplies gradually run out, the cost of some materials will rise so much that it will be more economic to start mining on the Moon. Tests carried out on rocks brought back from the Moon have shown that it contains elements that are relatively rare to Earth. These include chromium, titanium, zirconium and the radioactive elements uranium and thorium. All these elements seem to occur in much greater amounts on the Moon than on the Earth. But the Moon also has large amounts of common elements, such as aluminium.

Mining tests for minerals on the Moon will probably lead to the setting up of permanent laboratories on the lunar surface.

Laboratories on the Moon would be sealed and air conditioned, so that scientists could work there without having to wear space suits. They would have special living, eating and leisure areas. Over the years, man's activities on the Moon would increase, and the small lunar bases would gradually expand to become large towns. Mines would be established in areas with rich mineral deposits. Refineries would be built near them, for it would generally be cheaper to refine minerals on the Moon than to transport large quantities of ore back to the Earth.

Other important activities on the Moon would include exploring its surface and setting up observatories for studying the universe. Unlike the Earth, the Moon has no atmosphere. So observers would always have an extremely clear view of the stars and planets—even in the daytime.

As well as the Moon, there are other places in the Solar System suitable for our colonization.

Left: An artist's impression of a possible future environment for man. This is part of the interior of the 'Island Three' space community project. For some years, scientists have been considering this and other proposed schemes for setting up colonies in space. Man may be forced to live in space if the Earth becomes overcrowded. It is possible that today's children may be alive when construction work begins on the first space colony.

Left: The living area of a future space colony may be shaped like a wheel. It would rotate slowly to produce an outward force. This would act as 'artificial gravity'.

Below: The interior of a wheel-shaped space station could be made to resemble the Earth in many ways. But there would be no horizon. And the 'artificial gravity' acting outwards would give the surface of still water a noticeable curve.

Mars is the most suitable of the major planets for our colonization. Although it is our neighbour in space, Mars is much farther from the Sun. Even during its summer, temperatures are like those in Antarctica, but vary much more during the day. However, such conditions are excellent compared with the hostile environments of the other major planets. Jupiter, for example, consists mainly of liquid hydrogen. But it does have several moons, two of which are larger than the planet Mercury. These, and the moons of other planets, are likely targets for manned missions after the exploration of Mars.

Even people who do not work on space technology will, one day, leave the Earth to form colonies elsewhere. This could become necessary if the population grows so much that our planet is overcrowded. Once away from the Earth, man has to live in conditions which match those of earth. So there would be no great advantage in going to another planet, or one of the moons, just to house the excess population. Instead, giant space stations could be assembled in orbit around the Earth. In order to make conditions as natural as possible, the space stations would be made to spin. The centrifugal (outward) forces produced would act as 'artificial gravity' and prevent objects from floating around.

Whatever else happens, the whole human race will have to leave the Earth before the Sun runs out of hydrogen fuel. Enormous nuclear-powered spaceships will then take man to a distant part of the universe.

Above: A manned spaceship blasts out of Earth orbit and heads towards Mars. The Americans made detailed plans for a manned mission to Mars, commencing in April 1985. But it will probably be many years before the American government decides to approve such a costly space project.

Left: Part of the proposed 'Island Three' space station, which may become man's first permanent home in space. The complete structure would extend over many kilometres.

Below: This Jupiter spaceship was featured in the film 2001*: A Space Odyssey***. To reduce danger from radiation, the nuclear engine (left) is kept away from the spherical crew quarters.**

Index

Acknowledgements

The photographs in this book are used by courtesy of the following people and organisations:

Victoria and Albert Museum (page 9); Ken Merrylees (page 14 top); Mansell Collection (pages 14 (bottom), 15 (top), 82 (top right and bottom), 84 (top), 93, 101); British Museum (page 20 top); National Research Development Council (page 22 top left); Swiss National Tourist Office (page 23 top right); Air France (page 23 bottom); N.A.S.A. (pages 24, 25, 105, 107, 111, 114, 116, 127, 129); New Zealand High Commission (page 37); Atomic Energy Authority (page 42; Robin Kerrod (pages 44, 46 (bottom), 101, 108); Michael Chinnery (pages 46 (top), 55, 90); Zefa/Photri (page 49); P. Morris (page 53 top); B.O.C. (page 53 bottom); Zefa (pages 54, 59); Yachting World (page 57); London Transport (page 74); Peabody Coal Co. St Louis, Missouri (page 75); Maritshuis, The Hague (page 82 top left); K. Moreman (page 84); Transworld Feature Syndicate (page 91); Mary Evans Picture Library (page 92); Max Planck Institute for Radio Astronomy (page 95); Science Museum (pages 96, 97 (bottom), 122 (top right); Fox-Rank (page 97 top); Royal Astronomical Society (pages 98, 99, 118); Ann Ronan Picture Library (page 100); Patrick Moore (page 109 bottom); Lockheed Solar Observatory (page 109 top); California Institute of Technology (pages 120 (left), 122 (top left), 125); Michael Holford (page 120 right); Kitt Peak Observatory (pages 121 (top), 123); American Meteorite Laboratory (page 121 bottom).